D1716966

DESIGNING THE OFFICE OF THE FUTURE

THE JAPANESE APPROACH TO TOMORROW'S WORKPLACE

DESIGNING THE OFFICE OF THE FUTURE

THE JAPANESE APPROACH TO TOMORROW'S WORKPLACE

Volker Hartkopf
Vivian Loftness
Pleasantine Drake
Fred Dubin
Peter Mill
George Ziga

Advanced Building Systems Integration Consortium
The Center for Building Performance and Diagnostics
Carnegie Mellon University

JOHN WILEY & SONS, INC.
New York • Chichester • Brisbane • Toronto • Singapore

This text is printed on acid-free paper.

This publication is designed to provide accurate and
authoritative information in regard to the subject
matter covered. It is sold with the understanding that
the publisher is not engaged in rendering legal, accounting,
or other professional services. If legal advice or other
expert assistance is required, the services of a competent
professional person should be sought.

Library of Congress Cataloging in Publications Data:

Designing the office of the future : the Japanese approach to tomorrow's workplace / Volker
    Hartkopf... [et al.].
        Includes bibliographical references.
        ISBN 0-471-59569-1
        1. Office building — Japan. 2. Architecture, Modern — 20th century — Japan. 3. Interior
    architecture — Japan. 4. Engineer design — Japan. I. Hartkopf, Volker. II. Japanese approach to
    tomorrow's workplace.
        NA6234.J3J37   1993   92-45225
        725'.23'095209048—dc20

Printed in the United States of America

10 9 8 7 6 5 4 3 2 1

In memory of Dr. Kei Mori — scholar, economist, engineer, inventor, and master builder—who dedicated himself to creating better environments for people.

Contents

Appendices

Preface

There are many titles used to describe the new office settings designed to incorporate the latest in technologies — the intelligent office, the smart office, the office of the future, the electronically enhanced office, the automated office, the high-tech office. Overuse of these terms has blurred their meaning and burdened them with ambiguity. Yet the understanding of new approaches in office design is critical to the creation of more appropriate settings for present and future office technologies and activities. The "workplace of the future" or the "intelligent office" must be defined as more than the assembly of a long list of new products in telecommunications, electronics, security, automation, and building control systems. Indeed, the "workplace of the future" must provide for unique and changing assemblies of new technologies and work styles in *appropriate physical, environmental, and organizational settings*, to enhance worker speed, understanding, communication, and overall productivity.

In 1988, the Advanced Building Systems Integration Consortium, an industry-university partnership, was established at Carnegie Mellon University, and dedicated to researching and developing the quality of the workplace through the innovative use of advanced technologies. This Consortium has defined a number of activities critical to the development of advanced workplace settings:

- first, anticipating the range of new technologies that will be developed for the workplace;
- second, understanding the physical and environmental responses and controls that will be needed for these technologies;
- third, integrating building systems to provide the necessary spatial, thermal, visual, acoustic, air quality, and long-term integrity; and
- fourth, rethinking the building delivery process to deliver high-performance environments capable of accommodating changing technologies, while maintaining time, cost, and energy effectiveness.

In-depth building studies, viewed from the range of building disciplines, offer a major opportunity to define and compare the performance of advanced office buildings and the impact of advanced technology on these buildings. With a multidisciplinary field team performing two-day studies of intelligent buildings, ABSIC has been able to address such issues as closed versus open offices; three-dimensional cable management; central versus distributed mechanical systems; movable/tether lights and air supply; individual occupant control; and advanced materials and equipment at the workstation. These efforts bridge the normal disciplinary boundaries of architects, engineers, interior planners, and facilities managers — becoming the most critical areas of development needed for the advanced workplace.

The ABSIC building studies began in Japan — in part due to the level of investment that the Japanese building industry is making toward the creation of new office environments. Since 1988, the studies have been pursued in Germany, the United Kingdom, North America, and France. This book, the first in a series of ABSIC publications on the international "Office of the Future," reports the major findings of the multidisciplinary field team in the study of a few key Japanese office buildings. Rather than presenting a survey of the contemporary Japanese office, or its evolution over time, the authors have focused on a selected set of design features — components and integrated systems — that herald innovative future trends and stand the test of occupancy evaluation.

The book is divided into three parts. Part I provides the general approach of the Advanced Building Systems Integration Consortium to the building studies and their use toward the development of advanced products and workplaces. Chapter 1 reports generalized findings from the international buildings studies in four countries. Chapter 2 explains the intellectual framework of the team's approach to defining advanced workplaces, and chapter 3 presents the details of the actual building evaluation process.

Part II begins with an overview of Japanese trends drawn from the in-depth building studies and other building visits, as well as critical readings and discussions with Japanese leaders in intelligent building design. The next four chapters present the selection of innovative components, systems, and processes identified by the multidisciplinary team in four Japanese buildings — Toshiba Headquarters, NTT Twins Regional Headquarters, the ARK Mori Building, and the Umeda Center building. The final chapter of Part II captures glimpses of other Japanese innovations and approaches introduced since the 1988 study, which individual team members have observed in subsequent visits to Japan.

Part III provides a list of major design changes to be introduced into the advanced workplace — a list that will be modified with future building studies. In creating this "environment for innovation," the issue must not be which present technologies should be integrated into the advanced workplace, but which physical, environmental, and organizational settings will best accommodate today's, and tomorrow's, technologies.

VOLKER HARTKOPF
VIVIAN LOFTNESS
PLEASANTINE DRAKE
FRED DUBIN (DECEASED)
PETER MILL
GEORGE ZIGA

Pittsburgh, Pennsylvania
March 1993

Acknowledgments

Just as the design and realization of a building is a team effort, so has been the creation of this book. The authors would like to acknowledge and thank the following team members for their contributions to this project.

The continuing support of the ABSIC industry partners — both financial and intellectual — has been germaine to the success of the international building studies. We thank the corporate members of ABSIC: AMP Incorporated, American Bridge Company/Continental Engineering Corporation, Armstrong World Industries, Bechtel Corporation, Bell of Pennsylvania, Duquesne Light Company, Johnson Controls Incorporated, The Knoll Group, Miles Inc., PPG Industries Incorporated, and Westinghouse Electric Corporation.

We also acknowledge the contributions of other individuals involved in ABSIC: Jim Posner, George Rainer, and Herb Rosenheck. The organization of site visits was managed by Steve Lee and Yoko Tai, aided by Ichinowatari Katsuhiko and Makiko Miwa of Epoch Research Corporation. Simultaneous interpretation during the building studies was performed by Yoko Tai, Michi Kimura, and Noriko Kobayashi.

We thank Anne Garvin for editorial contributions, copyediting, desktop publishing, and coordination of the book production. We thank the staff of John Wiley & Sons, in particular Everett Smethurst and Linda Bathgate. We thank Richard Rush for his encouragement and support of this project. We also thank Paul Mathew for desktop publishing and graphic support, and Susan Cullen, Andrew Booth, Laura Booth, Henry Kim, and Laura Vinchesi for contributions to the project.

We are grateful for the efforts of the Japanese company representatives — listed below — involved in the building studies.

IBM: Takashi Hakka, Facilities Project Specialist; Motosugu Nakatsu, Manager, Real Estate.

LaForêt Engineering & Information Service Co., Ltd: Kei Mori; Koichi Sato, Managing Director; Magoichiro Chatani, Adviser; Peter Siekmeier.

Mori Building Development Co., Ltd.: Minoru Mori, President; Yoshio Kamata, General Manager.

NEC: Yasushi Sakakibara, General Manager; Motozo Kojima; and Kevin Chase.

Nihon Sekkei, Inc.: Takekuni Ikeda, President; Koi Tsukamoto, Senior Engineer; Ki-Chul Kim, Engineer; Tomatsu Taiki.

NOPA: Hideo Minagawa, Secretary General; Shigeya Yoshise, President; Hideaki Ishida, Tooru Kumaki, Tathuo Komori, Akiharu Kioka, Shoji Wakoh, Researchers.

NTT: Kunihiko Yoshida, General Manager; Masao Kimura, Chief Architect, Division Manager; Masahiro Yamagami, Engineer; Sugi Ura; Masanori Nakazawa, Senior Manager; and Kenichi Arakawa, Research Engineer in NTT Human Interface Laboratories.

Shimizu: Tadashige Sengoku, Chief Architect, General Manager; T. Adachi; Yutaka Kamiya; Junichi Yagi; Kazuhiro Yamao; Yanagisawa Yoshimo; Syozo Yoshikawa.

Taisei: Haruo Nabeshima, General Manager.

Takenaka: Masato Ujigawa, Chief Research Engineer; Jota Shimazaki.

Toshiba: Ufo Mohri, Senior Manager; Syoutarou Saitou, Chief Engineer; Katsumi Hiramoto, Facilities Manager; Kenichi Hosaka; Yokoyama.

TRON: Ken Sakamura, Computer Architect.

Uchida Yoko Co., Ltd.: Akio Kondoh, General Manager.

Umeda: Haruhiko Kiji, Deputy Manager.

Other individuals who contributed greatly to this project include Yoshisugu Aoki of Tokyo Institute of Technology; Sugehiro Hosono of Keio University; Kazuo Noda of Japanese Research Institute; Shigeyuki Inubushi of Nippon Univac Kaisha; and Soichiro Okishio of the Science University of Tokyo.

Part I

Part I introduces the major issues that need to be addressed in the Office of the Future, including building performance, systems integration, and the building delivery process.

1

An International Perspective on the Office of the Future

Learning from the Present

This chapter offers a broad brush overview of the international building evaluation studies performed by the authors.

The "intelligent office building" traditionally has been defined by a long list of new products in telecommunications, electronics, security, automation, and building control systems. Although the United States has been a leader in the development and packaging of high-tech products and images, the buildings to house these technologies have not advanced significantly. Indeed, after ten years of use, the original definition of the intelligent building has proven insufficient, given the high-tech work environments anticipated by building owners and building occupants.

A better definition for the intelligent office building would be one that provides for the unique and changing assemblies of recent technologies *in appropriate physical, environmental, and organizational settings*, to enhance worker speed, understanding, communication, and overall productivity (Loftness, Hartkopf, and Mill 1990). Three critical conditions must be met to fit this definition.

First, the intelligent office building must accommodate a compatible package of recent technologies, resolving the full range of hardware for managing external signal propagation; external power; telephone systems; internal signal propagation; computers (capacity, speed, and networking); peripheral "inputters," processors, and "outputters"; environmental management systems; personnel management systems; building management systems, including diagnostics and maintenance automation; and command centers.

Second, the intelligent office building must provide appropriate physical and environmental settings for this hardware. This involves the design of structure; enclosure (walls, windows, roofs); building geometry, including massing, orientation, horizontal and vertical plenum space, and overall spatial organization; major conditioning services such as heating, ventilation, and air conditioning; major support services such as data, voice, power, lighting, and fire protection; and interior elements such as ceilings, partitions, floors, and furniture systems. The 1985 BOSTI study and the 1985 ORBIT-2™ study were the first to identify the building and organizational responses necessary to accommodate intelligent-building products (Brill et al. 1985, Davis et al. 1985).

Third, the intelligent office building must address crucial environmental conditions such as spatial quality, thermal quality, air quality, acoustic quality, visual quality, and building integrity versus rapid degradation (Hartkopf, Loftness, and Mill 1986). The "high-tech" building must provide the appropriate setting to accommodate immediate electronic enhancements, as well as future technologies and the anticipated level of long-term user requirements. The National Academy of Sciences report, "Electronically Enhanced Office Buildings," explores this relationship between intelligent building products and the necessary physical and environmental responses (National Academy of Sciences 1988).

To achieve these three conditions (indeed, these levels of innovation), the design and delivery of an intelligent office building must take an unprecedented series of steps. A long-term mission statement must be written, with expert input, that anticipates the capacity for technological and organizational change. Clear goals for short- and long-term budgets must be formulated. Building design must be delivered through a team decisionmaking process, involving a range of experts (including telecommunications and high-technology HVAC experts as well as facilities managers) from the project's outset. A performance-based design and construction contract with testable specifications must exist, along with a controlled building diagnostics process for quality assurance through design and construction. An expert commissioning stage must follow construction, to fine tune systems and train personnel for long-term expert maintenance and operation. Finally, field evaluation techniques and user questionnaires should be used with increased frequency to assess the overall performance of the integrated system for the building occupancy over time (Loftness, Hartkopf, and Mill 1989).

Most critically, however, the intelligent office building must clearly improve the quality of the workplace for the individual, representing a major philosophical change in office design. After all, what is the electronically enhanced office intended to facilitate, if not the effectiveness, productivity, and well-being of the worker, and the ultimate effectiveness of the organization?

Developing an Evolving List of Major Design Changes

In 1988, the Advanced Building Systems Integration Consortium (ABSIC) was established at Carnegie Mellon University (CMU) to pursue a better understanding of the international advances in commercial building design (ABSIC 1989-1990). A university-industry partnership, the Consortium conducts research, development, and demonstrations for the purpose of increasing the quality and user satisfaction of commercial buildings and integrated building systems, while improving long-term cost, time, and energy effectiveness. The research carried out by the CMU Center for Building Performance and Diagnostics, through the sponsorship and participation of the ABSIC industrial members, is developing new approaches

to the complex system problems that exist in the design, construction, commissioning, and use of future buildings.

The Advanced Building Systems Integration Consortium is built on the foundations of performance, systems integration, and better building delivery processes, as described in chapter 2. Although ABSIC is pursuing a number of major goals ranging from educational programs to demonstration buildings, one of the significant efforts of the Consortium is building an international knowledge base about new developments in office design.

To compile this international knowledge base, the Consortium's building evaluation team has developed field evaluation procedures for the multidisciplinary evaluation of advanced office buildings around the world. To date, fifteen advanced buildings have been studied in depth in four countries (see figure 1.1).

Japan
Umeda Center Building, Osaka
NTT Twins Regional Headquarters, Tokyo
Toshiba Headquarters, Tokyo
ARK Mori Building, Tokyo

Germany
Institute of Applied Microelectronics, Braunschweig
Colonia Insurance Headquarters, Cologne
Nixdorf Regional Offices, Cologne
Daimler-Benz AG Headquarters, Stuttgart

United Kingdom
Lloyd's of London Headquarters, London
United Distillers Headquarters, Edinburgh
Grianan Building, Dundee High Technology Park

North America
York Mills Centre, Toronto, Ontario
TRW, Cleveland, Ohio
Pacific Bell Headquarters, San Ramon, California
Lockheed Building 157, Sunnyvale, California

Figure 1.1 To date, most buildings studied by the ABSIC team were studied in-depth over two days with follow-up, a few in one-day walkthroughs.

Expert walkthroughs (simultaneous and multidisciplinary), field checklists, questionnaires, and simple instrumentation techniques are combined to ensure that the field studies uncover building system innovations that truly improve the quality of the workplace. (Chapter 3 provides details of the field evaluation process.) These studies have led to an evolving list of major changes and trends in office design, contributing to an understanding of new materials, products, and integrations needed for improving office environments over time.

With the input of developments in North America, Germany, the United Kingdom, and Japan, the international studies have added strength to early National Academy of Science findings on changes in the workplace, and have contributed a range of new options for consideration in the design of tomorrow's workplace (see figures 1.2 and 1.3). Although the list of major design changes in the office of the future is still evolving, some general findings in each country are described in the following sections. These international studies are a first step in the university-industry consortium's long-term effort to research, develop, and demonstrate office environments for innovation.

The Advanced Office in North America: A Focus on the Workstation

The greatest developments in advanced office settings in North America center around the workstation (ABSIC, *North American Studies I*, 1990;

Major Design Changes Towards the Electronically Enhanced Office

	Japan				Germany				United Kingdom			N.America	
	Toshiba	NTT	ARK Mori	Umeda	Colonia	Nixdorf	IAM	Diamler-Benz	Lloyd's	Distillers	Grianan	York-Trillium	TRW
1. 3-D cable network	●	●	●	●	●	●	⊕	●	●	●	⊕	●	●
2. Multiple-zone HVAC network	●	●	●	●	●	●	⊕	●	●	⊕	⊕	●	●
3. Increased shared facilities	⊕	⊕		⊕	●	⊕	⊕	⊕	⊕	⊕	⊕	●	●
4. Improved lighting/daylighting control			⊕	⊕	⊕		●	⊕	⊕	⊕	●	⊕	⊕
5. Improved noise/ pollution isolation					⊕		⊕	⊕	●	⊕		⊕	⊕
6. New, redesigned workstations		⊕		●	⊕	⊕	⊕	⊕	●			⊕	●
7. Individualized environmental control		⊕		●	●	⊕	⊕	⊕	●	⊕		●	⊕
8. Effective interior/envelope interface					●		●	●	●	●	⊕	⊕	●
9. More social settings, visual diversity	●	⊕	●	●	●	⊕	●	●	●	⊕			●
10. Management trio with CAFM				⊕	⊕	⊕	⊕	⊕	⊕	⊕			⊕

● Fully implemented   ⊕ Partially implemented

Figure 1.2 The international building studies confirmed the significance of the ten major design changes for the electronic office identified by the National Academy of Sciences report "Electronically Enhanced Office Buildings" (National Academy of Sciences 1988).

ABSIC, *North American Studies II*, 1991). Each individual workstation now includes a vast range of electronic peripherals (phones, personal computers, printers, faxes), which are housed in newer ergonomic and computer-capable furnishing systems and supported by cable management floor systems. Also, for the first time in modern offices, workstations include systems for individual environmental control.

The list of major design changes in the North American office building consistently includes the introduction of a three-dimensional cable network, involving both vertical and horizontal cable distribution plenums. U.S. manufacturers and designers have developed a range of solutions for horizontal distribution, from cable trays overhead, to "poke-throughs," trench systems, and raised floors below. However, further development is needed in flexible and expandable horizontal cable management technologies and their effective connection with the work surface. In addition, building-wide vertical distribution — with inadequate vertical chase space, that is inappropriately located and accessed — has not been satisfactorily considered in the early design stages.

Second, designs have shifted away from four- or five-zone systems with VAV controls, toward multiple-zone HVAC systems with local fan-coils and heat pumps, or at least multiple VAV controls that offer more local variation in temperature delivery. The development of the multiple-zone heating, ventilation, and air conditioning system has instigated a renewed development in individual environmental control technologies for personally setting light, heat, fresh air, and air conditioning levels. The most significant product

Additional Design Directions Identified in the Japanese Advanced Office

	Japan				Germany				United Kingdom			N.America	
	Toshiba	NTT	ARK Mori	Umeda	Colonia	Nixdorf	IAM	Diamler-Benz	Lloyd's	Distillers	Grianan	York-Trillium	TRW
1. 3-D service "trees" estab. before design	●	●	●	●	⊕	⊕	⊕	⊕	●	⊕		●	●
2. "Fresh air architecture"	●	●	●	●	●	●	●	●	●	⊕	⊕		●
3. Resource conservation	●	●	●	●	⊕	⊕	⊕	⊕	⊕	⊕	⊕	⊕	⊕
4. Electronic boardroom (fixed/ mobile)	●	●	●	●	⊕	⊕	⊕	⊕	●				⊕
5. Articulated ceiling for light / sound mgmt.	●	⊕	⊕	⊕	●			⊕	●	⊕		⊕	⊕
6. Accessible floors: "fat" tiles, raised	⊕	⊕	⊕	●	●	●		●	●			●	●
7. Open fire stairs to minimize elevator use	⊕	●	⊕	●	⊕	⊕		⊕	⊕	●	●		●
8. HVAC/PLEC integration w/ envelope	⊕	●	⊕	●	●		●	●	●				
9. Window-washing systems (incl. robotic)	●	●	●	●	⊕		⊕	●	⊕				⊕
10. Interior diagnostic system (incl. robotic)			●					⊕	⊕				⊕

● Fully implemented   ⊕ Partially implemented

Figure 1.3 The Japan studies highlighted additional critical design changes for the "Office of the Future," of significance in other countries as well (ABSIC, Japanese Studies, 1988).

development in this area is the Personal Environments™ system by Johnson Controls, in which fresh air is ducted to each desk in an open office environment, with dimmer controls for cool air, radiant heat, task light, and even white noise (see figure 1.4).

In addition, the American intelligent office is beginning to show the effects of the increased memory capability of personal computers, with mainframe rooms being replaced by minicomputers and microprocessors at every workstation, linked through local area networks. However, the shift away from mainframes and dummy terminals has not diminished the number of shared facilities. Group spaces for printers, fax machines, copiers, electronic conferencing, and socializing have grown.

Finally, there are some indications of a shift in the building design process in North America, toward team decisionmaking to ensure the creation of a truly intelligent office. Most notable is the TRW Headquarters project in Cleveland (see fig-

ure 1.5), where a full-time project manager coordinated a team of peer decisionmakers including exterior architects, interior architects, mechanical engineers, telecommunications engineers, and the building constructor. This design team was fully involved from early conceptual design *through* one year of commissioning to ensure an office headquarters with the latest in technology and the physical and environmental setting needed to support the technology over time.

The Advanced Office in Germany: A Focus on the Shell

Although the ABSIC team's intention was not to highlight polar differences in the international studies, they did find that the German intelligent office designs focused far more on the building shell than on either the core emphasized in Japan or the workstation emphasized in North America (see figure 1.6). Many intelligent office buildings in Germany are shifting toward six- or seven-story buildings (rather than high-rises), with greatly in-

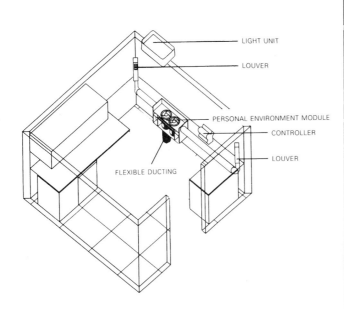

Figure 1.4 Personal Environments™ system by Johnson Controls allows the individual to control light, heat, and fresh air settings.

Figure 1.5 The TRW Headquarters building in Cleveland, Ohio, had a most outstanding team design process, which in no way compromised the aesthetics of the building.

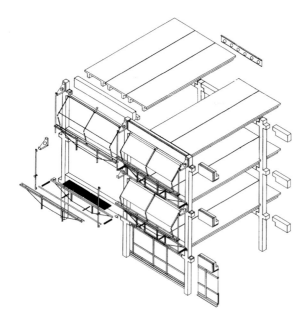

Figure 1.6 The IAM building in Braunschweig, Germany, shows a layered facade for sun control, daylight management, natural vegetation, fire egress, and maintenance. (photo, Schulitz and Partner)

creased exposure to the landscape through campus planning, green atria for social spaces and circulation, and much smaller floor plates.

Design innovations explored in intelligent German office buildings include daylight and artificial light interfaces, as well as management systems such as exterior sunshading devices and distributed lighting controls. Gartner Industries, Siemens, and the Fachhochschule Köln are developing window "lenses" to eliminate glare and to evenly distribute daylight for working light levels deep into office bays. Air flow windows and water-heated framing technologies use waste heat from the highly automated office to minimize energy loads, building degradation, and human discomfort at the envelope (see figure 1.7). The Germans have also explored the interface of mechanical ventilation and operable windows to allow natural ventilation at the workplace. Climate sensors inform the central system and the occupant about the timing for open windows (see figure 1.8). There is increasing interest in natural products, with heightened concern about the use of "unhealthy" building products.

This emphasis on environmental interface has led to a broad range of intelligent office technologies, including distributed lighting systems on movable tethers in the ceiling, and distributed air systems on movable tethers in the floor. The movable air supply ports are fed by central systems with distributed controls or by individual heat pumps. The interest in individual air supply has led to the simultaneous development of raised floor technologies for air and cable management. Early raised floors were acoustic failures (due to vibration, drum, and squeaking sounds). However, new technologies are emerging, including the Schmidt-Reuter "eggcrate" floor system, to provide structural soundness and adequate air and cable management space.

New cabling technologies, new computer technologies, and new desktop peripherals have been developing. However, the German intelligent

Figure 1.7 Water-heated framing technologies by Gartner Industries use waste heat to balance perimeter/core load differences, without compromising aesthetics and view. Exterior glass sunshades reflect daylight onto the ceiling plane for deeper distribution. (photo, Josef Gartner & Co.)

office focuses less on the rapid development of computer hardware and more on providing the vertical and horizontal plenum space and the environmental systems needed for the introduction of future hardware. Indeed the intelligent office concept has fostered unique industry growth — in quiet individual heat pumps, in lighting and shading systems, and in accessible and easily modifiable mechanical and electrical concepts.

In contrast to Japan and the United States, the German building delivery process consistently involves the ultimate users of the building from the project outset. These long-term building users are responsible for directing the German intelligent office toward "fresh air architecture." As a result, a high-quality work environment for each individual is pursued, with more individual or small group offices, and direct access to daylight, fresh air, and landscaped gardens and courts (ABSIC, *German Studies*, 1989).

Figure 1.8 Colonia Insurance responded to occupant desires for operable windows by reducing building height and redesigning HVAC controls to allow natural ventilation.

The Advanced Office in the United Kingdom: A Focus on Material and Detail for Aesthetic and Performance Qualities

The United Distillers, the Grianan, and the Lloyd's of London office buildings in the United Kingdom revealed a fascination with material and detail for their aesthetic qualities, justified through potentially higher performance qualities.

In all three buildings, the designers selected a restricted number of high-integrity materials — lead for roofs, stone, stainless steel, aluminum, glass, and natural woods — to create an enduring modern aesthetic. Working with the manufacturers, the designers developed the material and component details critical to ensuring immediate high-performance quality and long-term integrity. Once details were resolved and appropriately integrated with other systems, the architects maximized the visibility of these select materials and details, through highly articulated building forms and interior cutouts (courts and atria), toward increasing overall surface exposure as well as daylight accessibility.

A very significant development in the United Kingdom is the engineering expressionism demonstrated in the Lloyd's of London building, designed to ensure accessibility and expandability of servicing systems in order to accommodate major changes in technology. Each subsystem — mechanical supply and return, electrical, telecommunication, and transportation — is run independently on the exterior of the building. These exposed service cores create the building aesthetic and its long-term adaptability (see figure 1.9), and are reminiscent of the large, accessible interior cores in Japan and Germany, though far more expressive and expandable.

Interior design in Lloyd's also demonstrates the selected use of high-quality materials and well-resolved details, with performance as a justification. Highly engineered ceiling insets provide glareless light and individual control in a heavily automated workplace, high acoustic absorption with modest sound reflection, and effective return air in a very high density workplace. Air flow windows were engineered for using waste heat to minimize poor mean radiant temperatures and condensation at the envelope. This technology too was used to provide an aesthetic both inside and out, with supply and return ducts exposed on the facade.

Finally, the significant cultural and political tradition in the U.K. in the form of "right-to-light" laws continues to positively affect the design of modern high-tech buildings (see figure 1.10). Workstations are designed with direct visual access to windows; building depths are controlled; and courts and atria are designed to maximize sun-

Figure 1.10 England has traditionally valued daylight access for the workplace, as shown in the United Distillers Headquarters.

Figure 1.9 Lloyd's has the mechanical and telecommunications cores on the outside of the building, in recognition that these systems require greater access, change, and growth.

Figure 1.11 The Grianan building provides glare-free daylight with inwardly sloping glass and upwardly sloping ceilings.

Results of a British Study on Building Sickness

Building Code No.	Sickness Score*	Organization	Ventilation	Humidity Controls	Openable Windows	Tinted Glazing	Age	% in 1-2 Person Offices	% Clerical Staff
HEALTHIEST BUILDINGS OF THOSE STUDIES									
081	1.25	Private	Mechanical	●	Yes	No	1980's (refurb)	95	22
141	1.52	Private	Mechanical	●	Yes	No	1980's	90	43
021	1.53	Public	Natural	●	Yes	No	1950's	80	73
053	1.54	Private	Natural	●	Yes	No	1960's	20	38
151	1.63	Private	Natural	●	Yes	No	1920's	65	23
HEALTHIEST AIR-CONDITIONED BUILDINGS OF THOSE STUDIES									
211	2.12	Private	VAV	Steam	Yes	No	1980's	50	27
051	2.25	Private	VAV	●	Yes	No	1980's	30	14
251	2.60	Private	VAV	Evaporative	No	No	1980's	90	60
LEAST HEALTHY BUILDINGS OF THOSE STUDIES									
161	4.25	Public	Induction	Spray	No	Yes	1970's	12	23
102	4.29/72	Public/ Private	Induction	●	No	Yes	1970's	20/30	60/64
141	4.76	Public	VAV	Spray	No	Yes	1970's	9	45
293	4.91	Public	Induction	Spray	No	Yes	1970's	1	93
291	5.08	Public	VAV	Spray	No	Yes	1970's	1	86

* sickness score = mean number of symptoms, out of ten, complained of per person in building

Figure 1.12 British studies reveal occupancy concerns about sealed, air-conditioned buildings with reflective glass (Wilson and Hedge 1987).

light penetration (with "cones" of sunlight such as in the United Distillers Headquarters). Clear glass with overhangs continues to be the norm. The two-story Grianan building in the speculative Dundee High Technology Park effectively provides working daylight for deeper open office areas through the use of clear glass, sloped inward to the sill, and a corresponding upwardly sloped ceiling (see figure 1.11). These examples build on the tradition in the U.K. of using daylight as the primary source of working light in shallow-plan buildings.

The United Kingdom also continues to show interest in passive solar designs for heating, cooling, and lighting commercial buildings. There is some speculation that the U.K. will enter a period of sealed, air-conditioned buildings and reflective glass, in response to global warming trends and greatly increased internal heat gains. However, this trend is already being challenged by building research groups (see figure 1.12) and by the office workers who presently benefit from access to windows, clear views, and sunshine.

One can argue that "aesthetics" dominated the system design process at some point, leaving weaknesses in the independent or integrated performance of components. Nonetheless, major lessons can be learned from the careful and limited selection of materials (including daylight), as well as the careful resolution of details and integrations (with the support of industry), toward creating durable and flexible settings for increasing and ever-changing electronics (ABSIC, *U.K. Studies*, 1989).

The Advanced Office in Japan:
A Focus on the Core

When looking at Japanese intelligent office buildings (including the Toshiba Headquarters, the NTT Twins Regional Headquarters, the ARK Mori Building, and the Umeda Center Building), it is clear that the advanced design of the building core and its servicing systems has been emphasized rather than workstations or building enclosures.

One major intelligent design change in the Japanese office building is a rethinking of the 3-D cable network, as in the United States. However, the vertical distribution is far better resolved through distributed cores than the horizontal distribution, which is often excessively confined in trenches and thin raised floor plenums. The assumption appears to be that the workstation arrangement will remain static, while the workstation hardware will change.

The use of multiple-zone HVAC has also been embraced in the Japanese office, but through distributed mechanical systems rather than space-by-space mixing devices. The distribution of mechanical rooms varies from one every three floors, to four per floor, providing for more thermal variation and control in the constantly changing office setting.

The Japanese have significantly developed technologies for resource conservation (energy, water, and air) including gray water management, thermoelectric cooling, load balancing, and off-peak storage. There is also far-reaching development of systems for fire and earthquake management, and systems for vertical transportation (elevator and "communicating" fire stairs), all located in the carefully planned core.

Most unprecedented are the developments in post-occupancy robotics, ranging in use from continuous environmental testing of temperature, air quality, and noise, to unmanned window-washing systems.

Japan is a leader in team decisionmaking. The design process encourages team decision strategies from the outset, between architects, engineers, constructors, and facilities managers. A missing link, however, is the organized introduction of occupant input into workstation design and servicing and into individual environmental requirements for light, heat, air, and sound control.

Part II of this book will clarify these claims about the Japanese emphasis in new office design, as well as provide additional insights into the Japanese approach to tomorrow's buildings. But first, the following two chapters will present the conceptual framework for field evaluations and the process by which the field team conducts its international evaluations of advanced workplaces.

References

(ABSIC, *German Studies*, 1989)
ABSIC, *German Building Studies*, research report presented at the February 14, 1989, meeting of the Advanced Building Systems Integration Consortium, Pittsburgh, PA.

(ABSIC, *Japanese Studies*, 1988)
ABSIC, *Japanese Building Studies*, research report presented at the October 4, 1988, meeting of the Advanced Building Systems Integration Consortium, Pittsburgh, PA.

(ABSIC, *North American Studies I*, 1990)
ABSIC, *North American Building Studies I*, research report presented at the May 30, 1990, meeting of the Advanced Building Systems Integration Consortium, Pittsburgh, PA.

(ABSIC, *North American Studies II*, 1991)
ABSIC, *North American Building Studies II*, research report presented at the March 6, 1991, meeting of the Advanced Building Systems Integration Consortium, Pittsburgh, PA.

(ABSIC, *U.K. Studies*, 1989)
ABSIC, *U.K. Building Studies*, research report presented at the July 20, 1989, meeting of the Advanced Building Systems Integration Consortium, Milwaukee, WI.

(ABSIC 1989-1990)
"The ABSIC Mission," *ABSIC News*, No.2, 1989-1990.

(Brill et al., 1985)
Brill, M., with S. Margulis, E. Konar, and BOSTI, in association with Westinghouse Furniture Systems, *Using Office Design to Increase Productivity*, Vol. 1. Buffalo: Workplace Design and Productivity, Inc., 1985.

(Davis et al., 1985)
Davis, G., F. Becker, F. Duffy, and W. Sims, *ORBIT-2™ Overview Report*, Norwalk: Harbinger Group, Inc., 1985.

(Loftness, Hartkopf, and Mill 1989)
Loftness, V., V. Hartkopf, and P. Mill, "Critical Frameworks for Building Evaluation: Total Building Performance, Systems Integration, and Levels of Measurement and Assessment," in *Building Evaluation*, New York: Plenum Press, 1989.

(Loftness, Hartkopf, and Mill 1990)
Loftness, V., V. Hartkopf, and P. Mill, "The Intelligent Office," *Progressive Architecture*, September 1990.

(Hartkopf, Loftness, and Mill 1986)
Hartkopf, V., V. Loftness, and P. Mill, "The Concept of Total Building Performance and Building Diagnostics," in *Building Performance: Function, Preservation, and Rehabilitation*, Philadelphia: ASTM, STP 901, 1986.

(National Academy of Sciences 1988)
National Academy of Sciences, Building Research Board, *Electronically Enhanced Office Buildings*, a joint report by the Committee on Technologically Advanced Buildings and the Committee on High Technology Systems for Buildings, Washington, DC: National Research Council, 1988.

(Wilson and Hedge 1987)
Wilson, S., and A. Hedge, *The Office Environment Survey: A Study of Building Sickness*, London: Building Use Studies Ltd., 1987.

2

A Framework for Designing and Managing the Office of the Future

This chapter presents the basic tenets of the professional research team toward defining advanced work environments as distinct from "equipped" workplaces.

The early efforts at widespread office automation recognized the cost of the technologies but not the cost of the necessary connectivity, the result being a shockingly underestimated total cost for automation, as shown in figure 2.1 (Wall Street Journal 1987). Moreover, these estimates still do not include the costs of the physical and environmental responses needed for a truly productive office automation effort. Owners and designers collectively must recognize that office automation includes not only the planned introduction of new peripheral technologies, but also the modification of the physical and environmental settings to accommodate those technologies (figure 2.2) (Mill, Hartkopf, and Loftness 1986).

Indeed, the Office of the Future must emphasize three specific areas beyond the introduction of new electronic products:

1. a definition of the critical environmental performance qualities needed in today's intelligent workplace;
2. the systems integration needed to achieve these performance qualities; and
3. the changes in the building delivery process needed to ensure integration for performance.

By incorporating these three conditions, the Office of the Future will provide for "unique and changing assemblies of recent technologies and work styles in *appropriate* physical, environmental, and organizational settings, to enhance worker satisfaction, understanding, communication, and overall productivity" (ABSIC 1989-1990).

The Total Cost of a PC

Based on 100 personal computers shared by 300 users	ANNUAL COST PER PC
Hardware ($5,000 system amortized over 3 years)	$1,667
Software	1,200
Technical support (2 people for a total of $80,000)	800
General support (1 person at $40,000 for every 50 users)	2,400
Diskettes (100 diskettes per user annually)	900
Other supplies (paper, ribbons, etc.)	180
Maintenance	300
Total annual cost per computer	**$7,447**

•Source: Nolan, Norton & Co.

The Price of Networking

Based on annual costs on a 40-computer, local area network, excluding cost of personal computers	ANNUAL COST PER PC
Hardware and software and installation	$ 567
Startup planning and analysis	823
Systems management	2,708
User training	2,812
Unproductive time	1,800
Total annual cost per computer	**$8,710**

•Source:Ferrix Corp.

Figure 2.1 The "connectivity" or networking of peripherals costs as much as the new technologies themselves (Wall Street Journal, June 12, 1987. ©1987 Dow Jones & Co., Inc.). The authors contend that physical and environmental modifications necessary to accommodate these new technologies will cost yet again an equal amount.

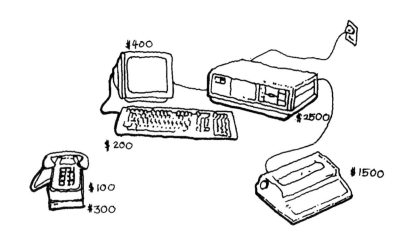

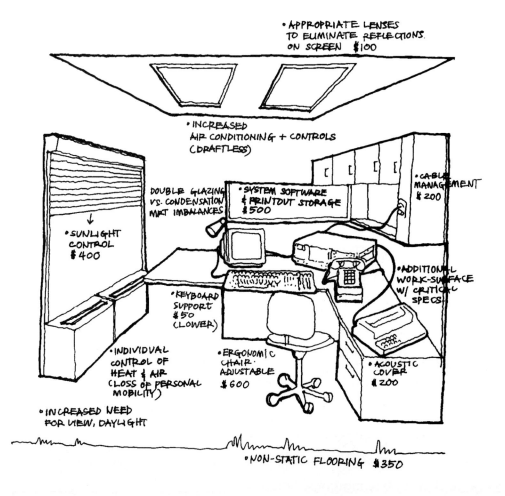

Figure 2.2 Office automation is not just the planned introduction of new "peripherals," but the necessary modification of the physical and environmental settings. (sketch, Azizan Aziz)

Problems In Existing Work Environments and the Impact of New Technology

In extensive commercial building performance evaluations, the Architectural and Building Sciences Directorate of Public Works Canada, under the direction of Peter Mill, repeatedly found the following serious problems in occupied buildings (Public Works Canada 1983):

- spatial problems of cabling, storage, privacy, and wayfinding;

- acoustic problems of people and equipment, untempered (if not amplified) by building interiors;

- thermal problems of excessive heat, of unbalanced mean radiant temperatures, of local controls not adjusted for the occupancy, and of local sensors not corresponding with local controls (due to frequent spatial/layout changes);

- air quality problems due to low air changes per hour for energy conservation, outgassing from materials and equipment, and short-circuiting from air supply to air return above poorly designed interior systems; and

- visual problems of glare, brightness contrast, and flicker from overpowering arrays of light fixtures and unmanaged windows.

These conditions affect workers to various degrees of seriousness, depending on occupant activity and sensitivity. The composite of these problems contributes to building-related illnesses and to concerns regarding the "sick building syndrome."

Imagine, then, what happens when extensive office automation is added to the picture. If current centrally managed environmental control systems have not successfully coped with major changes in building functions and occupancies, or rapid changes in exterior environmental conditions (such as the sun coming out), these systems certainly will fail in the face of new and ever-changing office

automation loads. Indeed, performance problems such as those identified in figure 2.3 are significantly worse in the high-tech workplace (Mill, Hartkopf, and Loftness 1986). Even in office settings that are effectively designed for their specific occupancies and functions, the introduction of office electronics creates unexpected stresses, de-

Spatial quality problems	• Tripping, ducking cables and cable changes • Pile-ups of print-out and computer peripherals • Work surface now covered by equipment • Neck strain from screens on conventional desk • Tired arms, backache from keyboards on desk • Sitting long hours in "dining room" chairs
Visual quality problems	• Glare from windows without controls • Reflections of light fixtures/windows on screens • Coping with contrast ratios (from black-on-white text, to white-on-black screen) • Headaches, eyestrain from focusing on screen
Thermal quality problems	• Overheating from equipment, hotspots (500-1000 W each) • Radiant heat effect near equipment • No heat, air when high partitioning is introduced
Air quality problems	• Outgassing from some equipment and wiring • No control of fresh air, removed from windows (because of glare) • Need for more environmental change and control owing to reduced mobility
Acoustic quality problems	• Printers without acoustic covers (sold separately) • Annoyance from some keyboards (clicks) and disk drives (whirrs) • Modified mechanical systems with greater noise • Future voice-activated technologies
Building integrity problems	• Unanticipated weight of equipment and paper • Heightened need for dust-free environment

Figure 2.3 Common performance problems in the electronic workplace.

manding a greatly improved understanding of the environmental quality needed by the office worker.

The most common performance problem in the electronic office is glare. Arrays of ceiling light fixtures are often superimposed on the computer screen. Uncontrolled sunshine reflects off computer screens and paper, or shines into the eyes of the typist. However, eliminating the window — which offers visual relief, a sense of time and environmental dynamics, and contributes to air and thermal quality — is an unacceptable solution in our increasingly immobile jobs.

Spatial quality also suffers in most electronic offices. Extensive cabling on the floor makes tripping inevitable and mobility difficult, while cabling from the ceiling is typically unsightly. Rarely can the available work surface accommodate the terminal, screen, printer, modem, fax, and the papers and personal belongings of the worker, not to mention the reams of printout stacked around the desk of a serious computer user. Poor spatial and ergonomic decisionmaking can result in muscular problems (e.g., carpel tunnel syndrome), especially when conventional desk heights are maintained. Trapping the worker in more constrained sitting positions, the conventional workstation's low screens cause neckaches and raised keyboards cause wrist, arm, and back problems.

Acoustic quality, thermal quality, and air quality also suffer significantly in the electronic office, given that they were already poor in most conventional open office areas. Even building integrity is a concern, due to continuous recabling, additional loads on the structure and the material finishes, and due to the heightened need for dust- and static-free environments.

Buildings must be conceived as totally integrated and dynamic systems. From the very first conceptual ideas, building design and subsequent management must ensure that the final integrated setting is continually responsive to the increasingly variable and stressful needs of the office worker.

Design for Total Building Performance

A Discrete Number of Critical Performance Qualities

To create the high-quality setting needed for worker productivity and user satisfaction, it is necessary to define a manageable list of critical performance qualities for office environments — for their evaluation, programming, design, construction, maintenance, and use. Significant precedent has been set in defining a discrete list of building performance requirements, by the National Bureau of Standards (GSA *Peach Book* 1975), Centre Internationale de Batiment (CIB 1982), and International Standards Organization (ISO 1980; ISO 1981). Figures 2.4a and 2.4b offer examples of such lists. To provide a manageable list of discrete criteria, however, six performance qualities, based on the fundamental human senses and their protection over time, could capture the performance qualities we want to find in the workplace today:

1. spatial quality,
2. thermal quality,
3. air quality,
4. acoustic quality,
5. visual quality, and
6. building integrity over time.

First, there are a series of mandates relating to interior occupancy requirements (human, animal, plant, artifact, machine) and their elemental needs for health, safety, and welfare (comfort and protection for the five senses in the case of human occupancies).

In addition, there has been a fundamental mandate over the centuries for building integrity, or the protection of the building's appearance and critical properties from degradation through moisture, temperature shifts, air movement, radiation, chemical and biological attack, human attack, and natural disasters (fire, flood, earthquake). Established by concerns for health, safety, welfare, resource management, and image, the requirements for building integrity are bound by

						1. STRUCTURE	2. HVAC	3. ELECTRICAL DISTRIBUTION	4. LUMINAIRES	5. FINISHED FLOOR	6. FINISHED CEILING	7. SPACE DIVIDERS
	BUILDING PROCESS	QUALIFYING										
		MANUFACTURE						*THE PROCESS*				
		SHIPPING										
		CONSTRUCTION										
SUPPORT						**BUILT ELEMENTS: HARDWARE**						
LIFE	TASK	PYSCHOLOGICAL										
			ATTRIBUTES	CONDITIONED AIR	A							
				ILLUMINATION	B							
	THE USER			ACOUSTICS	C			*BUILDING "IN USE"*				
				STABILITY AND DURABILITY	D							
				HEALTH & SAFETY	E							
				MAINTENANCE	F							
				PLANNING	G							

Figure 2.4a   Significant precedent toward defining building performance requirements includes this table from the National Institute of Standards and Technology (GSA Peach Book 1975).

limits of "acceptable" degradation—ranging from slight decay (of the building's visual, mechanical, and physical properties), to debilitation in the ability to provide weathertightness or environmental conditioning for the function (Lemer and Moavenzadeh 1972), to total devastation.

For the office environment, therefore, "total building performance" is the simultaneous provision of these five qualities, and the provision of building integrity for the integrated "system" over time, as outlined in figure 2.5 (Hartkopf, Loftness, and Mill, *Building Performance,* 1986). The programming, design, construction, and operation of buildings for total building performance is intended to ensure the immediate suitability of the integrated setting for the building occupancies and functions (all performance qualities); the long-term reliability of the integrated setting to perform as intended through the life of the facility (given appropriate maintenance and use); and the long-term adaptability to accommodate changing functions and occupancies, toward maintaining suitability throughout the building's life-cycle.

**Performance Standards in Building —
Principles and Factors to be Considered**

I.   USER REQUIREMENTS
    A.   Stability
    B.   Fire Safety
    C.   Safety in Use
    D.   Tightness
    E.   Hydro-Thermal
    F.   Air Purity
    G.   Acoustical
    H.   Visual
    I.   Tactile
    J.   Anthropodynamic
    K.   Hygiene
    L.   Suitability of Spaces for Specific Uses
    M.   Durability
    N.   Economic

II.   SUB-SYSTEMS OF THE BUILDING FABRIC
    A.   Structure
    B.   External Envelope
    C.   Spatial Dividers Outside the Envelope
    D.   Spatial Dividers Inside the Envelope
    E.   Services (water, HVAC, PLEX, transport, protection)

Figure 2.4b   The International Standards Organization established another definition of critical building performance requirements (ISO 1980).

Total Building Performance

I.   SPATIAL QUALITY
    A.   Workstation Layout
    B.   Workgroup Layout
    C.   Conveniences and Services
    D.   Amenities
    E.   Occupancy Factors and Controls

II. THERMAL QUALITY
    A.   Air Temperature
    B.   Mean Radiant and extreme radiant temperature
    C.   Humidity
    D.   Air Speed
    E.   Occupancy Factors and Controls

III. AIR QUALITY
    A.   Fresh Air
    B.   Fresh Air Distribution
    C.   Restriction of Mass Pollution — gases, vapors, micro-organisms, fumes, smokes, dusts
    D.   Restriction of Energy Pollution — ionizing radiation, microwaves, radio waves, light waves, infrared
    E.   Occupancy Factors and Controls

IV. ACOUSTIC QUALITY
    A.   Sound Source — Sound Pressure Levels and Frequency
    B.   Sound Source — Background Noise
    C.   Sound Path — Noise Isolation (air and structureborne)
    D.   Sound Path — Sound Distribution; absorption, reflection, uniformity, reverberation
    E.   Occupancy Factors and Controls

V.   VISUAL QUALITY
    A.   Ambient Light Levels — artificial and daylight
    B.   Task Light Levels — artificial and daylight
    C.   Contrast and Brightness Ratios
    D.   Color Rendition
    E.   View, visual information
    F.   Occupancy Factors and Controls

VI. BUILDING INTEGRITY
    A.   Quality of Mechanical/Structural Properties — compression, tension, shear, abuse
    B.   Quality of Physical/Chemical Properties — watertightness, airtightness transmission, reflection, absorption of heat, light and sound energy, fire safety
    C.   Visible Properties — color, texture, finish, form, durability, maintainability based on knowledge of loads, moisture conditions, temperature shifts, air movement, radiation conditions, biological attack, man-made and natural disasters

Acceptable Limits for Environmental Quality in the Workplace

Codes and standards are the traditional guarantee of environmental quality in the workplace, embracing certain aspects of spatial, thermal, air, visual, and acoustic quality, as well as building integrity. However, these limits of acceptability present some severe shortcomings. First, they focus primarily on physiological (health, safety) limits of acceptability. Second, the standards are set, measured, and assessed for one performance quality at a time, whereas the occupant senses all environmental qualities simultaneously. Third, they do not quickly reflect state-of-the-art understanding of conditions below which spatial quality, thermal quality, visual quality, acoustic quality, and building integrity are known to be unacceptable.

Today, limits of acceptability for environmental quality can be discussed in terms of physiological, psychological, sociological, and economic (resource) needs of the occupants and surrounding community (see figure 2.6). With regard to human occupancy, physiological requirements aim to ensure health and safety, protection against such conditions as fire, building collapse, poisonous fumes, high and low temperatures, and poor light. Psychological requirements aim to support the individual's mental health through appropriate provisions for privacy, interaction, status, and change. Sociological requirements (also termed socio-cultural requirements) aim to support the well-being of the community within which the individuals act, relating the needs of the individuals to those of the collective. Finally, economic requirements aim to allocate resources in the most efficient manner with the overall goal to serve user needs within the wider social context.

Figure 2.5 It is critical to define a discrete number of building performance qualities to be achieved in design (Hartkopf, Loftness, and Mill, The Building Systems Integration Handbook, ©1991, The American Institute of Architects, Reproduced with permission under license number 91069. ALL RIGHTS RESERVED).

Organizing Performance Criteria for Evaluating the Integration of Systems

	PHYSIOLOGICAL NEEDS	PSYCHOLOGICAL NEEDS	SOCIOLOGICAL NEEDS	ECONOMIC NEEDS
	PERFORMANCE CRITERIA SPECIFIC TO CERTAIN HUMAN SENSES, IN THE INTEGRATED SYSTEM			
SPATIAL QUALITY	Ergonomic comfort handicap access functional servicing	Habitability, beauty, calm, excitement, view	Wayfinding, functional adjacencies	Space conservation
THERMAL QUALITY	No numbness, frost-bite, no drowsiness, heat stroke	Sense of warmth, individual control	Flexibility to dress with the custom	Energy conservation
AIR QUALITY	Air purity; no lung problems, no rashes, cancers, no outgassing	Healthy plants, not closed in or stuffy, no synthetics	No irritation from neighbors, smoke, smells	Energy conservation
ACOUSITICAL QUALITY	No hearing damage, music enjoyment speech clarity	Quiet, soothing, or active, exciting "alive"	Privacy, communication	First costs
VISUAL QUALITY	No glare, good task illumination, way-finding, no fatigue	Orientation, cheer-fulness, calm, inti-mate/spacious, alive	Status of window, daylit office "sense of territory"	Energy conservation
BUILDING INTEGRITY	Fire safety; struct. strength+stability; weathertightness	Durability, sense of stability, image	Status/appearance quality of construction "craftsmanship"	Material / labor conservation
	PERFORMANCE CRITERIA GENERAL TO ALL HUMAN SENSES, IN THE INTEGRATED SYSTEM			
	Physical comfort Health Safety Function Appropriateness	Psychological comfort Mental health Psychological safety Aesthetics Delight	Privacy Security Community Image/status	Space conservation Material conservation Time conservation Energy conservation Money conservation

Figure 2.6 Standards should be set for these key building performance qualities to address the physiological, psychological, sociological, and economic needs of the occupant (Hartkopf, Loftness, and Mill, The Building Systems Integration Handbook, ©1991 The American Institute of Architects. Reproduced with permission under license number 91069. ALL RIGHTS RESERVED).

Integrate Building Systems for Total Building Performance

For the most part, successes and failures in building environments are not the result of individual components or assemblies but of the effectiveness of those components within their integrated setting. An acoustic ceiling system may have excellent noise reduction (NRC) ratings, but be rendered ineffective by the extensive introduction of flush lens light fixtures, plastered ceiling areas for decorative effect, or fresh paint applied in routine maintenance. Similarly, the cost and success of an office automation effort lie not only with the selection of desktop hardware, but with the associated modification of other systems that form the integrated, physical, and environmental setting.

Just as a manageable list of performance mandates is needed, so is a manageable but comprehensive list of building systems and subsystems. At a minimum, one should consider five basic system groups: structural systems; envelope or enclosure systems; interior systems; mechanical/electrical systems; and telecommunication systems (Hartkopf, Loftness, and Mill, *Handbook*, 1986). The impact of various subsystem decisions on building performance must be understood (see figure 2.7 and expert checklists in Appendix A). More significantly, however, the impact of the *integration* of various systems on building performance must be pursued (see figure 2.8), and the building delivery process must be modified to ensure the necessary integrated, multidisciplinary decision-making.

Examples of Envelope System Design Decisions Affecting Performance

ENVELOPE	SPATIAL QUALITY	THERMAL QUALITY	AIR QUALITY	ACOUSTIC QUALITY	VISUAL QUALITY	BUILDING INTEGRITY
Wall / roof / exterior floor						
Exterior surface, material properties		○				●
Composite materials, thickness	●	○	○	○		●
Interior surface	○	○	○	●	●	○
Form: planar, curved	●	○		●	○	○
Slope, orientation	●	○		●	●	○
Module size, shape	●	○				●
Connection to other envelope components	○	●	○	○		●
Windows / openings						
Material properties	●	●		●	●	●
Size, shape, spacing	●	●	●	○	●	
Orientation		●	●	○	●	○
Control systems, sunshading	○	●		○	●	●
Control systems, heat loss		●				○
Control systems, ventilation	○	●	●		○	●
Frame connections, plan / section	○	●	○	○	●	●
Access, visual and physical	●	○	○		●	●
Expansion potential (vert / horiz.)	○				○	
Change potential for access and image	○				○	○
Color, texture, ornament	○		○		●	●

● Critical implications for the delivery of this performance mandate

○ Some implication for the delivery of this performance mandate

Figure 2.7 Total building performance is affected by the design and specifications of subsystem components and assemblies, as idenified in relation to enclosure decisions here (Hartkopf, Loftness, and Mill, The Building Systems Integration Handbook, ©1991, The American Institute of Architects. Reproduced with permission under license number 91069. ALL RIGHTS RESERVED).

The performance of a system cannot be studied or developed in isolation from other systems, or from the building occupancies and their sensitivities. Consequently, the framework for design innovation must demonstrate expertise in all of the system areas, their generic choices, and their history of performance in the integrated setting.

Designing for Office Automation Within the Integrated Setting

Whether the focus of a particular product or building design is a single performance agenda, such as visual quality, or a single subsystem design, such as the lighting system, the designer must resolve the introduction of new office technologies within the integrated setting. Yet, the task of defining the subset components of new office automation technologies, their interrelationships with other systems, and the generic design alternatives is not a trivial one. For example, the common focus of office automation studies is the impact of the peripherals that sit on the worker's desk. Although some studies may broaden to look at mainframes and even cabling architecture, few of them look at the full range of office automation technologies that exist in the intelligent office (National Academy of Sciences 1988). Moreover, the impact of these office automation technologies must be studied in relation to the other building systems forming the physical and environmental setting. It is in this realistic "morass" of integrated systems that one finds the critical conditions for success and failure in the occupied setting.

First, the high-performance office building must assemble a flexible and adaptable package of recent technologies, resolving the full range of hardware for managing: 1) external signal propagation; 2) external power; 3) telephone systems; 4) internal signal propagation; 5) computers — capacity,

Examples of Integrated Decisionmaking Critical to Performance

Integrate Mechanical and Interior Systems for :

SPATIAL QUALITY	• service module for present use and flexibility • space volume and ceiling height, functional identity • individual space layout, compartmentalization & flexibility • suitable servicing to individual space and aggregated space • expansion and change potential • individual control/space management
THERMAL QUALITY	• balanced mean radiant temperatures • air distribution, heating and cooling effectiveness, comfort • humidity impact on interior components • volume to be heated, stratification • mechanical efficiency from source to task
AIR QUALITY	• fresh air distribution effectiveness • flushing vs. outgassing • protection from radiant pollution • individual control, compartmentalization vs. pollution migration
ACOUSTICAL QUALITY	• background noise coordinated with appropriate room absorption • minimization of mechanical noise disturbance • minimization of vibration disturbance • effective acoustical compartmentalization around mechanical components
VISUAL QUALITY	• adequate light distribution balance • mechanical components for lighting dispersion, reflection • integration for space/function identity • lighting efficiency from source to task • flexibility potential • individual control, compartmentalization
BUILDING INTEGRITY	• humidity and temperature controls to support components, machines and comfort • staining and dirt buildup on interior from mechanical • vibration disturbance/destruction • mechanical accessibility, maintenance and repair • fire safety

Figure 2.8 Total building performance is also affected by the integration of these subsystem components and assemblies, as shown here for mechanical and interior system interfaces (Hartkopf, Loftness, and Mill, The Building Systems Integration Handbook, ©1991, The American Institute of Architects. Reproduced with permission under license number 91069. ALL RIGHTS RESERVED).

speed, and networking; 6) peripheral "inputters," processors, and "outputters"; 7) environmental controls and energy management; 8) security and fire safety systems; and 9) transport systems (see figures 2.9 and 2.10).

Then, the intelligent office building must ensure the appropriate physical and environmental set- tings for the range of hardware anticipated, thereby resolving the level of adaptability needed in each of the major building subsystems: 1) structure; 2) enclosure, including walls, windows, roofs, basement; 3) building geometry, from massing to orientation to horizontal and vertical plenum space to overall spatial organization; 4) major heating, ventilation, and air-conditioning services; 5) ma-

**Sets of Technological Choices for the
High-tech Building**

I.   EXTERNAL SIGNAL PROPAGATION
     (Outside Communication Links)
     A. Microwave
     B. Satellite (dishes)
     C. Copper Wire Networks
        (Landline: copper T-1,coax, 'campus')
     D. Fiber-optic Network
     E. Two-way Radio
     F. Public Network Interfacers, Multiplexers

II. EXTERNAL POWER
     A. Capacity (two grids, additional, cogeneration)
     B. Quality (grounding, spikes, interference)
     C. Reliability (UPS)

III. CONTROL SYSTEMS
     A. EMCS
     B. Fire/Life Safety
     C. Vertical transport
     D. Security
     E. Lighting
     F. Personnel Management

IV. TELEPHONE SYSTEM
     A. PBX
     B. Key
     C. Centrex

V.   INTERNAL SIGNAL PROPAGATION
     (Cabling Network for Inside Communication Link)
     A. Copper Twisted Pairs
        Flat Wire — Non twisted Cable
     B. Coaxial Cables
     C. Fiber-optic Cables
     D. Universal Wiring
     E. Wireless — Radio Frequencies
     F. Multiplexers, Concentrators
     G. Termination Hardware, Ground Cables
     H. Architecture: LAN — Hardware and Software
     I. Wire Management — Hardware and Software
     J. ISDN, Smart Wiring

VI. COMPUTERS AND NETWORKING
     A. Mainframes and Super Mainframes
     B. Minis and Super Minis
     C. Micros and Super (enhanced) Micros
     D. Controllers
     E. Architecture

VII. PERIPHERALS AND NETWORKING
     A. Inputters (data, voice, video/graphics,
        environmental sensors)
     B. Processors
        (read/process, compute, file/store, transfer)
     C. Outputters (tapes/disks, printers, plotters,
        projectors, voice, commands)
     D. Services & Service Architecture
        (e.g., electronic mail, video teleconferencing,
        electronic data base services, security)

VIII. COMMAND CENTERS
     A. InformationTechnology Management
        Center; Computer Aided Wire Management
     B. Energy/Facilities Management Center
        with CAFM Capability
     C. Personnel/Technology Training Center

jor power, lighting, electronics, and communication services; and 6) interior elements such as ceilings, partitions, floors, and furniture systems (see figure 2.10).

In the intelligent office building, these two sets of physical components should be designed and evaluated not only independently but also in their integrated state, to ensure that all crucial environmental qualities are provided — spatial, thermal, visual, acoustic, and air quality as well as long-term building integrity (see figure 2.10). The usefulness of this framework for high-performance design innovation has been tested both through the field studies in part II of this book and through the development of new major design concepts for the Office of the Future, described in part III.

Develop a Team Building Delivery Process with Follow Through

Performance failures can result from decisions made at any stage in the building delivery process that reduce the alternatives for each succeeding stage, such that the final product has less chance for success. This concept might be titled "stress factors" or the introduction of decisions in one stage of the building delivery process that significantly narrow the range and success of possible decisions in successive stages. This narrowing of alternatives ultimately affects the delivery of suitable spatial, thermal, air, acoustic, and visual quality, as well as long-term building integrity. Indeed, a major percentage of the performance failures that occur in buildings results from stress factors introduced at the design conception stage of the project. If the range of professionals involved in the building delivery process are unable to contribute to early conceptual design ideas, it becomes increasingly difficult for each succeeding decisionmaker to ensure performance. The lack of adequate front-end knowledge-building and the

Figure 2.9 Shake the high-tech building and a host of complex technologies fall out, well beyond the PC on the desk (National Academy of Sciences 1988).

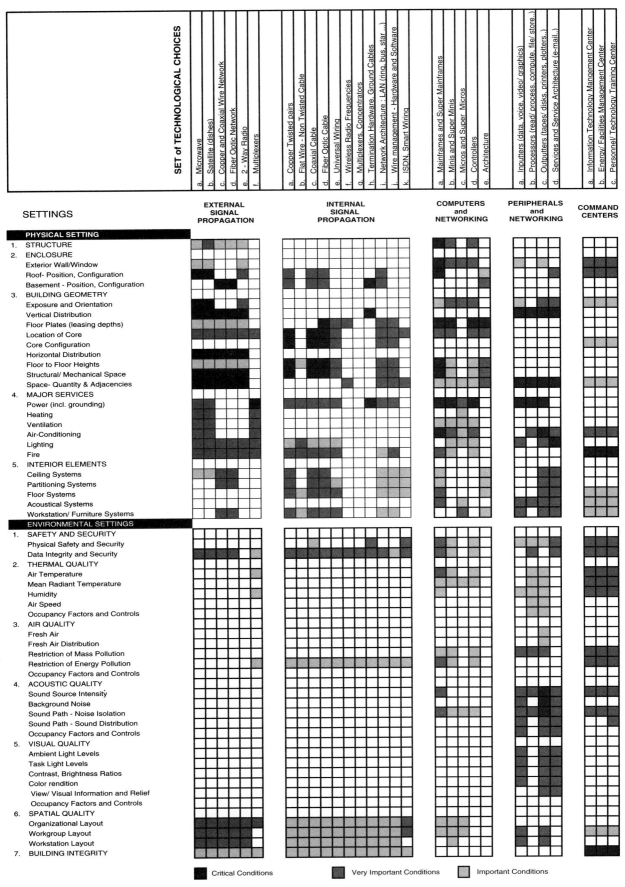

Figure 2.10 A review of the design implications of introducing new technology reveals, for example, critical conditions for structure and building geometry in relation to external signal propagation, and critical conditions for acoustical and visual comfort in the selection of peripherals (Loftness and Hartkopf 1989).

heavy reliance on the architect as the integrated knowledge base from which conceptual ideas must develop are beginning to take their toll.

The most serious concern in this division of responsibility for building production is the lack of "teeth" (testable limits of acceptable performance quality) and the lack of continuous responsibility of any one player throughout the process (see figure 2.11). Consequently, it is critical that the building delivery process reflects more collective or team front-end decisionmaking, and possesses a continuous structure of accountability, to meet the conditions stipulated in the definition of the intelligent office. Indeed, the building delivery process should incorporate several new steps toward creating high-performance, integrated designs:

1) a long-term mission statement and performance program written with expert input, anticipating the capacity for change;
2) clear goals for short- and long-term budgets;
3) a team decisionmaking process involving a range of experts with decisionmaking power, from the project's outset (for cost effectiveness and performance);
4) a performance design and construction con-

tract with negotiated bidding and testable specifications;
5) a controlled building diagnostics process for quality assurance throughout design and construction;
6) an expert commissioning stage, to lead into long-term expert maintenance and operation; and
7) a growing use of field evaluation techniques and user questionnaires (post-occupancy evaluations) to assess the overall performance of the integrated system for the needs of the building's occupants.

Two of these steps — the critical need for team decisionmaking and building diagnostics throughout the building delivery process — will be discussed below.

Team Decisionmaking to Ensure Design Performance

A team decisionmaking process, with built-in quality assurance procedures, is critical to the building design process today — given the range and complexity of the potentially intelligent sub-

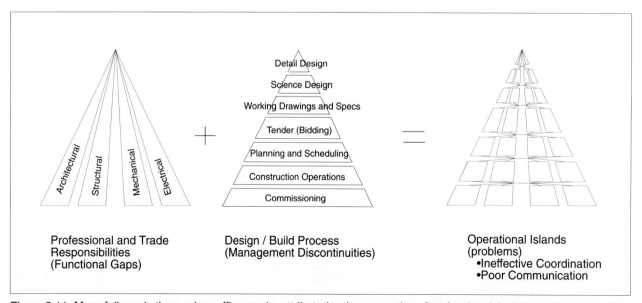

Figure 2.11 *Many failures in the modern office can be attributed to the separation of professional decisionmaking and to the "hands-off" approach to the building delivery process (sketch by A.G. Mattar, Public Works Canada, from The Building Systems Integration Handbook, ©1991, The American Institute of Architects. Reproduced with permission under license number 91069. ALL RIGHTS RESERVED).*

systems available, as well as the responsiveness and dynamics needed to accommodate change and provide environmental quality. The members of this "transdisciplinary" design team must rise above their traditional associations with building product lines (such as enclosure systems or mechanical systems) to address the delivery of each of the six building performance mandates in the integrated setting (see figure 2.12). This design team must also maintain involvement for the duration of the project and transcend the typical boundaries drawn between decisionmakers for conceptual design and those for working drawings, construction, and facilities management. Once in place, this transdisciplinary design team can begin the process of identifying the performance issues for electronic offices, setting the integrated standards, and profiling innovative solutions to ensure that the stress factors so obvious in present-day workplaces are not perpetuated.

One key addition to this list of front-end requirements is the introduction of a full-time project manager with extensive facilities management and building construction expertise, as a single line of authority. At a relatively minimal cost to a multimillion-dollar building, this project manager represents the client's best interests, and manages the stages of the building delivery process from conception through occupancy. This ensures accountability and continuity in the building project, and effective multidisciplinary decisionmaking by the design team. The addition of a project manager in no way diminishes the critical contribution of the project architect to the building's overall quality, particularly its formal, spatial, and functional performance.

Building Diagnostics for Ensuring Performance in the Occupied Setting

The development of field evaluation techniques and instrumentation is greatly needed for several purposes: for assessing the building performance of similar building types in the conceptual design stage; for use as a communication tool between

Traditional Accountabilities for Building Performance

	SPATIAL QUALITY	THERMAL QUALITY	AIR QUALITY	ACOUSTIC QUALITY	VISUAL QUALITY	BLDG. INTEGRITY
ARCHITECT	●			○	○	●
MECHANICAL ENGINEER		●	●			
ELECTRICAL ENGINEER	●			○		
LIGHTING EXPERT	○				●	
ACOUSTICAL EXPERT						
STRUCTURAL ENGINEER	○					●
INTERIOR DESIGNER	●			○	○	●
ENERGY CONSULTANT		●	○		●	

Necessary Accountabilities for Building Performance

	SPATIAL QUALITY	THERMAL QUALITY	AIR QUALITY	ACOUSTIC QUALITY	VISUAL QUALITY	BLDG. INTEGRITY
ARCHITECT	●	●	●	●	●	●
MECHANICAL ENGINEER	●	●	●	○	○	●
ELECTRICAL ENGINEER	●				●	○
LIGHTING EXPERT	●	○	○	○	●	○
ACOUSTICAL EXPERT	●			●		○
STRUCTURAL ENGINEER	●	○	○	○	○	●
INTERIOR DESIGNER	●	●	●	●	●	●
ENERGY CONSULTANT	○	●	●	●	●	●

● Primary Responsibility/Accountability Taken for Building Performance

○ Secondary Responsibility/Accountability

Figure 2.12 The old design approach of "territorial" decisionmaking, with accountability only for specific subsystems, must be replaced by a team decisionmaking process to ensure total building performance (Mill, Hartkopf, and Loftness, The Building Systems Integration Handbook, ©1991 The American Institute of Architects. Reproduced with permission under license number 91069. ALL RIGHTS RESERVED).

professionals during the design development stages; for use as an evaluation tool during the working-drawings and specifications stage; and for monitoring performance during the construction, occupancy, and one-year commissioning stages.

Although there has not been much development in team decisionmaking processes (for building conception, design, construction, and operation), progress has been made in the development of quality assurance testing and building evaluation. Traditionally, the evaluation of occupied buildings has relied heavily on experts and expert instruments for field measurement, with laboratory support for data assessment and knowledge development. This approach has limited the number of buildings evaluated, and allows only the most acute problems to be addressed, with minimal out-of-house information transfer.

Today, a new field is developing known as "building diagnostics" (National Research Council 1985), marrying simplified objective instrumentation procedures with subjective (occupancy) evaluation procedures for the diagnosis of buildings from conception through occupancy. It is critical for the design community to realize the potential of field diagnostics for studying overall performance in the integrated and occupied setting (see chapter 3). Building diagnostics will greatly enhance conceptual design, design development and specification, construction acceptance procedures, and project commissioning through the years of "office churn" and modifications.

Forecasting Major Design Changes in the Office of the Future

Many decisionmakers in the building sector, including owners and architects, envision the creation of a high-tech building as the introduction of the appropriate portable "baggage" into a traditionally well-designed office. A few more boxes here, a few more outlets and wires there, a few more computer-intertwined control systems, and one inner office adapted for housing the main

frame, printers, and supplies: presto, an instant high-tech office. Today's owners and architects for the most part have not grasped the significance of the changes demanded in designing high-tech spaces: changes in the design process, changes in the physical setting, and changes in the delivery and operation of the building. If one could imagine designing a hospital today for the old black-bag doctor and then converting it for contemporary use by patching in all of today's high-tech equipment as if it were baggage dropped into each room, you would be imagining the process by which high-tech offices are currently designed.

Both the Building Research Board at the National Academy of Science and the Center for Building Performance and Diagnostics at Carnegie Mellon University have studied in-depth the impact of electronic enhancements on the office environment (see figure 2.10). A careful study of these relationships reveals major areas for design innovation that emerge from an understanding of the most significant physical and environmental features in the electronic or intelligent office (see figure 2.13).

These areas of potential innovation include three-

Major Office Design Changes

1. Three Dimensional Cable Network
2. Multiple Zone HVAC Network
3. Increased Shared Facilities
4. Improved Lighting/Daylighting Control
5. Improved Noise & Pollution Isolation
6. New, Redesigned Workstations
7. Individual Environmental Controls
8. Effective Interior/Envelope Interface
9. More Social Settings/ Visual Diversity
10. Building Management Trio:
    Facilities Manager
    Technology Manager
    Personnel Manager

Figure 2.13 An early identification of major design changes for the Office of the Future (National Academy of Sciences 1988).

dimensional cable networks so massive and so heavily used that they must be treated like a structural system during the conceptual design stage; an associated HVAC network flexibly subdivided into dozens of zones (instead of five or six) with modularized horizontal and vertical duct plans and individualized controls; demand for much more effective interior-envelope design interfaces for daylight and fresh air; a major increase in the amount of shared facilities (well beyond the coffee pot and copy machine) to house main frames, telephone and data closets, uninterrupted power supplies, printing rooms, and teleconferencing rooms, on a building-wide or floor-by-floor level; and a major rethinking of workstation design to incorporate cabling, adequate work surface and storage, adjustability, and improved environmental controls for temperature, light, air, and acoustics. Chapter 10 will expand on these major design opportunities for the Office of the Future.

To reiterate, *intelligent office buildings will provide for unique assemblies of current technologies and work styles in appropriate physical, environmental, and organizational settings to enhance worker speed, understanding, communication, and overall productivity.*

References

(ABSIC 1989-1990)
"The ABSIC Mission," *ABSIC News*, No. 2, 1989-1990.

(CIB 1982)
CIB Working Commission W60, "Working with the Performance Approach in Building," International Council for Building Research Studies and Documentation, Publication 64, January 1982.

(*GSA Peach Book* 1975)
GSA Peach Book, or *The PBS Building Systems Program and Performance Specification for Office Buildings, Third Edition*, Washington, DC: Public Buildings Service, General Services Administration, 1975.

(Hartkopf, Loftness, and Mill, *Building Performance*, 1986)
Hartkopf, V., V. Loftness, and P. Mill, "The Concept of Total Building Performance and Building Diagnostics," in *Building Performance: Function, Preservation, and Rehabilitation*, Philadelphia: ASTM, STP 901, 1986.

(Hartkopf, Loftness, and Mill, *Handbook*,1991)
Hartkopf, V., V. Loftness, and P. Mill, "Integration for Performance," in *The Building Systems Integration Handbook*, ed. Richard A. Rush, Washingtion, D.C.: The American Institute of Architects, 1991.

(ISO 1980)
Performance Standards in Buildings: Contents and Presentation; ISO 6240, Geneva, Switzerland: International Standards Organization, 1980.

(ISO 1981)
Performance Standards in Buildings: Principles for Their Preparation and Factors for Inclusion, ISO/DP 6241, Geneva, Switzerland: International Standards Organization, 1981.

(Lemer and Moavenzadeh 1972)
Lemer, A.C., and F. Moavenzadeh, "Performance of Systems of Constructed Facilities," in *Proceedings, Performance Concept in Buildings*, NBS 361, Gaithersburg, MD: National Bureau of Standards, 1972.

(Loftness and Hartkopf 1989)
The Electronically Enhanced Office, Pittsburgh, PA: Carnegie Mellon University Technical Report, Pittsburgh, PA, 1989.

(Mill, Hartkopf, and Loftness 1986)
Mill, P., V. Hartkopf, and V. Loftness, "Evaluating the Quality of the Workplace," in *The Ergonomic Payoff: Designing the Electronic Office*, ed. Rani Lueder, New York: Nichols Publishing Co., 1986.

(National Academy of Sciences 1988)
National Academy of Sciences, Building Research Board, *Electronically Enhanced Office Buildings*, a joint report by the Committee on Technologically Advanced Buildings and the Committee on High Technology Systems for Buildings, Washington, DC: National Research Council, 1988.

(National Research Council 1985)
National Research Council, Building Research Board, Commission on Engineering and Technical Systems, *Building Diagnostics: A Conceptual Framework*, Washington, DC: National Academy Press, 1985.

(Public Works Canada 1983)
Public Works Canada, Architectural and Building Sciences Division, *Stage I in the Development of Total Building Performance, Summary Report*, Volume I, 1983.

(Wall Street Journal 1987)
"Uncovering the Hidden Costs," *Wall Street Journal*, June 12, 1987, Northeast edition.

3

A Process for the Field Evaluation of Advanced Office Environments

There is a significant difference between two-hour, two-day, and two-week field evaluations of buildings. This chapter describes key conditions for effective two-day field evaluations, as applied in the studies of advanced buildings in Japan, Germany, the U.K., and North America.

ABSIC and the Center for Building Performance and Diagnostics initiated international studies of the performance of advanced office buildings in 1988. These field studies focused on evaluating the impact of new technologies and new integrated systems on the quality of the workplace for building occupancies. The in-depth studies began in Japan, with four buildings recognized as among the most technically advanced in the world: the Toshiba Headquarters, the NTT Twins Regional Headquarters, the ARK Mori Building (ARK Hills Complex), and the Umeda Center Building.

Many rapid building study tours are taking place around the world, evaluating various building types including intelligent office buildings. Often in these studies, a large group of similarly educated professionals, touring a facility in two to three hours, is led to a dozen predefined building highlights. However, we argue that a small multidisciplinary group (from key professions) is more appropriate to define a list of truly successful innovations in the advanced office building. To understand the overall performance of integrated systems, this group must incorporate all key professionals — interior and exterior architect, mechanical engineer, telecommunications expert, personnel/occupancy expert, and a facilities manager. The team needs an adequate length of time to investigate the building collectively and separately, with measurement and assessment tools tuned to the building type, and with field input

from the range of building decisionmakers and users. Moreover, this multidisciplinary group must collectively debate whether the innovations they have identified are successful from the perspectives of each discipline and of the building's occupants.

Indeed, the ABSIC building evaluation strategy relies on a series of critical requirements:
- first, the use of an approach focused on the imperatives of total building performance for the building occupant; the integrated systems rather than component parts; and the modified design process toward achieving systems integration for performance;
- second, the creation of a transdisciplinary team and team evaluation process; and
- third, the development of a field evaluation package to help document the full range of advances in building technology and component integration, as well as their contribution to higher quality working environments.

An Evaluation Approach Focused on Total Building Performance, Systems Integration, and Innovative Design Process

Addressing Total Building Performance

As described in chapter 2, field evaluations should focus on all performance areas simultaneously, should evaluate the performance of both the components in isolation and the integrated systems, and should document the building delivery process supporting successful performance (Loftness, Hartkopf, and Mill 1989).

To this end, the ABSIC field evaluation team developed the manageable yet comprehensive list of the six performance mandates previously discussed. As the 1970s demonstrated, an isolated emphasis on one performance area, such as energy, often negatively affects other performance areas, e.g., causing serious air quality and degradation failures. To avoid associated failures, the emphasis on office automation carries with it the need for a total building performance approach to building evaluations. Conventional offices already stretch the limits of humane working conditions: vast, open floor areas; high-density layouts; inadequate surface and storage; an army of fluorescent light fixtures marching flush across an "acoustic" ceiling; and such unresponsive or untouchable environmental controls as zone thermostats, floor light switches, and fixed windows. The haphazard introduction of computer equipment with office automation will make these already trying conditions intolerable. In addition, the retrofit measures that have been recommended as solutions (acoustic equipment covers, parabolic louvers, glare screens, additional air conditioning) solve the performance problems of one component at a time, without recognition of the implications for other performance areas and other components.

Yet building evaluations continue in singular performance areas — such as studies of acoustics in factories, lighting in offices, heat loss in old buildings — with recommendations for action that may solve one performance problem, yet create two more.

The evaluating community can greatly improve field evaluations of buildings by adopting a comprehensive outline of total building performance, finite enough to be manageable in the field, yet developed enough to represent the "integrated multi-sensory evaluator" known as the human. "Aesthetics" to the building occupant comprises a thermal, air quality, acoustic, visual, and spatial experience. Although a building evaluation may not emphasize all performance areas equally (an acoustic emphasis or lighting emphasis may be critical to a specific building type), its framework

and its recommendations must consider all of the building performance areas in an integrated fashion.

In addition, the field evaluations must measure not only physiological limits of acceptable performance, but also the psychological, sociological, and economic limits of acceptability. Research efforts and resultant codes and standards tend to focus on physiological limits, aimed at ensuring the physical health and safety of the building's occupants. Given the "hidden cancers" in today's working and living environments, we can benefit from a more refined definition of physiological "comfort," and an additional emphasis on psychological and sociological "comfort."

Addressing the Integrated Setting

The second imperative for building evaluation is the need to study performance qualities in the integrated setting. The focus of an evaluation can not be the success (or failure) of office automation systems alone, but those systems within their integrated setting of interior, structural, enclosure, mechanical, and telecommunication systems, as well as building occupancies. This implies that the building evaluator must have a working knowledge of the generic choices in each of those system groups, and their effectiveness in relation to office automation. Alternatively, the building must be evaluated by an expert team capable of covering those knowledge areas.

Just as a manageable list of performance mandates is needed, a manageable but comprehensive list of building systems and subsystems is needed. At a minimum, five basic system groups must be discussed: structural systems, envelope (or enclosure) systems, interior systems, mechanical/electrical systems, and telecommunication systems. The expert checklist that was developed for the ABSIC field studies is divided into systems, subsystems, components, and materials (see figure 3.1). This checklist also evaluates component interfaces with other subsystems and their impact on overall performance (see Appendix A). Again, team evaluations are critical for identifying the

Expert Checklist Outline

1.   ENVELOPE SYSTEM INNOVATIONS
1.1   Exterior wall
1.2   Window glazing
1.3   Roof
1.4   Subgrade
1.5   Notable overall performance
1.6   Systems integration

2.   STRUCTURAL SYSTEM INNOVATIONS
2.1   General system
2.2   Notable overall performance
2.3   System integration

3.   INTERIOR SYSTEM INNOVATIONS
3.1   Ceiling
3.2   Floor
3.3   Fixed interior wall
3.4   Furnishings

4.   MECHANICAL SYSTEM INNOVATIONS
4.1   Heating, Ventilating, and Air Conditioning
       Service generators, conduits and terminals
4.2   Energy management control system (EMCS)
       Central and Local management system
4.3   Lighting
       Service generator, conduits, and terminals
       Lighting/ dynamic control systems
4.4   Plumbing
       Service generator, conduits, and terminals
4.5   Fire safety
       Service generator, conduits, and terminals
4.6   Vertical transportation
4.7   Notable overall performance
4.8   System integration

5.   POWER & TELECOMMUNICATION
5.1   Service generator(External Signal)
       Power
       Data/video
       Telephone
5.2   Service conduits (Internal Signal)
       Power
       Wire management systems
       Telephone
5.3   Service terminals
       Power
       Telephone
       Computers & Peripherals
5.4   Dynamic controls
5.5   MIS/ Telecommunications planning module
5.6   Notable overall performance
5.7   System integration

6.   PHYSICAL SECURITY SYSTEMS
6.1   Security system
6.2   Notable overall performance
6.3   System integration

7.   OVERALL BUILDING PERFORMANCE

Figure 3.1 ABSIC's expert checklist for the field evaluation of components, systems, and integrations (see Appendix A).

successes and failures in integration between systems and their subsets.

One purpose of the in-depth study of innovative buildings is to increase the understanding of advancements in components and assemblies *as they perform* in the occupied setting. This book translates the results of a planned package of measurement and assessment procedures, in relation to advancements in structural, enclosure, interior, mechanical, and telecommunications systems, and their integration into high-quality work environments.

Addressing the Building Delivery Process

In addition to addressing overall performance of the fully integrated system in the field evaluation of buildings, it is equally important to study the process whereby the innovative decisions were introduced. Not all building delivery processes are equal by any means, as is witnessed by the cornerstone of the NTT building (see chapter 10, figure 10.12) — displaying individual photos of the design team members — as compared to a typical one name cornerstone on a new U.S. office building. The widespread variations in managing building programming, design delivery, commissioning, and operation are especially noticeable in innovative buildings, and in buildings that are considered very satisfying to the building occupants. Variations from conventional design processes range from the input of facilities management and occupants into the conceptual design, to the planned continuum or "accountability" of all of the design players through the first years of occupancy.

Most critical, however, is the level of team decision-making used throughout the design process to ensure the overall performance of the integrated setting. The field studies of innovative buildings must examine the process that led to success as well as the success itself, documenting the range of activities that could be introduced into today's conventional building delivery processes. The international field evaluations of buildings presented in this book and subsequent books of this series represent an effort to document and identify a number of innovative steps, toward creating advanced, high-performance buildings (see figure 3.2).

An Evaluation Approach Relying on a Transdisciplinary Team

Team evaluation is critical to the accurate assessment of a building. Developing the makeup of the field evaluation team and ensuring expertise in critical areas are strategic efforts. Most importantly, the team must work interactively and strongly debate issues across disciplinary boundaries — an ability of major importance to the evaluation and design of advanced workplaces.

The evaluation team is described as "transdisciplinary," as distinct from "multidisciplinary," to emphasize the interactive process whereby the team reaches consensus decisions on building innovations. Team members are skilled in and adamant about contributing to building design decisions outside the traditional boundaries of their own experience.

As depicted in figure 3.3, the team must be small enough for interactive field studies and communication, and yet large enough to provide expertise in:

- each of the six performance areas — spatial, thermal, acoustic, visual, and air quality as well as long-term building integrity;
- each of the major building systems, with up-to-date knowledge about generic alternatives, subsystem components, and their performance in integrated settings; and
- the decisionmaking process whereby those settings were delivered and are maintained.

The team must also have experience in various levels of evaluation measurement and assessment, in order arrive at reliable conclusions with ease during the evaluation.

Finally, the team must be capable of working in an interactive manner. It is necessary to establish a

Steps Toward Creating Highly Innovative Buildings that Perform for the Building's Occupancies

1. Mission statement and performance budget
2. Performance program
3. Collective client problem identification for up-front decisionmaking
4. Specification of a project manager (in addition to architect of record)
5. Performance selection of entire design team
6. Creation of team decisionmaking process
7. Integrated performance studies of existing advanced buildings and building delivery processes
8. Team concept development for innovation
9. Design development testing through expert analysis/peer review
10. Working drawing testing through expert analysis/ peer review
11. Full-scale mock-up testing of repetitive, highly innovative configurations
12. Diagnostics against standards through the construction process
13. One-year commissioning, including expertise and accountability carryover
14. Integrated building management: facilities, technology, and personnel

Figure 3.2 Field evaluations should also attempt to uncover the innovative building delivery processes that result in high-performance settings (ABSIC 1988-1989).

workable team decisionmaking process for the exchange of ideas and for arguing through the ramifications of decisions on the effective design and integration of building subsystems for each performance quality.

In the Japan studies, the ABSIC team devoted the entire first day to a group walkthrough, to understand the full range of technologies in the building, and their effectiveness as integrated systems in the eyes of the full team. The evening offered team members time to discuss their impressions and establish fundamental questions (surround-

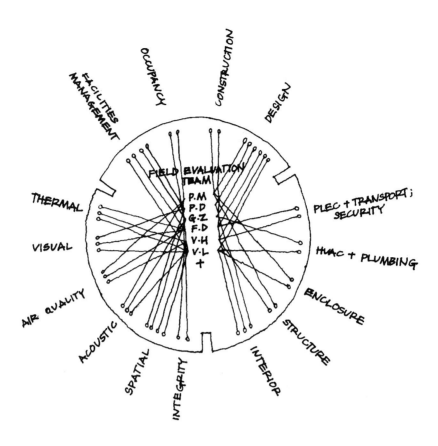

Figure 3.3 The ideal team should be small enough to interact yet large enough to provide full performance and systems expertise. (sketch, Azizan Aziz)

ing innovations and concerns) for the second day of study.   On the second day, team members worked one-on-one with the building decisionmakers and occupants most versed with their areas of expertise (enclosure, mechanical, telecommunications, interiors, facilities management, personnel management).   At the end of the second day, the team gathered for three to four hours to debate the extensive expert checklist records, toward identifying innovations that span systems and performance areas.   The building studies in part II of this book highlight the five to ten building features per building that were judged most innovative by the team members as a result of their collective debate and eventual consensus.

Field evaluations of buildings must encompass the full range of performance qualities, and their limits of acceptability, within the *occupied* setting of integrated systems. Although emphasis may be placed on one performance area, or one building

system, the field methods must cover all performance requirements, such that recommendations for action do not lead to other failures. The most viable, informative approach to field evaluations of buildings involves a team of experts measuring and assessing the range of systems and performance areas.

An Evaluation Approach Spanning Subjective and Objective Measurements and Assessments

There has been heated discussion over the past few years about the need for both objective and subjective field evaluation methods (Zeisel 1981; *Methods* 1987; Preiser, Rabinowitz, and White 1988). Professional organizations such as the Environmental Design Research Association (EDRA) have provided a forum for this debate, as is reflected in EDRA conference proceedings of past years. Despite the ongoing debate, adequate strategic packages including both methods for field evaluation of buildings have yet to be developed. A package combining objective and subjective evaluation is critical to document effectively total building performance, systems integration, and innovative process.

Exploration of the possible types of field measurement and assessment techniques will help promote the development and deliberate documentation of techniques, and offer a range of choices in the percentage of building covered; the cost, time, repeatability, and level of expertise needed for measurement; the level of expertise needed for assessment; the depth of evaluation; and the assurance of results. A distinction must be made between levels of evaluation measurement (data collection) and levels of evaluation assessment (data interpretation or diagnosis), as they lead to recommendations that vary from specific to global. With further development of these performance measurements and assessment procedures, the field evaluation of buildings can be organized into strategic packages that respond to client needs and resources, as well as available equipment and expertise.

In each evaluation package, some level of subjective and objective evaluations is combined to enhance the objective understanding of occupant comfort, satisfaction, and productivity, and to clarify the subjective responses of occupants to the quality of their built environment.

Levels of Evaluation Measurement

If one assumes that both subjective and objective field evaluation procedures contribute to measuring the quality of a built environment, at least five levels of evaluation measurement can be developed: 1) plan/archive analysis; 2) expert walkthrough analysis; 3) occupancy and use analysis; 4) simple instrumentation; and 5) complex instrumentation (see figure 3.4). To evaluate whether innovations truly improve the quality of the workplace for the individual occupants, the ABSIC team relies on the full range of field mea-

surement techniques to ensure breadth and depth in both objective and subjective evaluations.

In the *plan/archive analyses*, the field team evaluates a range of available documents to ascertain whether such performance criteria as spatial, thermal, air, acoustic, and visual quality, as well as building integrity, are assured for the building occupancies and their activities (see figure 3.4). The evaluators make scalar measurements, counts, tracings, pattern comparisons, and specification/detail comparisons to determine innovative or problematic components and component interfaces for various occupancies and functions.

In the *expert walkthroughs*, the ABSIC team (with expertise spanning the range of major building systems and building performance mandates) studies the occupied building in depth to identify potential innovations. Team members use an extensive expert checklist (see Appendix A), photography, and knowledge-based sensory evaluation — sight, hearing, touch, smell, even taste — within the integrated setting of the occupied building.

For *occupancy and use measurements*, the transdisciplinary team relies on four techniques — physical trace observations, behavioral observations, interviews, and questionnaires — to collect adequate data for evaluation. Physical trace records capture the consequences of interactions between occupants and their settings, including remnants of use (wear and tear, labeling) and adaptations for use (furniture rearrangements, fans, humidifiers, space heaters, taped-over air diffusers). Behavioral observations concentrate on the occupants' activities within their setting (adjusting blinds, whispering, putting on sweaters). Both behavioral observations and physical traces are recorded on graphic checklists (see figure 3.5).

The questionnaire and interview techniques that are used to assess the overall quality of the workplace from the occupant's point of view are included in Appendix B. The statistical analysis of the questionnaire results is critical, enabling the

Field Measurement Techniques

1. PLAN / ARCHIVE ANALYSIS
    a. Plans, specifications, photographs
    b. Building budgets, implementation history
    c. Occupancy management records

2. EXPERT WALKTHROUGH ANALYSIS
    a. Ear: listening
    b. Eye: seeing
    c. Nose: smelling
    d. Hand, body: touching, feeling
    e. Mouth: tasting

3. OCCUPANCY AND USE ANALYSIS
    a. Questionnaire
    b. Interview
    c. Behavioral mapping, physical traces

4. SIMPLE INSTRUMENTATION ANALYSIS

5. COMPLEX INSTRUMENTATION ANALYSIS

PLAN / ARCHIVE ANALYSIS INCLUDES STUDIES OF:
1. Project Brief and/or Program
2. Working Drawings and Specifications
3. As-built Drawings and Shop Drawings
4. Fit-up Drawings and Specifications
5. Project Management and Cost Breakdown Records
6. Field Photographs
7. Work Orders
8. Building Operating Manuals
9. Building Maintenance Manuals and Repair Records
10. Energy Consumption and Utility Bills
11. Occupant Health / Complaint Records
12. Previous Studies

Figure 3.4 Field measurement techniques can encompass both subjective and objective procedures. The first logical step in assessing innovation is the plan/archive analysis of a building's drawings and records (Mill, Hartkopf, Loftness 1986).

field team to merge objective and subjective assessments of the building. The widespread distribution of questionnaires and the structured use of interviews and observations are invaluable steps in the assessment of the overall performance of the advanced components and systems integration in the modern office, and of the effectiveness of the ongoing building delivery process (Rubin and Elder 1980).

Simple instrumentation is also critical to the merging of objective and subjective assessments (Ventre 1983). During building studies, the ABSIC team carries inexpensive, portable equipment, including a temperature measurement probe, a sound level meter, a light meter, a smoke pencil kit, and a sling psychrometer. This instrumentation is used to grossly quantify performance in four areas: thermal quality, visual quality, acoustic quality, and air quality (see figure 3.6). Since misinterpretation is easy, simple instrumentation techniques

must rely heavily on the building science expertise of the team. Nonetheless, the use of simple instrumentation in combination with expert walkthroughs provides consistent and quantified assessments for effective comparison with occupancy and use assessments. The next level of objective measurement, *complex instrumentation*, would involve using portable equipment over longer time periods, with built-in assessment capability, an effort beyond this level of field evaluation, budget, and time frame.

Each level of evaluation measurement is fed directly into records, or combined with other levels and other performance qualities. Checklists, counts, annotated plans, photos, videos, graphs, and tables may be carried away from the field measurements. Preparing all record sheets in advance greatly simplifies the evaluation assessment. For example, CO_2 measurements can be plotted on a scalar chart already indicating the

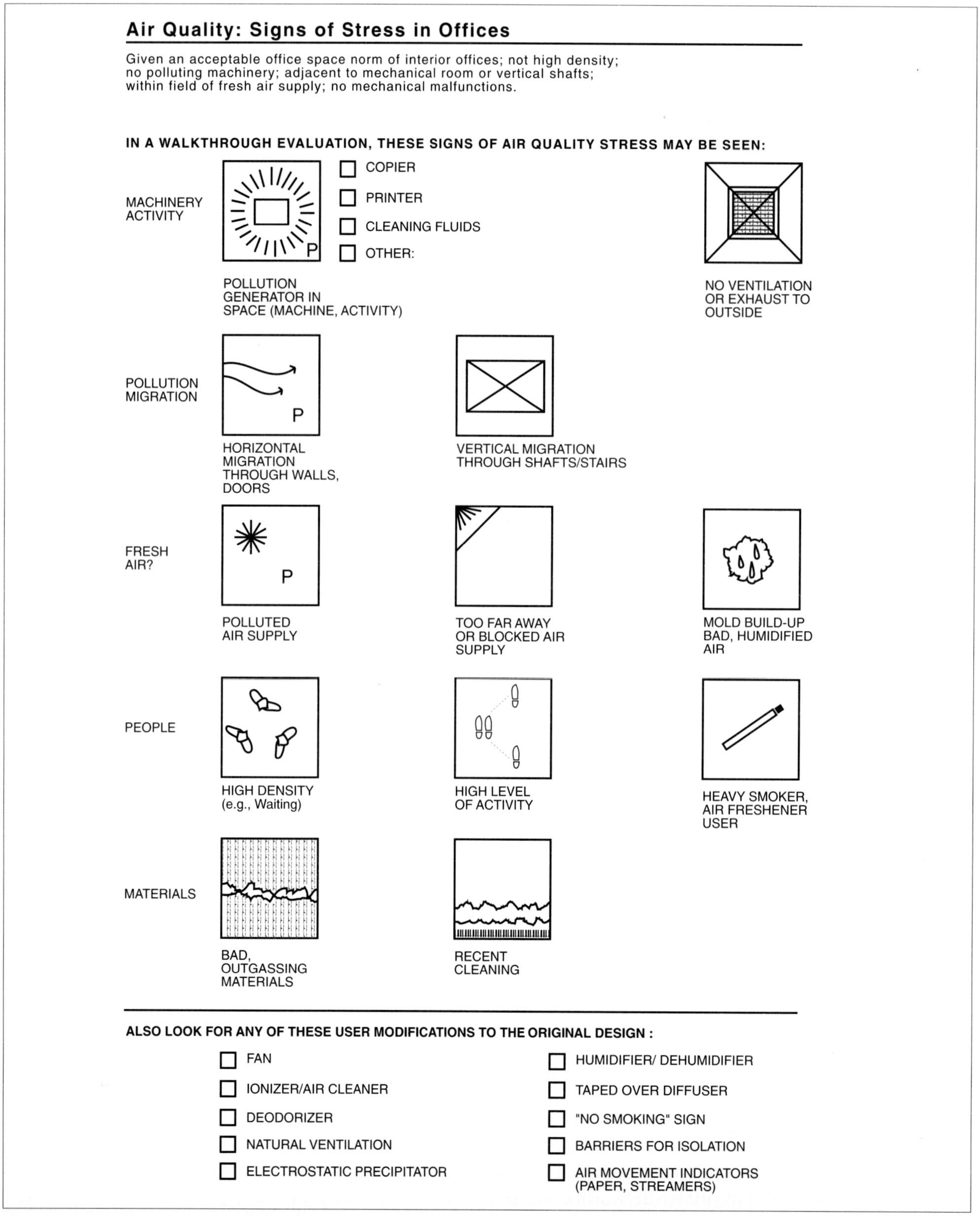

Air Quality: Signs of Stress in Offices

Given an acceptable office space norm of interior offices; not high density;
no polluting machinery; adjacent to mechanical room or vertical shafts;
within field of fresh air supply; no mechanical malfunctions.

IN A WALKTHROUGH EVALUATION, THESE SIGNS OF AIR QUALITY STRESS MAY BE SEEN:

MACHINERY
ACTIVITY

☐ COPIER
☐ PRINTER
☐ CLEANING FLUIDS
☐ OTHER:

POLLUTION
GENERATOR IN
SPACE (MACHINE, ACTIVITY)

NO VENTILATION
OR EXHAUST TO
OUTSIDE

POLLUTION
MIGRATION

HORIZONTAL
MIGRATION
THROUGH WALLS,
DOORS

VERTICAL MIGRATION
THROUGH SHAFTS/STAIRS

FRESH
AIR?

POLLUTED
AIR SUPPLY

TOO FAR AWAY
OR BLOCKED AIR
SUPPLY

MOLD BUILD-UP
BAD, HUMIDIFIED
AIR

PEOPLE

HIGH DENSITY
(e.g., Waiting)

HIGH LEVEL
OF ACTIVITY

HEAVY SMOKER,
AIR FRESHENER
USER

MATERIALS

BAD,
OUTGASSING
MATERIALS

RECENT
CLEANING

ALSO LOOK FOR ANY OF THESE USER MODIFICATIONS TO THE ORIGINAL DESIGN :

☐ FAN
☐ IONIZER/AIR CLEANER
☐ DEODORIZER
☐ NATURAL VENTILATION
☐ ELECTROSTATIC PRECIPITATOR

☐ HUMIDIFIER/ DEHUMIDIFIER
☐ TAPED OVER DIFFUSER
☐ "NO SMOKING" SIGN
☐ BARRIERS FOR ISOLATION
☐ AIR MOVEMENT INDICATORS
(PAPER, STREAMERS)

Figure 3.5 Occupancy and use measurement techniques, such as these used to evaluate air quality, include records of physical traces and behavioral observations, as well as expert knowledge of component and system conditions contributing to performance (Hartkopf, Loftness, and Mill, The Building Systems Integration Handbook, ©1991, The American Institute of Architects. Reproduced with permission under license number 91069. ALL RIGHTS RESERVED).

Spot Measurements in the NTT Building

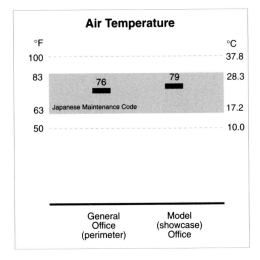

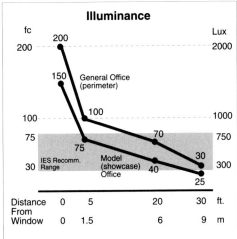

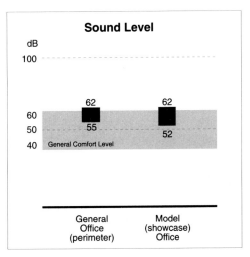

Figure 3.6 Field team members took spot measurements using simple instrumentation to compare subjective and objective evaluation.

standards and guidelines of acceptable limits against which the data are to be assessed.

Rather than being self-contained categories, the five levels of evaluation measurements often work in concert, i.e., in such areas as sequencing (one clearly depending on another); filtering capability (in revealing the scale of the problem or giving identical results a majority of the time); and modification capability (results of one allowing quantifiable enhancement of another). The field evaluation team is charged with developing an effective and strategic field measurement package for the problem at hand.

Strategic Packaging of Measurement and Assessment Procedures

In the past, data assessment procedures for interpreting the data collected were inseparably tied to the measurement procedures. However, to ensure reliable performance evaluations and recommendations within budgetary and time constraints, measurement procedures clearly should be developed independently from assessment procedures. The range of assessment procedures might include expert/informed judgment, pattern recognition, simple algorithms, statistical assessment, complex algorithms, expert systems, and mock-up/sensory assessment (a statistical form of expert judgment). Depending on the scale or complexity of the building issue or problem under evaluation, a focused complex instrumentation might be paired with a quick expert judgment, or a widespread plan/archive measurement might be paired with a complex algorithm assessment (such as the energy simulation program DOE2). Independent measurement and assessment procedures enable the field evaluation to be tailored for appropriate building coverage, depth and focus of search, repeatability of evaluation, and reliability or confidence in the results, given the constraints of time or money.

The challenge of completing cost-effective field evaluations of occupied buildings lies in packaging appropriate measurement procedures with assessment procedures to respond to client issues, demands, and resources. Working from a measurement and assessment "menu" such as that displayed in figure 3.7 (Mill, Hartkopf, and Loftness 1986), and a clearly stated level of recommendation or conclusion, the ABSIC team evaluates innovations in the workplace. To go beyond the first round of measurements and assessments, the evaluating team would develop a filter strategy for uncovering conditions in various performance areas, with increasing investment of time and resources only where merited (see figure 3.8). Regardless of the specific issue or problem under evaluation, the strategic package must still address a full set of performance criteria and the full set of building systems for ensuring recommendations that will improve the working environment, without side effects.

Packaging various levels of measurement and assessment techniques for the evaluation of total building performance in the integrated setting, the authors have studied modern offices, museums, laboratories, and courthouse settings. With various assembled teams of building performance and building systems experts, they have set goals to uncover performance successes, failures, and calls for action, in an effort to promote better environments for building occupants. The results of these studies have led to specific retrofit measures as well as to general maxims. Through these building studies, the ABSIC team has begun to formulate a series of design maxims that would greatly resolve the flaws and enhance the performance of the advanced workplace (see chapter 10).

Introducing Field Evaluations Throughout the Building Delivery Process

The results of these field evaluations of occupied buildings, however, go beyond maxims for the design of future spaces to a rethinking of the design

Levels of Evaluation Measurement

1. Plan/archive analysis
2. Expert walkthrough
3. Occupancy and use analysis
4. Simple instrumentation
5. Expert instrumentation
   assign $/time/level of confidence

   What is looked at:
1. Documentation
2. Component - component interface
3. Occupant - component interface
4. Occupant - occupant interface
   % of building
   % of occupancy

   Records kept :
1. Checklists
2. Counts
3. Annotated plans
4. Photos/videos
5. Plots
6. Tables
   total $/time/level of confidence

Levels of Evaluation Assessment

1. Expert/Informed judgement
2. Pattern recognition
3. Simple algorithms (scalar, curve fit)
4. Statistical assessment
5. Complex alogrithms
6. Expert systems
7. Mock-up sensory assessment
   assign $/time/ level of confidence

   Thresholds compared to :
1. Codes/standards
2. Guidelines
3. Project brief
4. Norms
5. Research results

   Recommendation type:
1. Specific retrofit
2. Organizational change
3. Maintenance operation change
4. General retrofit
5. Project delivery system change
6. Codes and standards change
7. Data base development
8. Further testing

Figure 3.7   Given a measurement and assessment "menu," the field evaluation team can develop a cost-effective strategy for studying innovations and their performance (Mill, Hartkopf, and Loftness 1986).

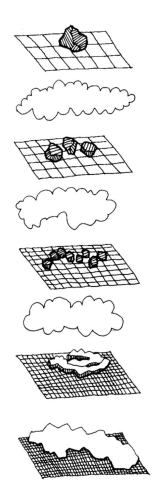

Figure 3. 8 Given the resources and time available, as well as the goals of the field study, a filter strategy for field evaluation can be developed. (sketch, Azizan Aziz)

process. If we are to get any closer to ensuring quality in the built environment, at least three steps must be reconsidered in regard to the development of field evaluation methods: predesign programming, team decisionmaking in design, and field diagnostics in the construction, commissioning, and operation of buildings.

Public Works Canada has instituted a well-defined Project Delivery System outlining the deliverables and criteria for ten stages in building production (*Project Delivery System* 1983): 1) identification of needs and opportunities; 2) option analysis and selection; 3) project definition; 4) design; 5) working documents; 6) contracting; 7) construction; 8) commissioning; 9) occupancy; and 10) evaluation. Given this definition of process, or a parallel definition, field evaluations can enhance the building delivery

The Use of Field Evaluation Packages in Various Stages of the Building Delivery Process

STAGE 1 IDENTIFICATION OF NEEDS AND OPPORTUNITIES
- Establish clients total performance needs and concerns
- Test existing/own facilities against these needs
- Test state-of-the-art facilities against these needs
- Establish programming team and transdisciplinary method

STAGE 2 ANALYSIS AND SELECTION
- Gather performance standards and test packages
- Complete transdisciplinary building visits
- Complete site/environmental impact testing

STAGE 3 PROJECT DEFINITION
- Write and test performance specifications for function/use
- Establish building delivery process' stress factors for each performance area
- Establish performance checks for each design stage
- Establish design team and transdisciplinary method

STAGE 4 DESIGN
- Establish advocacy approach to concept development (to reduce stress factors in each performance area)
- Test concept against performance standards
- Establish hierarchical and advocacy approach to preliminary design
- Test preliminary design against performance standards
- Establish hierarchical and advocacy approach to final design
- Test final design against performance standards

STAGE 5 WORKING DRAWINGS
- Establish detail/specification and transdisciplinary methods
- Test working drawings against performance standards

STAGE 6 CONTRACTING
- Set up construction performance tests before tender
- Tests performance of various contractors' buildings

STAGE 7 CONSTRUCTION
- Test performance quality against project brief regularly
- Supervise known stress factors for performance
- Ensure as-builts are completed
- Install performance "tattletales"

STAGE 8 COMMISSIONING
- Avoid early occupancy; Debug base building
- Establish maintenance, operation, user's manuals
- Establish one-year training/turnover design and construction to maintenance and operation
- Balance building to occupancy/functions, to meet project brief performance specifications
- Test performance given occupancies/functions

STAGE 9 MAINTENANCE AND USE
- Monitor preventative maintenance
- Establish "belt-tightening" operations programs and fine tuning
- Initiate staged mini-test packages to avoid problems and failures

STAGE 10 EVALUATION
- Identify transdisciplinary nature of issues/problems
- Develop cost/benefit transdisciplinary test "menu" package
- Develop transdisciplinary recommendations without side effects
- Feedback into building delivery process
- Institute post-failure evaluation

Figure 3.9 Field evaluations can enhance the building delivery process in a number of stages.

process in several areas (figure 3.9), with marginal increase in front-end time and cost compared to the massive increase in down-the-line time and cost to the building.   Not only is field evaluation critical in early studies of similar building types (for assessing overall performance of the integrated systems), the project team needs it as a communication tool in the conceptual development stage.   Field evaluation will also be needed to support the working drawing and specification stage, and most critically in the construction, commissioning, and occupancy stages.

In conclusion, *building diagnostics* is the measurement and assessment of a building's ability to provide thermal comfort, acoustic comfort, lighting comfort, air quality, and spatial comfort for its occupancy, as well as to provide building integrity

(National Research Council 1985). Effective diagnostics implies that the measurements and assessments must be completed in a transdisciplinary manner for each of the six performance areas, in relation to established standards or limits of acceptability, for the specific occupancy and function.   Building diagnostics establishes, at various stages during the building delivery process, the suitability of a building and its component parts to serve occupancy needs in the present; the reliability or probability that the service will continue to be suitable through the life of the building (dependent on the appropriateness of the maintenance and operation practices); and the flexibility or adaptability of the building and its component parts to provide long-term suitability given changing occupancies and functions.

The ABSIC field team in Japan

References

(ABSIC 1988-1989)
ABSIC, *ABSIC News*, Vol.1, No.1, 1988-1989.

(Loftness, Hartkopf, and Mill 1989)
Loftness, V., V. Hartkopf, and P. Mill, "Critical Frameworks for Building Evaluation: Total Building Performance, Systems Integration, and Levels of Measurement and Assessment," in *Building Evaluation*, New York: Plenum Press, 1989.

(*Methods* 1987)
Methods in Environmental and Behavioral Research, ed. Robert B. Bechtel, Robert W. Marans, and William Michelson, New York: Van Nostrand Reinhold Co., 1987.

(Mill, Hartkopf, and Loftness 1986)
Mill, P., V. Hartkopf, and V. Loftness, "Evaluating the Quality of the Workplace," in the *Ergonomic Payoff: Designing the Electronic Office*, ed. Rani Lueder, New York: Nichols Publishing Co., 1986.

(National Research Council 1985)
National Research Council, Building Research Board, Commission on Engineering and Technical Systems, *Building Diagnostics: A Conceptual Framework*, Washington, DC: National Research Council, 1985.

(Preiser, Rabinowitz, and White 1988)
Preiser, W., H. Rabinowitz, and E. White, *Post-occupancy Evaluation*, New York: Van Nostrand Reinhold Co., 1988.

(*Project Delivery System* 1983)
Project Delivery System, Stages 1-10, Ottawa, Canada: Departmental Planning and Coordination Branch, Public Works Canada, 1983.

(Rubin and Elder 1980)
Rubin, Arthur, and Jacqueline Elder, *Building for People: Behavioral Research Approaches and Directions*, Special Publication 474, Washington, DC: National Bureau of Standards, 1980.

(Ventre 1983)
Ventre, Francis T., *Documentation and Assessment of the GSA/PBS Building Systems Program: Final Report and Recommendations*, Washington, DC: National Bureau of Standards, 1983.

(Zeisel 1981)
Zeisel, J., *Inquiry by Design: Tools for Environment-behavior Research*, Monterey: Brooks/Cole Publishing Co., 1981.

Part II

Part II introduces the Japanese approach to the Office of the Future, and presents case studies of four advanced buildings in Japan, with an emphasis on innovative products and assemblies.

4

Japan's Rapid Approach to the Office of the Future

Although by no means a comprehensive survey of the advanced Japanese office or its evolution over time, this chapter offers some insights into the overall directions and innovations in Japan.

Many visitors and distant critics of Japan are shocked by the shop floor quality of the typical Japanese office: rows of four-foot desks lined up perpendicular to the window, from where supervisors survey worker diligence; parallel rows of bare-bulb light fixtures; and insufficient clusters of office automation equipment with long, polite lines awaiting access (see figure 4.1). Many are equally shocked by the long working hours (12 hour days) and six-day work weeks, mandated by peer pressure (see figure 4.2). But look again. The newer Japanese office provides amenities that are both physical and socio-intellectual. The building

cores and services are excellently engineered, providing high-quality services with long-term adaptability. The peer respect that suffuses throughout the organizations ensure that knowledge development, communication, and even decisionmaking is widespread, flowing from the top down and from the bottom up. Moreover the quality of the individual workstation is improving rapidly as well, approaching the spatial amenities of the West, with the additional provision of environmental amenities.

Although Japan constitutes only 3% of the world's population, it produces more than 10% of the world's total annual product, 16% of which is generated in its massive construction industry. Indeed its construction industry is as large as that of the U.S. or the European community and steadily

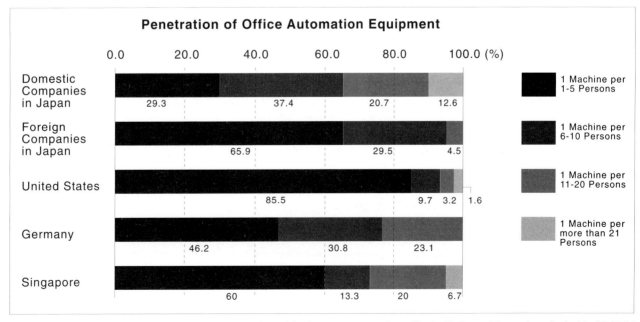

Figure 4.1 No country comes close to the penetration of desktop computers found in the U.S., and Japan lags far behind (NOPA 1988).

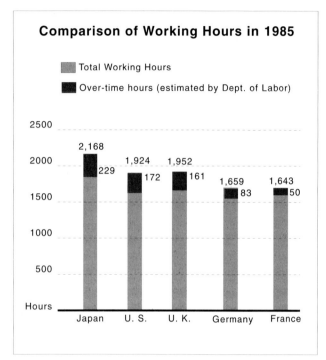

Figure 4.2 Working hours are longer in Japan than in any
Western industrialized nation (Umeda Intelligent Building
1988).

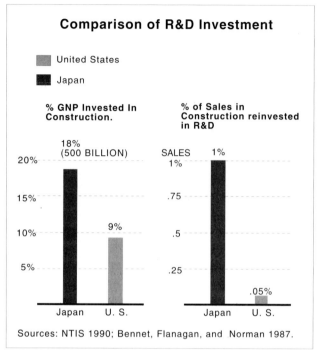

Figure 4.3 An unparalleled percentage of industry profits are
reinvested in long-term building research.

growing (Bennett, Flanagan, and Norman 1987).
The Japanese have targeted their construction industry as key to improving quality of life and to
long-term manufacturing competitiveness.
Moreover, this construction industry contributes
a significant percent of its GNP to the research,
development, and demonstration of advanced office environments (see figure 4.3). And yet we
know surprisingly little about what contributes to
this building industry's success and its long-range
impact for the design, use, and management of
tomorrow's workplace (*Officing* 1988). While the
West undertakes independent, mostly short-term
research into new intelligent products and markets, the major Japanese construction companies
are each undertaking long-term research into integrated products and systems toward the creation
of fully intelligent buildings. In a report on the
Japanese construction industry, Bennett, Flanagan,
and Norman describe this long-term research as
"based on the idea that buildings should 'know'
what is happening inside and immediately outside themselves, and 'decide' the most efficient

way of providing a convenient, productive environment for the users" (page 62).

Therefore, even though examples of what would
be considered unacceptable working conditions
still exist in Japanese buildings, in-depth field
evaluations have revealed that these conditions
are quickly disappearing. During the field
evaluations, the ABSIC team identified a number
of trends in the Japanese development of the
modern office. The following six of these trends
should provide further insights into the international pursuit of advanced workplaces.

An Interactive Demonstration Process with Comparative Products

The Japanese building industries are engaged in
an internal race to develop the highest quality and
most advanced intelligent buildings. To achieve
this they have established five-year demonstration project cycles for their regional headquarter

buildings, with each new project advancing beyond the successes (and weaknesses) of the previous buildings.

For example, the Toshiba Headquarters, one in a series of collaborative projects by the Shimizu Construction Company, houses distributed mechanical (HVAC) systems from four competitive industries in various sections of the building, for long-term comparison of comfort, energy, and cost. Then, studies of the peak electrical load conditions in the Toshiba building have led to the research and imminent demonstration of a Canadian ice storage system for the next Shimizu project. Each completed project is carefully fine tuned and studied, toward achieving a long-term goal of excellence in design, construction, maintenance, and operation of tomorrow's office buildings.

The NTT design division also demonstrates this interactive pursuit of better performance through comparative and iterative projects. In the model office area in their Tokyo headquarters, the NTT design team is studying the impact of new office furniture and servicing system concepts on comfort, satisfaction, and productivity. The design division — a team of architects, engineers, constructors, and facilities managers — actively pursues high-performance building products and integrations (see figure 4.4). This knowledge-building approach enables the NTT design unit to market their design/engineering skills as professional services, supported by a planning and design guidebook for intelligent buildings and a companion volume for product specifications of intelligent building components (see figure 4.5).

Formalizing an iterative learning cycle for building design, construction, and operation is largely unprecedented in the world today, and is founded on several conditions:

1) Senior managers in the client industries (those commissioning the buildings) have predominantly engineering backgrounds (versus business or law), promoting the sponsorship of high-tech innovations and R&D investment.

2) Major construction firms lead the pursuit of high-performance buildings, investing extensively in research, development, and demonstration. (The "big six" Japanese construction firms include Ohbayashi, Kajima, Shimizu, Takenaka-Komuten, Taisei, and Kumagai-Gumi.) These firms have well-established research centers, with more than 300 staff members and budgets of $40 million, pursuing both fundamental (with no near-term benefits) and applied research. These firms employ university-trained planners, architects, engineers, and construction managers in extensive up-front design processes within a multidisciplinary team of peers.

3) Architects have extensive building engineering training and are capable of collective team decisionmaking. This orientation prepares the architect to deal with such issues as energy and earthquake demands, the integrations of new technologies and systems, the quality of building systems

Figure 4.4 NTT investigates a wide range of products to provide state-of-the-art design throughout Japan (Nation's Business, January 1984. © 1984 U.S. Chamber of Commerce).

NTT Technologies Supporting Building Intelligence

Office Automation

- LAN construction
- Text processing
- Decisionmaking process support

- Schedule control and support
- Information management
- Office task processing
- On-line services

- CAD and CAM
- Public-oriented information services
- Software support
- External data base access support

Building Control Systems

- Optimal control of heat source and air conditioning facilities
- Automatic control of temperature and humidity
- Operation and control by schedule

- Control of intake air
- Elevator bank control
- Elevator voice response control
- Monitoring of building environment and facilities status

- Energy consumption metering and billing
- Telecontrol
- Automatic parking control

Security Systems

- Video observation
- Entry control
- Tele-locking control
- Fire detection, alarm, extinguishing control

- Smoke control and automatic evacuation
- Gas leakage detection and alarm
- Water leakage detection

- Automatic monitoring of fire protection
- Earthquake response
- Power failure response

Energy Saving Systems

- Automatic lighting adjustment and on/off adjustment
- Centralized automatic blinds control
- Energy management

- Water-efficient, hygienic
- Solar energy power supply
- Outdoor air cooling
- Heat reclamation for air conditioning

- Automatic small-zoned, controlled air conditioning
- Energy-efficient heat transfer

Telecommunications

- In-building telephone system and PBX
- High-speed digital data transfers
- Memo-pad communications

- Electronic mail
- Video conferencing, voice messaging
- Graphic communications, moving and still pictures

- Satellite communications
- Teleport systems
- Automatic tenant billing

Environmental Planning

- Flexible planning systems — Zoning-related planning procedures,flexible office layouts, lighting,HVAC planning
- Office furniture systems — Office furniture layout procedures, workstation layout procedures
- Ergonomic planning systems — Color strategies, increase of greenery, OA lighting & control, noise strategies

- Amenity planning, systems planning — Hall and lounge, atrium and airshaft void, restaurant, lounge, rest area
- Maintainability planning systems— Building systems, preventive maintenance strategies; failure diagnosis procedures
- Life-cycle planning systems

   Life-cycle cost computation procedures, cost-efficiency evaluation procedures
- Public communication space systems — Rental intelligent offices; intelligent building information and showroom services

Intelligent Building Construction System

- LAN configuring — Cable shaft, PBX site and node accommodation space planning
- Floor wiring — Under-carpet cable and cellular floor duct techniques; double layered OA flooring

- Wall wiring — Panel and cable-pole wiring
- Ceiling wiring — Ceiling and cable-rack wiring; optical star links
- Flexible air conditioning (AC) — Task-oriented, distributed, VAV, condensationless air conditioning

- Flexible lighting circuit switching
- Document conveying - Document transfer robots, vertical conveyors - linear motors, compressed air
- Seismic design - Free access seismic design - floor strengthening, piping, equipment installation
- Prevention of electromagnetic interference

Figure 4.5 Through in-house demonstration projects and market research, NTT now offers full design services for intelligent buildings with professional guidebooks (NTT Guidebook 1987).

NOPA Description of the Intelligent Office

Basic Systems

OA & Communications
- Digital PBX
- Local Area Network
- Satellite Communication
- TV Conference System
- Closed-circuit TV
- Flexible Wiring System

Building Automation
- Operation Management
  HVAC, Lighting, Transport
- Conservation
  Energy, Manpower
- Security Control
  Fire, Crime, Data, Access

Additional Amenities

Identity & Amenity
- Status, Individuality
- Space Planning
  Modularization, Atrium, Lounge
- Refreshment
  Cafeteria, Fitness, Clinic, Greenery
- Air Quality, Odor, Temperature-
  Control

Office Service
- Information
- Stationery Supply
- Print, Word Processing
- Consultation
- Renew, Remodel, Removal

Figure 4.6 The New Office Promotion Association (NOPA), sponsored by 40 organizations and 247 corporate members, focuses on developing the intelligent office (Rubin 1991).

(i.e., structure, enclosure, mechanical, interior systems), buildability, and maintenance.

4) Building maintenance and operation staffs are university-educated and highly trained on the job to manage the optimization of built environments in response to new technologies.

5) Government is also actively involved in the pursuit of better performing buildings, investing in construction research through Tsukuba Science City. Government also sponsors NOPA (New Office Promotion Association) to support multiple industry collaboration toward ensuring new product development and systems integration for building performance and effectiveness (see figure 4.6).

Japan has a reputation of assimilating, modifying, and adapting ideas from other countries. Today, however, Japan is *initiating* major high-tech innovations, and is willing to develop and demonstrate products and product integrations that Western markets have not supported.

A Team Decisionmaking Process from the Outset

The Japanese encourage cooperative decisionmaking by establishing the entire building team (architects, interior planners, engineers, constructors, and facility managers) at the outset of a project. The team is a group of highly-educated peers, capable of cooperatively identifying and structuring problems, developing all stages of the design (concepts, specifications, and working drawings), and assuring quality throughout construction and operation.

The team decisionmaking process is built on the Japanese strengths of group-oriented work with long-term views, and decisionmaking by consensus and consultation, versus top-down decisionmaking. Each team player feels responsible for the quality of the whole, such that if any one player sees a problem, he or she will take responsibility for its solution.

The major construction firms, acting as project managers and even clients, provide a focal point for the management of the team decisionmaking process. At the outset, they establish a lateral team structure of peers, including many architects and engineers, eliminating the multiple accountability gaps that result from divided responsibility (compare figure 4.7 and figure 2.11). This project management style ensures the maximum intellectual contribution of all the individual workers, including the building industry, manufacturers, and contractors, who consequently are involved in the design, manufacturing, and installation of a wide range of products.

This team decisionmaking environment seems to have had no negative impact on construction time, real costs, or strength of image of the finished building. Indeed, cost is kept within ten percent of initial estimates; design and construction time is not longer than in the West; quality control is greatly improved in envelope and servicing system design; and the approach lends a cohesiveness to the overall appearance, detail, and finish.

Distributed and Highly Accessible Servicing Systems

New Japanese office buildings demonstrate highly rationalized servicing systems or cores. The multiple cores are distributed to minimize vertical and horizontal maneuvering, and to improve local management, control, and maintenance. Moreover, all of the building service systems — mechanical, telecommunications, fire, security, and elevators — are easily accessible throughout their runs to ensure long-term serviceability and change.

First, the new Japanese office has a greatly increased percentage of floor area committed to electrical/telecommunication and mechanical rooms (see figure 4.8). The building cores are stretched across east and west facades, with direct access to outside walls for air (see figure 4.9). In addition to the increased space allocated to a greater number of vertical service cores, the horizontal plenum space has been reallocated, shifting from conventional commitments of hung ceilings alone to combination ceiling and floor plenum areas.

In the service cores of the Japanese office, innovations include integrated "trees" for HVAC, structure, and cable management; direct access from HVAC rooms to outside walls; rigid frame design

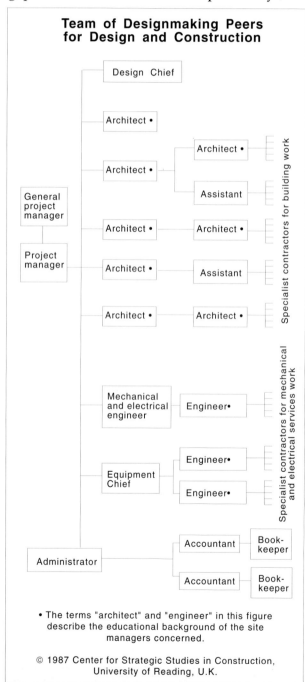

Team of Designmaking Peers for Design and Construction

• The terms "architect" and "engineer" in this figure describe the educational background of the site managers concerned.

© 1987 Center for Strategic Studies in Construction, University of Reading, U.K.

Figure 4.7 Architects with building science, structural, interior, and enclosure design expertise work side by side in design decisionmaking under a project manager (Bennett, Flanagan, and Norman 1987).

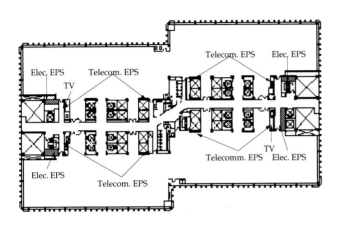

ARK Mori Building

Figure 4.8 The new Japanese office has an increased percentage of floor area committed to electrical, telecommunications, and mechanical systems. (sketch, Mori Biru Architects and Engineers Co., Ltd.)

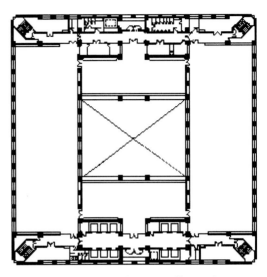

NTT Twins Building - Office Wing

Figure 4.9 Building cores are stretched across (or to) east and west facades with direct access to outside air. (sketch, NTT)

of elevator cores and envelope structure for earthquake resistance; compartmentalized fire management zones; "access carpeting" for cable management; continuous corridor cabinet doors for service core and closet access; and intelligent elevator cores that tally the number of people waiting, for efficient elevator management.

In each case, the Japanese intelligent office building manifests a major commitment to integrating the systems that will share distributed core spaces, refining the integrated system designs for performance, and creating distributed and highly accessible servicing systems for present serviceability and future adaptability.

Rapidly Improving Quality of Life

Although the conventional Japanese office tends to have a recognizable layout of long double rows of desks facing each other, lined up perpendicular to the window wall, with inadequate space and antiquated furniture (see figure 4.10), many organizations are experimenting with very different office layout concepts.

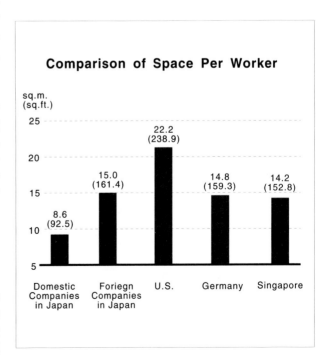

Figure 4.10 The traditional Japanese open office with minimal work space and amenities is rapidly being replaced (NOPA 1988).

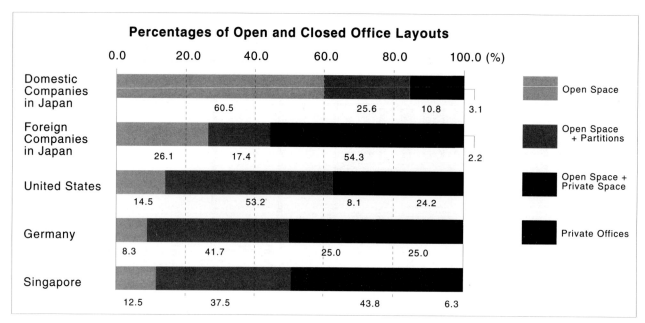

Figure 4.11 *The commitment to open office planning versus closed offices remains strong, but with far greater amenities (NOPA 1988).*

In the NTT, Umeda, and Toshiba buildings, there are model office areas under study with very Western amenities and open office furniture systems (see figure 4.11). These work areas not only feature ergonomic furniture for spatial quality, they incorporate acoustic screens and individually controlled mechanical systems for acoustic, thermal, and air quality.

Beyond the introduction of furniture systems and individual environmental controls, the Japanese building industry is investing heavily in more amenities for the office worker, and surveying their needs and dissatisfactions (see figure 4.12). As a result, extensive outdoor garden areas with adjacent eating facilities and cafés, technical training areas, conference suites, meeting areas, smoking areas, tea rooms, fountain courts, and shops can be found in each new intelligent office building, designed to enhance worker communication and satisfaction.

The Takenaka-Komuten Company has set up a working office to study the interaction between building and user performance, by allowing for flexible light, sound, color, temperature, and humidity settings. Beyond these workstation op-

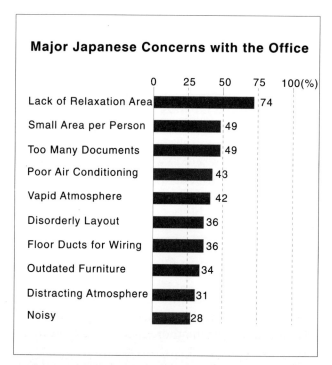

Figure 4.12 *Toward a better workplace, the Japanese building industry surveys the needs and dissatisfactions of office workers (NOPA 1988).*

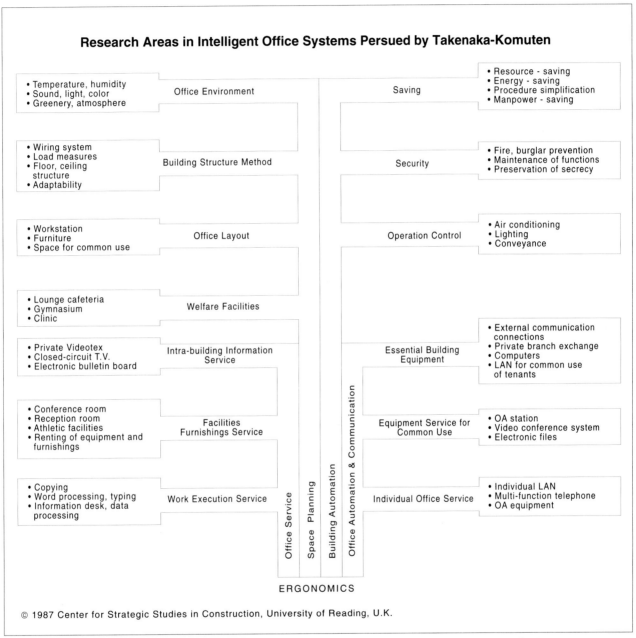

Research Areas in Intelligent Office Systems Persued by Takenaka-Komuten

- Temperature, humidity
- Sound, light, color
- Greenery, atmosphere

Office Environment

- Wiring system
- Load measures
- Floor, ceiling structure
- Adaptability

Building Structure Method

- Workstation
- Furniture
- Space for common use

Office Layout

- Lounge cafeteria
- Gymnasium
- Clinic

Welfare Facilities

- Private Videotex
- Closed-circuit T.V.
- Electronic bulletin board

Intra-building Information Service

- Conference room
- Reception room
- Athletic facilities
- Renting of equipment and furnishings

Facilities Furnishings Service

- Copying
- Word processing, typing
- Information desk, data processing

Work Execution Service

Office Service

Space Planning

Saving

- Resource - saving
- Energy - saving
- Procedure simplification
- Manpower - saving

Security

- Fire, burglar prevention
- Maintenance of functions
- Preservation of secrecy

Operation Control

- Air conditioning
- Lighting
- Conveyance

Essential Building Equipment

- External communication connections
- Private branch exchange
- Computers
- LAN for common use of tenants

Equipment Service for Common Use

- OA station
- Video conference system
- Electronic files

Individual Office Service

- Individual LAN
- Multi-function telephone
- OA equipment

Building Automation

Office Automation & Communication

ERGONOMICS

© 1987 Center for Strategic Studies in Construction, University of Reading, U.K.

Figure 4.13 The Takenaka-Komuten construction company is exploring all the attributes of the "intelligent office system" including sound, light, color, and atmosphere (Bennett, Flanagan, and Norman 1987).

tions, Takenaka-Komuten is studying a wide range of office amenities (see figure 4.13) to understand how offices behave as socio-technical systems. This construction company also created the "cell body" concept in the Umeda Center, which provides the individual worker with environmental control of light, air, and temperature settings.

Despite the fact that most workers will stay with the same firm most of their lives, and will voluntarily work long hours and six-day weeks, the Japanese industry realizes the long-term benefit of an increased quality of life for their workers, and today has the necessary resources to build these high-amenity workplaces.

A Continued Commitment to Resource Management

Japan continues a strong commitment to long-term resource management, responding to resource shortages, waste and pollution management concerns, and import dependencies. Not only does industry continue to pursue energy conservation efforts in production (see figure 4.14), the building sector pursues energy conservation in construction and building operation. Through legislation, financial incentives, and voluntary actions, the Japanese modern office has incorporated responses to energy, water, fresh air, peak power, materials, and manpower limitations.

The four Japanese intelligent buildings studied in depth demonstrated a range of these responses: water conservation with gray water processing systems (Toshiba) and a water recuperating robotic window-washing system (Umeda); energy conservation through fiber-optic "daylighting" (ARK Mori); fresh air conservation through exhaust scrubbers and heavily landscaped sites; land and energy conservation through mixed use planning (ARK Mori, Toshiba, and Umeda); and peak power conservation through energy management systems, as well as water and ice storage systems (Toshiba and NTT).

Beyond these four buildings, however, other projects bear out the Japanese commitment to resource management through effective design, engineering, operation, and maintenance. One outstanding example is the Super Energy Conserving Building by the Ohbayashi Construction Company. This building, both a working office and Ohbayashi's resource research institute, demonstrates a total of 98 energy conservation techniques. Undergoing testing for use in international projects funded and constructed by Ohbayashi, these techniques are expected to save *fifty percent* of the life cycle costs of a conventional building (see figures 4.15 and 4.16). The project is undergoing full monitoring, fine tuning, and development, so that researchers can learn how to design and run a building at lowest overall cost with maximum performance quality.

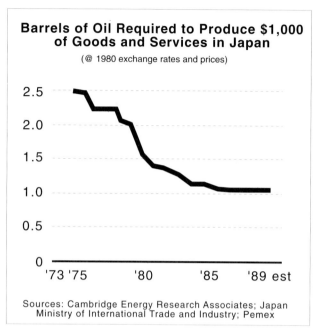

Figure 4.14 Japan maintains strong goals to limit energy use in production such that quality of life does not need to equate with a higher energy use.

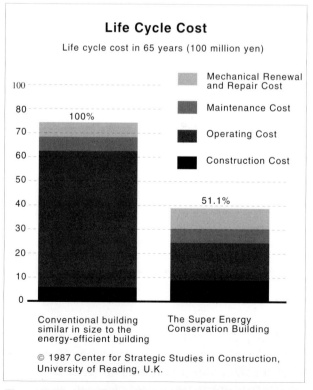

Figure 4.15 The Super Energy Conservation Building by Ohbayashi Corporation Technical Research Institute consumes 50% of the life cycle energy needed by a conventional building (Bennett, Flanagan, and Norman 1987).

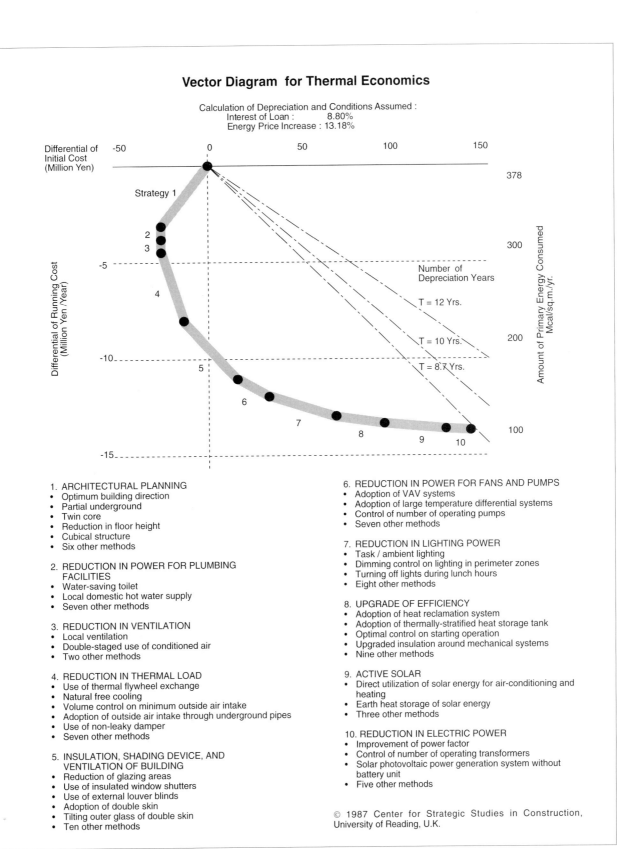

Vector Diagram for Thermal Economics

Calculation of Depreciation and Conditions Assumed :
Interest of Loan :   8.80%
Energy Price Increase : 13.18%

1. ARCHITECTURAL PLANNING
   - Optimum building direction
   - Partial underground
   - Twin core
   - Reduction in floor height
   - Cubical structure
   - Six other methods

2. REDUCTION IN POWER FOR PLUMBING FACILITIES
   - Water-saving toilet
   - Local domestic hot water supply
   - Seven other methods

3. REDUCTION IN VENTILATION
   - Local ventilation
   - Double-staged use of conditioned air
   - Two other methods

4. REDUCTION IN THERMAL LOAD
   - Use of thermal flywheel exchange
   - Natural free cooling
   - Volume control on minimum outside air intake
   - Adoption of outside air intake through underground pipes
   - Use of non-leaky damper
   - Seven other methods

5. INSULATION, SHADING DEVICE, AND VENTILATION OF BUILDING
   - Reduction of glazing areas
   - Use of insulated window shutters
   - Use of external louver blinds
   - Adoption of double skin
   - Tilting outer glass of double skin
   - Ten other methods

6. REDUCTION IN POWER FOR FANS AND PUMPS
   - Adoption of VAV systems
   - Adoption of large temperature differential systems
   - Control of number of operating pumps
   - Seven other methods

7. REDUCTION IN LIGHTING POWER
   - Task / ambient lighting
   - Dimming control on lighting in perimeter zones
   - Turning off lights during lunch hours
   - Eight other methods

8. UPGRADE OF EFFICIENCY
   - Adoption of heat reclamation system
   - Adoption of thermally-stratified heat storage tank
   - Optimal control on starting operation
   - Upgraded insulation around mechanical systems
   - Nine other methods

9. ACTIVE SOLAR
   - Direct utilization of solar energy for air-conditioning and heating
   - Earth heat storage of solar energy
   - Three other methods

10. REDUCTION IN ELECTRIC POWER
    - Improvement of power factor
    - Control of number of operating transformers
    - Solar photovoltaic power generation system without battery unit
    - Five other methods

Figure 4.16 Energy conservation efforts for the Ohbayashi building range from massing and planning decisions to construction details and new conditioning technologies (Bennett, Flanagan, and Norman 1987).

Introducing Robotics into Construction, Maintenance, and Operations

A final area of significant innovation in Japan is the development of building robots for quality assurance, speed, higher standards of safety and health, and for coping with manpower shortages. These developments range from tele-operated robots (human controlled) and programmed robots, to cognitive robots that can plan and act without human intervention.

In Japan, automated equipment can be found on most construction sites, for finishing concrete floors, applying paint and fireproofing, lifting ceiling and wallboard panels into place, and erecting structural steel work (see figure 4.17). Robots have been developed for construction and for building maintenance and operation, including such innovations as:

- the ARK Mori mobile environmental analyzer;
- the Takenaka-Komuten window-washing system;
- the Shimizu concrete finisher and a ceiling panel positioning robot;
- the Taisei exterior wall-painting robot and wallboard manipulator robot (Wright 1989);
- the Toshiba leakage monitoring system; and
- the NTT pass card for building entrance, telephoning, credit transactions, lunch billing, vending machine usage, conference room reservations, and access to computers.

Although the U.S. has been in the forefront of robot development, resources for the application of robots in building construction and operation have been inadequate, as is witnessed by the window-washing system developed in the U.S. but purchased and implemented by the Takenaka-Komuten construction company (see chapter 8).

With its team decisionmaking process and long-term financing and accountability approach to building, Japan is uniquely suited for introducing robots in design, construction, and operation.

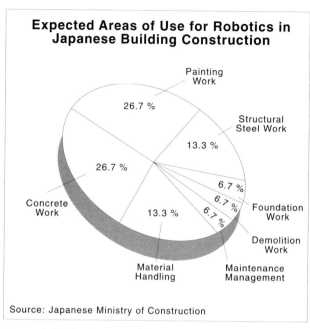

Expected Areas of Use for Robotics in Japanese Building Construction

Painting Work — 26.7 %
Structural Steel Work — 13.3 %
Foundation Work — 6.7 %
Demolition Work — 6.7 %
Maintenance Management — 6.7 %
Material Handling — 13.3 %
Concrete Work — 26.7 %

Source: Japanese Ministry of Construction

Figure 4.17 The Japanese Ministry of Construction estimates the potential automation of various construction tasks, based on a survey of Japanese contractors.

Fields for Employment of Robots Expected in the Near Future

CONSTRUCTION TECHNOLOGY

1. Robots for erecting steel structure
2. Robots for welding at site
3. Conveyor systems for precast concrete plants
4. Robots for finishing concrete floors
5. Robots for erecting and dismantling scaffolding
6. Robots for cleaning in site
7. Robots for applying sealant to exterior walls
8. Robots for painting exterior walls
9. Robots for decommissioning

SUPPLEMENTARY TECHNOLOGY

1. Systems for cleaning floor in factories
2. Robots for disaster prevention
3. Robots for extinguishing fires

Figure 4.18 The Taisei Construction profiles the company's projections for the use of robots in the near future (Suzuki 1983).

Figure 4.18 lists future robotic applications in construction projected by the Taisei Corporation (Suzuki 1983). There is no question that Japan intends to meet its manpower shortages, and to improve building construction quality, as well as long-term environmental quality and building integrity, through the introduction of robotics in design, construction, maintenance, and operation.

An Internal Race To Produce The Most Advanced Intelligent Buildings

The field evaluations in Japan have revealed that the Japanese building industries are engaged in an internal race to produce the most advanced intelligent buildings. These buildings are designed to go beyond a collection of high-tech systems to provide high-quality working environments for the Japanese office workforce. The race is being led by the major building construction firms in Japan, in joint venture with various building product manufacturers and their own internal product divisions. It is a long-term race, with the completion of each building conceived as only a milestone.

References

Chapter References

(Bennett, Flanagan, and Norman 1987)
Bennett, J., R. Flanagan, and G. Norman, *Capital & Countries Report: Japanese Construction Industry*, Reading, U.K.: Centre for Strategic Studies in Construction, University of Reading, 1987.

(NOPA 1988)
NOPA, *Results of Survey on Office Environments in Japan*, Tokyo, Japan: New Office Promotion Association, 1988.

(NTIS 1990)
NTIS, "Panel evaluates Japanese construction technologies," *Foreign Technology*, November 13, 1990, p. 1.

(*NTT Guidebook* 1987)
Planning and Designing Guidebook for Intelligent Buildings, First Edition, Tokyo, Japan: NTT Telecommunications and Architectural Research Division, 1987.

(*Officing* 1988)
Officing: Bringing Amenity and Intelligence to Knowledge Work, Osaka, Japan: Matsushita Electric Works and CRSS, 1988.

(Rubin 1991)
Rubin, Arthur, *Intelligent Building Technology in Japan*, NISTIR 4546, Washington, DC: U.S. Department of Commerce, April 1991.

(Suzuki 1983)
Suzuki, Etsuro, "The View from Japan of Future Building Programs," presented at the Fall Symposium of the Advisory Board on the Built Environment, Washington, DC , November 1983.

(*Umeda Intelligent Building* 1987)
Umeda Intelligent Building: Planning and Application, ed. Takenaka-Komuten Co., Tokyo, Japan: Sho-Koku Sha, 1988.

(Wright 1989)
Wright, Gordon, "Robots tiptoe onto the job site," *Building Design & Construction*, Vol. 30, No. 13, November 1989, p. 64.

Additional Major References

ARK Hills, Tokyo, Japan: Kogyo Chosakai Publishing Co., Ltd., 1987.

Becker F., *The Total Workplace: Facilities Management and the Elastic Organization*, New York: Van Nostrand Reinhold, 1990.

Duffy, Francis, "The emergence of intelligent office buildings in North America, Japan, and Europe," *Proceedings of the High-tech Buildings Conference*, London: Online Publications, 1987.

Intelligent Building, brochure published by the Shimizu Construction Co., Tokyo, Japan, 1986.

Intelligent Building, ed. Intelligent Complex Promotion Committee, Tokyo, Japan: Kabin Publishing Co., 1986.

Intelligent Buildings, ed. B. Atkin, New York: Halstead Press, 1988.

Mallery Stephen, "Catching Some Rays: New Device Delivers Filtered Sunlight Indoors," *Architectural Lighting*, October 1987.

NTT Twins, brochure published by NTT, Tokyo, Japan, 1986.

OA Furniture & Supplies '88, product catalog published by Kokuyo, Tokyo, Japan, 1988.

Office Renaissance, Beyond the Intelligent Buildings, ed. J. Lin, Tokyo, Japan: Sho-Koku Sha, 1986.

Office Today — Searching for a Richer and Better Environment, Takenaka-Komuten Co., Osaka, Japan (undated).

Planning and Detailing of Intelligent Buildings, Tokyo, Japan: Sho-Koku Sha, 1987.

Planning of Intelligent Building, Tokyo, Japan: Kajimi Publishing Co., 1986.

Rigg, David, "Intelligent Buildings—the Japanese Approach," *Proceedings of the High-tech Buildings Conference*, London: Online Publications, 1987.

Sakamoto, Nobuyuki, "The Intelligent Revolution Comes to Japan," *Japan Update*, Winter 1988.

Shimizu Corporation Brochure, Tokyo, Japan (undated).

"Sunlight Collection and Transmission System of the Himawari," brochure by La Foret Engineering and Information Service, Tokyo, Japan (undated).

Takenashi, M., "Intelligent Buildings in Japan," presented at the ASHRAE Forum on Advances in HVAC Systems in Japan, in Atlanta, GA, February 1990.

The Total Environment City — Ark Hills, Tokyo, Japan: Mori Building Co., Ltd., 1986.

Toshiba, brochure published by Toshiba Corporation, Tokyo, Japan (undated).

Umeda Center Building, brochure by Takenaka-Komuten Co., Ltd., Tokyo, Japan, 1987.

5

Toshiba Headquarters

Location:	Shibaru, Tokyo
Completed:	1984
First Occupied:	April 1984
Occupants:	70% Toshiba
	30% Miscellaneous tenants
Population:	7,600 Toshiba employees + tenants
Uses:	Corporate offices
Hours of Operation:	7:30 a.m. - 5:30 p.m.(standard)
	7:30 a.m. - 8:00 p.m. (extended)
Design:	Shimizu Construction Co.
Construction:	SKP (Shimizu & Kajima)
Construction Period:	August 1981 - March 1984
Site Area:	34,525 square meters
Building Footprint:	14,741 square meters
Plan:	H-shaped
Height:	166 meters
Depth:	18 meters
Stories:	40 above ground
	3 underground
Structural Span:	6 meters x 18 meters
	3 meters x 3 meters
Total Floor Area:	162,612 square meters
Floor-to-Floor Height:	3.78 meters
Ceiling Height:	2.56 meters
Typical Office Floor:	3,500 square meters
Office Area:	1,250 square meters/wing
	100 persons/wing
Computer Setup:	Extensive, sophisticated
	local area network (LAN)
	1,000 office automation (OA)
	workstations
Total Cost:	4 billion Yen
	(U.S.$1= 330 Yen, in 1984)

Figure 5.1 Toshiba was the first demonstration of the advanced Japanese workplace, integrating innovations in telecommunications as well as structural and mechanical systems. (photo, Toshiba)

Figure 5.2 A view of the Toshiba building through courtyard sculpture. (photo, The Japan Architect Co., Ltd.)

Profile

In 1984, the Toshiba Corporation, one of the world's largest manufacturers of electronics and communications equipment, completed their new headquarters in Shibaru, Japan, overlooking Tokyo Bay. The Toshiba Headquarters building represents an early implementation of the concept of intelligent buildings, and exhibits a number of innovative features. Most critically, the Toshiba building represents a major forerunner and catalyst to today's growth in the Japanese advanced office.

After a decade of preliminary studies, the designers of Toshiba Headquarters developed their solution for effective networking of operations and management, combining eleven scattered offices into this one building. Situated on the largely undeveloped waterfront of Tokyo Bay, where a factory and warehouses once stood, the Toshiba Headquarters comprises a 40-story headquarters building, a low-rise energy building, and a generous landscaped park that enhances both the aesthetics and air quality of that part of the city (figures 5.1 and 5.2). Although extremely close to the city center, the Toshiba building is removed from the crowded downtown landscape. In this respect, it is the first of its kind in Tokyo; unlike most other high-rise developments planned for dense city lots, the Toshiba building affords some of the luxuries of space and interaction with the natural landscape.

The Toshiba Headquarters building was first occupied in April 1984. At that time, it was the eighth highest building and had the largest average floor area of any office building in Tokyo. Toshiba occupies 70 percent of the 40 stories and rents the remainder to tenants. It was designed to contain 1,000 office automation (OA) workstations for a population of 7,600 employees. A typical office floor contains 3,500 square meters and consists of two wings, each 1,250 square meters of open unobstructed space. The office wings have long north and south facades of 60 meters, with a depth of 18 meters from the exterior wall to the central core. Continuous bands of windows span the exterior walls. The central core extends from east to west, and contains 24 elevators, a 3-meter-wide central corridor, washrooms, 2 fire stairs, mechanical rooms, and assorted small support rooms for tea and other services. Smoke-free (fire safe) lobbies are located at both ends of the central corridor and open onto egress balconies.

A 42-page occupancy manual was prepared prior to the move-in and still provides strict guidelines for how the building is to be used by the Toshiba staff. In addition to providing background information such as transportation alternatives in the area, services available in the complex, and facts about the building, the manual provides explicit instructions on various aspects of building use and was intended to assist occupants in understanding the operation of the building (figure 5.3). The preface, by the President of Toshiba, sets the tone: "Please think of this building as your home and therefore try to take responsibility for it. I believe thinking this way makes people more united."

The layout of the Toshiba offices is very similar throughout the building. Each of the two office wings is divided into two zones, with each zone accommodating about 100 people for a total of approximately 400 people per floor (figure 5.4). A total of 7,000 people work for Toshiba in this building. Within each wing, the layout is very similar, with rows of desks lined up underneath ceiling lighting fixtures, at right angles to the windows. Furniture is conventional and mostly older. Office automation (OA) work areas are shared and generally located close to the core of the building. The ratio of employees per OA unit varies somewhat, from 7 to 12 workers per OA workstation. There appears to be some movement toward the personal acquisition and use of portable desktop units.

Most of the innovations in the Toshiba building do not directly affect the comfort or well-being of workers at their individual workstations. Major innovations tend to center on the innovative design of the central and distributed systems as well as the building core. Large, well-planned core facilities demonstrate competitive, high-quality HVAC, structure, and fire systems with easy access for maintenance and adaptability. Energy management systems and gray water systems demonstrate an ongoing concern for resource conservation. And the electronic executive board room was one of the most advanced the field evaluation team has seen to date.

Although there is occupant dissatisfaction with the air and workstation quality, the expert walkthrough unveiled seven major innovations in component design, systems, and systems integration. One has only to approach the Toshiba Headquarters, through an arbor of trees and azaleas, glimpsing the extensive greenspace and mixed-use amenities, to realize that this building is a landmark in the Japanese advanced office.

Figure 5.3 Toshiba Building Occupancy Manual assists Toshiba employees in the efficient use of the building.

TABLE OF CONTENTS

-PREFACE FROM THE PRESIDENT
-GENERAL INFORMATION ON THE
  BUILDING
-THE PLAN OF OFFICES
-BUILDING EXITS
-ELEVATORS
-DETAILED PLAN AND LAYOUT
-GUIDELINES OF THE STANDARD OFFICE
  FLOOR
-RECEPTION, MEETING ROOM AND
  CONFERENCE ROOM GUIDELINES
-OFFICE SYSTEMS (INCLUDING
  INFORMATION EXCHANGE SYSTEMS)
-EMPLOYEE SERVICES AVAILABLE IN
  THE BUILDING
-FIRE PREVENTION AND MAINTENANCE
  OF COMPANY PRIVACY
-MISCELLANEOUS GUIDELINES
-CONTACTS AND EMERGENCY
  NAMES AND TELEPHONE NUMBERS

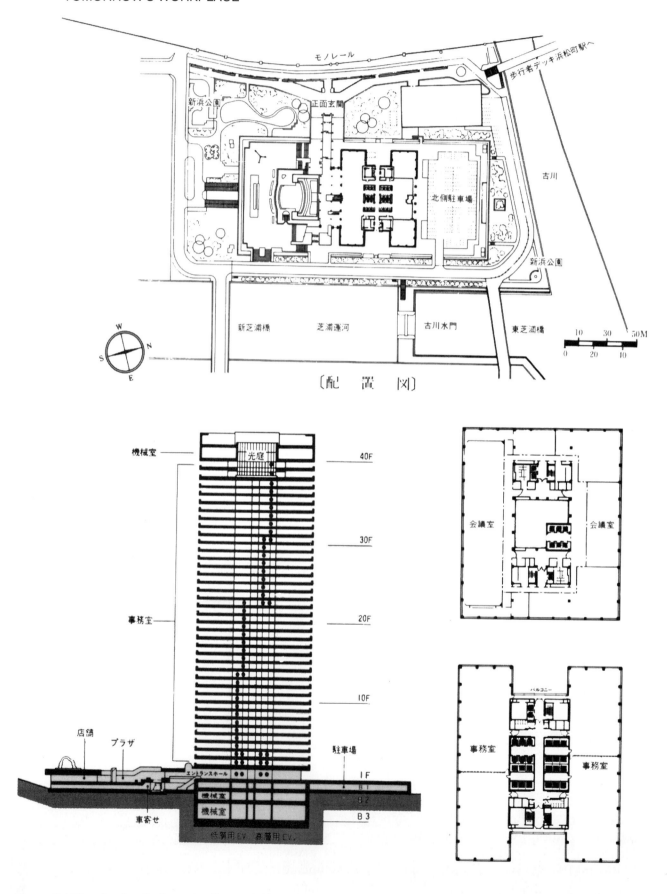

Figure 5.4 The site plan (top), section (bottom left), and typical floor plans (bottom right) of the Toshiba building. (sketches, Toshiba)

The Shimizu Construction Company, partners in the Toshiba Headquarters venture, clarifies the project's attributes:

" There is a growing demand within our society today for the reconsideration and improvement of every aspect of the environment in which we live, work, and play. Such simplistic attitudes that put technology and expense ahead of everything else in the field of construction will no longer be tolerated. Modern buildings should not be considered in terms of functional performance alone.... We are striving to create what we call a 'harmonious living environment,' the basis for a futuristic society that will have both a human and functional emphasis. The environment encompasses many components — cultural, economic, and industrial; ideally, it should consist of pleasant living and working spaces integrated with a solid basis of social services." (Shimizu Corp.)

Although close to the city center, the Toshiba building is situated on the Tokyo Bay waterfront, removed from the crowded downtown landscape.

Extensive Urban Greenspace Provides Occupants Quality Interaction with the Natural Environment

A major trend in intelligent building design in Japan, which was initiated with the Toshiba Headquarters, is increased exposure to urban, open-air greenspace, stretching from street to lobby, into atria and onto roofs. The Toshiba building leads this trend with its park-like setting and entry sequence, its village assembly of buildings surrounding a plaza and its elegant roof garden.

Extensive landscaping provides a meandering entry into the Toshiba Headquarters complex, with a number of distinct mini-park settings for midday walks, discussions, and lunch breaks (figure 5.5). A spacious entry lobby and atrium internally link the office high-rise with lower level support facilities (figure 5.6). The various facilities enclose an outdoor court and fountain, with direct access to a variety of eating establishments and shops. Unlike many single-client buildings, commitments from independent businesses were sought before construction, to ensure an effective multi-use complex.

Figure 5.5 An outdoor fountain and courtyard, surrounded by shops and eating facilities, provide inviting urban space for breaks and lunchtime. (photo, Toshiba)

Most unique is a traditional Japanese garden created in a cutout of the top two floors, where executives in the surrounding offices and conference rooms enjoy a view as though they were on ground level (figure 5.7). This courtyard displaces terminated elevator banks and servicing that is not needed on higher floors.

The focus on greenspace continues with the configuration of the building. "Thinner" floor plates provide more exposure to outdoor landscaped spaces for all employees, with a definite bias toward north and south window areas, where easily shaded visibility can be ensured.

Many studies have shown that quality greenspace areas such as those demonstrated in the Toshiba Headquarters are critical to the productivity and positive attitudes of building occupants. Given the increased immobility of workers due to heightened levels of office automation, the Toshiba building establishes a precedent by increasing environmental contact for all office workers (figure 5.8).

Figure 5.7 A traditional Japanese garden cut out of the center of the top two floors provides a serene view for Toshiba's top executives.

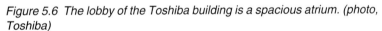

Figure 5.6 The lobby of the Toshiba building is a spacious atrium. (photo, Toshiba)

Figure 5.8 Outdoor circulation areas are sunlit and landscaped to encourage full use of the site and gardens.

Three-dimensional Trees for Structure, HVAC, Cabling, and Fire Systems Ensure Effective Integration for Suitability, Reliability, and Adaptability

The long-term need for vertical and horizontal plenum areas was clearly defined in the early conceptual design stages of the Toshiba building project. The conceptual design effort also profiled the desirable sub-zoning in HVAC, telecommunications, transport, structure and fire systems, and the interrelationships between these systems necessitating team decisionmaking.

The result is a spacious and clear three-dimensional tree in which the four major cable chases (telecommunications and electrical), four major HVAC chases and rooms, two major fire stairs, and 24 sets of elevator banks are integrated with the earthquake-resistant structural frame (figures 5.9 and 5.10). The multiple vertical networks are strategically located in relation to each other and the four major work areas. This multidisciplinary planning effectively anticipates such conditions as office subdivision changes, increased office automation and associated HVAC modifications, and serious fire, wind, and earthquake conditions.

Appendices C and D include the more detailed description and analysis of the mechanical and telecommunications systems.

The configuration of the building core in the early conceptual design stage — its location, dimension, systems integration, access, and modification potential — is key to the long-term performance and adaptability of the intelligent office.

The structure is further refined through the use of earthquake and sway monitoring systems that measure building movement and provide information to computers and systems which then counteract building sway.

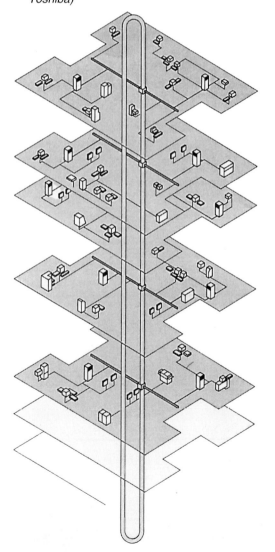

Figure 5.9 Information transmission channels extend to every corner of the building; vertical optical fiber cables and horizontal coaxial cables run like veins throughout the entire building, providing the lifeblood of the OA equipment. (sketch, Toshiba)

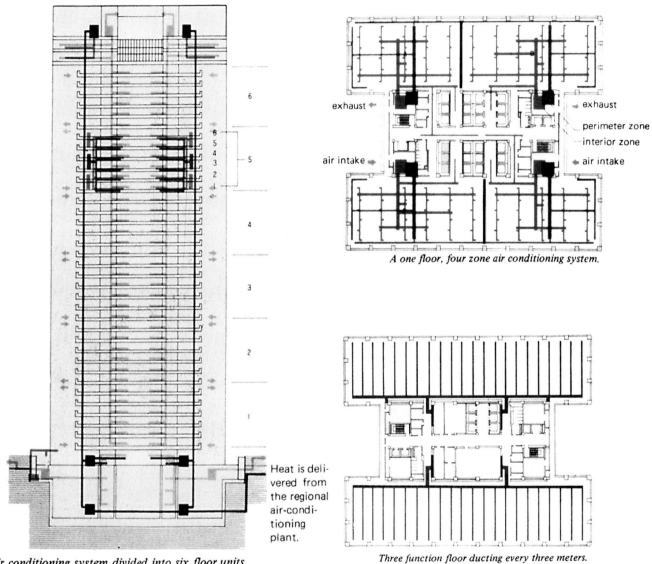

A one floor, four zone air conditioning system.

exhaust

exhaust
perimeter zone
interior zone
air intake

air intake

Heat is deli-
vered from
the regional
air-condi-
tioning
plant.

Air conditioning system divided into six floor units.

Three function floor ducting every three meters.

Figure 5.10 *The massive, distributed networks for structure, mechanical, and telecommunications systems ensure adequate service for the electronic workplaces as well as maintainability and adaptability. Vertically, the HVAC system is divided into units serving six floors (left). Horizontally, the HVAC system is divided into four zones on each floor (top right). The telecommunications network (bottom right) is also divided with four vertical chases on each floor, feeding horizontal floor trenches — spaced every three meters throughout the floor — to handle telephones, electricity, and the office automation system. (sketches, Toshiba)*

Figure 5.11 Core interior walls (top) of the Toshiba building are "cupboards" that house all cabling, and provide easy access to horizontal and vertical plenums, mechanical and electrical closets and rooms (bottom), as well as environmental and tele-communications control panels.

Continuous Interior Cupboard System for Core Walls Allows Easy Subsystem Access, Maintenance, and Modification

The corridor walls throughout the Toshiba building are modularized steel panels with key access. These modular panels provide direct access to all vertical and horizontal plenums, mechanical and electronic rooms, fire systems, plumbing, clocks, thermostats, light switches, emergency systems, elevator equipment, bathrooms, mini-kitchens, and storage (figure 5.11).

The modular "cupboard" system is continuous, lining all core walls in the circulation and office areas. The manageable access to small electronics such as clocks, thermostats, emergency systems, and light switches ensures easy maintenance and repair. The independent access to telephone, power, and data cable networks enables rapid expansion and change, as well as easy maintenance. Vertical plenum connections with horizontal floor trenches are easily accessed and conveniently aligned with the overhead lights. The cupboard doors also provide direct access to the major HVAC rooms and elevator control rooms, as well as bathrooms, mini-kitchens, and leftover storage space (figure 5.12).

The visible quality of the core walls is extremely high, having a continuous panel appearance. Coordinated and aligned controls or "punch outs" replace the conventional chaos of cutouts, doors, and fixtures installed in most office cores.

In contrast to the electrical and HVAC chases and controls that are buried in plaster and concrete, the "cupboard" wall approach to accessible and expandable systems is key to offices of the future, where technologies and environmental demands will be continuously changing.

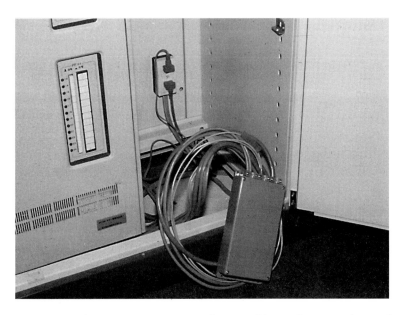

Figure 5.12 Space along the core walls is used for environmental control panels, telecommunication control panels, mechanical and electrical rooms, fire control systems, and even plumbing (above and right). The aesthetically and functionally designed cupboard walls (below) provide an innovative approach to the problem of access, maintenance, and modification to the building's mechanical and electrical systems.

Multiple and Distributed Mechanical Systems Showcase Competitive Manufactures to Meet Varying Thermal Demands

The typical floor in the Toshiba building is divided into four thermal conditioning quadrants in order to minimize the differential loads of north-, south-, east-, and west-facing office areas, typically serviced by one heavily dampered system. Six floors in each quadrant share a mechanical room and independent HVAC equipment. Additional mechanical systems handle the core loads for each set of four floors. This results in 50 independent systems within the building, representing a significant increase over conventional HVAC design in the number, type, and zoning of mechanical rooms and components. Figure 5.13 indicates the configuration of the mechanical and telecommunications systems within the Toshiba building.

The multiple distributed mechanical rooms are far better suited to deal successfully with the shifting environmental needs in offices. These shifts result from variations in working hours, internal loads, external (solar and wind) loads, and the environmental sensitivities of new occupant activities and equipment.

Further enhancing this innovation, Toshiba, along with the Shimizu Construction Company, has installed four different competitive manufacturer's HVAC systems in the building. This installation of competitive systems is designed to test for energy efficiency and thermal performance (but not air quality), in order to find the most effective and efficient products. Showcasing and studying competitive manufacturers is an innovative step in Toshiba's long-term quest for a more intelligent building.

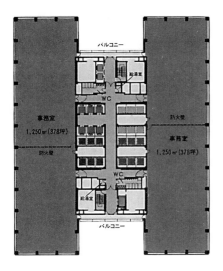

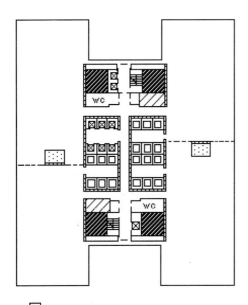

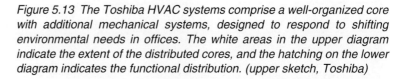

▤ Vertical chase

▨ Mechanical chases/rooms

▦ OA rooms/areas

▨ Electrical chases/rooms

Figure 5.13 The Toshiba HVAC systems comprise a well-organized core with additional mechanical systems, designed to respond to shifting environmental needs in offices. The white areas in the upper diagram indicate the extent of the distributed cores, and the hatching on the lower diagram indicates the functional distribution. (upper sketch, Toshiba)

Gray Water System Demonstrates Commitment to Water Conservation in Japan

Tokyo's large population and shortage of drinking water have led to the introduction of systems for capturing and filtering gray water in Japan's advanced office buildings. This resource conservation effort relies on all waste water, other than sewage water, that can be effectively filtered and reused for some secondary purpose, such as landscape irrigation and toilet water.

The Toshiba building has a particularly effective system with both anaerobic and aerobic filtering. After the water has been used for its primary purpose, e.g., as tap water, it is sent to a vast filtering plant in the second basement of the Toshiba building, where it is processed and then fed back up for secondary (non-drinking water) uses (figure 5.14).

The Toshiba building has also been designed to conserve primary (drinking) water demands through flow restrictors and pressurizers. There is much to learn from the present Japanese efforts, toward achieving truly intelligent office buildings that anticipate all of our resource shortages, including energy, peak power, fresh air, and water.

Figure 5.14 Management of resources, critical to preserving scarce natural resources, includes the recycling of water in the Toshiba Headquarters. After it has been used for its primary purpose, the water is filtered in the basement and then used for secondary purposes such as toilet water and landscape maintenance.

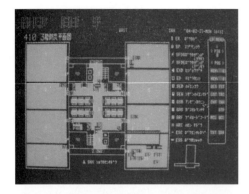

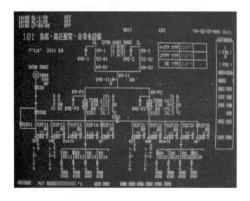

Figure 5.15 In the EMCS headquarters, schedules and status of all HVAC, security, and fire controls can be called up and easily modified. (Toshiba)

Extensive Energy Management Control Systems are Operated by Professional Engineers

The Toshiba building has the most extensive energy management and control system (EMCS) in all of the Japanese buildings studied. Manned by three licensed engineers, a series of independent building management programs are tied to a building computer-aided design (CAD) system. At the basement control center, the schedules and status of all fire, elevator, HVAC, and security controls can be called up, graphically displayed, and modified (figures 5.15 and 5.16). There is a continuous fire check, peak demand controls, equipment monitoring, demand control, light control (on/off), heat source control, office automation cooling control, and trend plotting (figure 5.17).

The energy management program ensures that all systems are in good working condition, and that optimization is being used whenever possible (e.g., economizer cooling and off-peak power). In addition, a field team tests all of the distributed equipment, sensors, and controls on a routine basis and feeds the status back into the EMCS program. However, local HVAC modification and control is still dependent on telephone complaints from the building's occupants, with no automated feedback methods or accumulated knowledge of environmental adequacies.

Nonetheless, the computerized control of the building's energy systems with the expertise of licensed engineers is critical to the effective and efficient use of both equipment and resources.

Figure 5.16 Licensed engineers monitor a sophisticated energy management system that provides a continuous check of all vital systems: fire, peak control demand, lighting, and heating source.

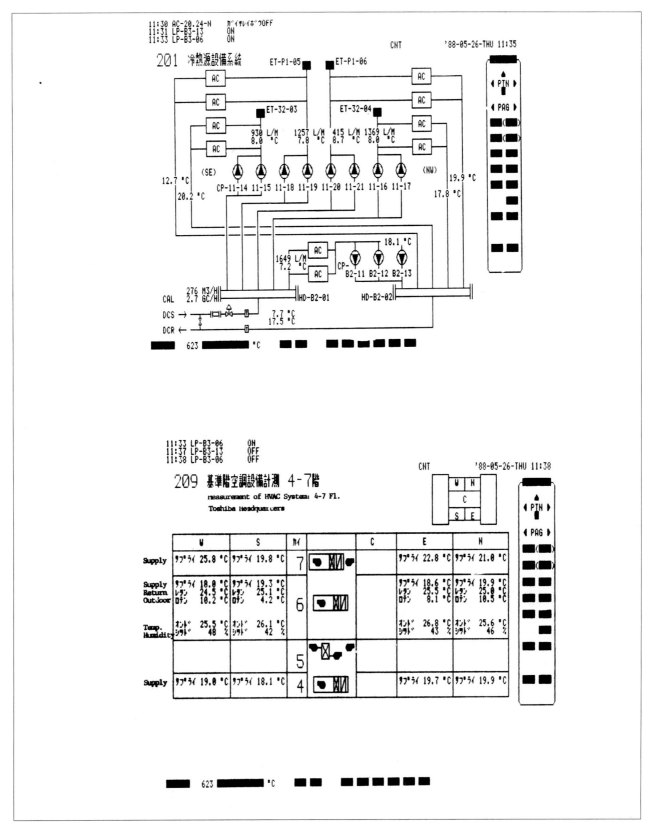

Figure 5.17 *Sample read-outs of heating and cooling systems and environmental status.*

Electronic Board Room Provides a Full Range of Communication Technologies and State-of-the-Art Environmental Controls

A close examination of the executive board room in the Toshiba building reveals a range of advanced systems for accommodating today's electronic communication equipment as well as for managing the thermal, visual, acoustic, and air quality environment.

The telecommunication equipment provides for all forms of presentation media through electronic networks. An audiovisual command table, tastefully designed in a wood enclosure, allows the speaker to project onto a screen any available medium, while standing in front of the audience (figure 5.18). Slides, videos, books pages, overheads, on-line computer screen information, and PC floppy disk information can each be projected from the acoustically and visually enclosed command center, and even graphically modified. The teleconference room also has the facilities to electronically transmit and receive all types of information from outside sources in real time, including video, data, and voice.

The command station also manages the microphones, speakers, curtains, lights, and thermal control in the conference room. A continuous microphone and amplification system

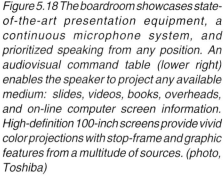

Figure 5.18 The boardroom showcases state-of-the-art presentation equipment, a continuous microphone system, and prioritized speaking from any position. An audiovisual command table (lower right) enables the speaker to project any available medium: slides, videos, books, overheads, and on-line computer screen information. High-definition 100-inch screens provide vivid color projections with stop-frame and graphic features from a multitude of sources. (photo, Toshiba)

has been discreetly integrated into the woodwork of the 40-person conference table, with automatic volume adjustment and prioritized speaking for the designated chairman at any position (figure 5.18). Excellent room acoustics is supported by an acoustic tile ceiling set into an elegant, curved three-dimensional configuration over the large, oval conference table (figure 5.19).

Visual performance is managed through both daylight and artificial light controls. Fully exposed, the windows allow a panoramic view of Tokyo and the landscaped gardens around the Toshiba building. Venetian blinds allow for diffuse light, reducing glare but not daylight ambience, while blackout curtains allow for projection when needed. The electric lights, blinds, and curtains are all controlled from the command table, along with room temperatures.

Because of the thoroughness with which this boardroom has been resolved electronically, acoustically, visually, and thermally, for changing occupancies, activities, and seasons, it should be a viewed as a significant forerunner in the development of the intelligent conference room.

Figure 5.19 Visual performance is supported by venetian blinds that reduce glare and curtains that provide blackout. Acoustic performance is supported by an articulated high-absorption ceiling and a continuous microphone system around the center of the table, which allows for prioritized speaking from any position.

Problems and Prospects

Although the Toshiba building showcases a number of innovative features, there are still many opportunities for improvement. The most serious problems in the Toshiba Headquarters building relate to the quality of the individual
workstations and the work area.

It was clear from both the interviews and questionnaire
responses that occupants have some concerns about the
building (figure 5.20). Slightly more than half of the
respondents disagreed with the statement that the building
was well ventilated. One third rated the building as usually

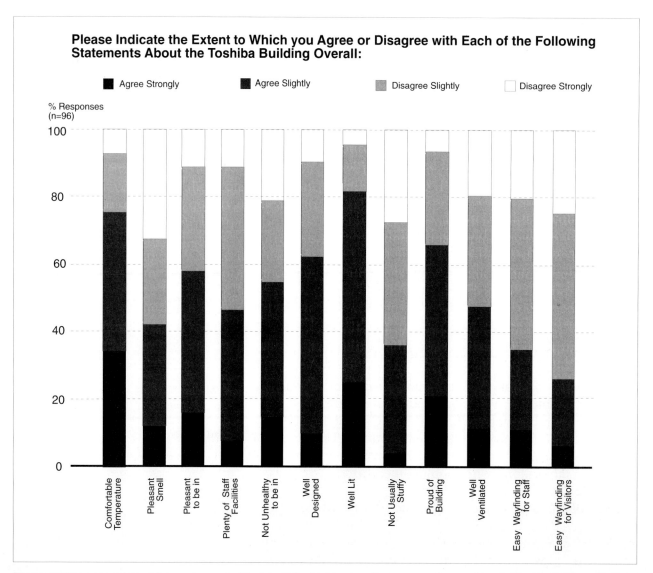

Figure 5.20 In general, Toshiba workers rated their building highly, despite concerns focused on stuffiness and "way finding."

stuffy, and about one quarter claim they are distracted from their work several times a day by too little fresh air and too little air movement. This did not appear to be a localized problem and was fairly consistent over the four zones surveyed. Just under one half rated air freshness as poor or very poor, and over one third rated air movement as poor or very poor.

Occupants are also concerned about the furnishings, which are outdated and constricting, with inadequate surface and storage, no acoustic and glare control, and no cable management (figures 5.21 to 5.23). Questionnaires completed by the occupants clearly reveal concerns about the furnishings. About one half rated their desk and their chair as inappropriate for their work. About the same proportion rated the size of their workspace as inappropriate and rated work storage as insufficient. Over one third are dissatisfied with their individual workspace and feel that the design does not help them work efficiently. Concerns were also expressed about the design of the OA workspaces. Over half the staff disagreed with the statement that the Toshiba building has ample facilities for staff. Especially given these concerns, it is not surprising that one third of all respondents felt the physical characteristics of their work area had a negative effect on their ability to do their work.

In the general office area, the window shading system is

Figure 5.21 Glare from the light fixtures and the windows, combined with a high density of furniture, creates a low spatial and visual quality work environment.

Figure 5.23 Minimal storage space creates cramped working conditions and worker dissatisfaction.

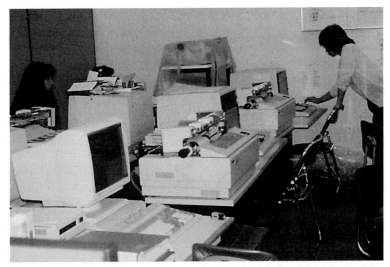

Figure 5.22 Inadequate acoustic covers for the numerous impact printers contribute to poor acoustic quality and the subsequent decrease in productivity levels.

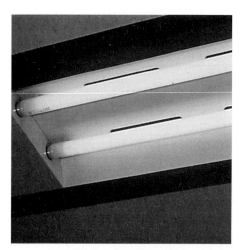

Figure 5.24 Bare-bulb light fixtures produce serious glare, decreasing the visual quality and spatial flexibility of the work environment.

incapable of managing glare while still providing the scenic view. Innovative glass types or exterior and interior systems for shading and diffusing are needed.

The overhead bare-bulb lighting fixtures cause serious glare for both computer (OA) and general office work (figure 5.24). In addition, the rows of fixtures, set up perpendicular to the window, do not allow for flexible furniture layouts. As a result, there is a single workable floor plan in all offices, regardless of activity. Although parabolic louvers have been introduced for glare management in other offices in Japan, no movable (tether or pigtail) lighting systems were seen, and split task-ambient systems are rare.

The horizontal cable distribution plan, relying on rows of floor trenches running parallel to the lights overhead, appears to be inadequate in volume or in accessibility, given the number of new cables strewn across the ceiling plenum and floor. It is clear that more accessible and manageable horizontal cabling alternatives are needed, not only in the Toshiba building but generally in all countries studied (figure 5.25).

These conditions should not be seen as atypical to modern office environments. Although temperature, light, and sound levels may fall within standards the lack of individual control of environmental conditions is a serious concern of workers (figure 5.26).

Figure 5.25 Trench space is both inadequate and improperly used; cables are strewn haphazardly across the ceiling tiles and the floor.

Clearly, these problems are also major market opportunities for new product development and marketing by manufacturers, and for better integration and resolution of existing products by building designers.

The variable air volume HVAC system configuration, used throughout the building for heating and air conditioning, provides uneven air distribution over the vast expanse of workstations, and uneven air quality. Even with one mechanical system for each quadrant (supporting six floors of that quadrant), the HVAC still cannot provide balanced temperature conditions for both exterior and interior desk positions. This is especially serious at interior desks and office automation workstations where more heat is generated than was expected in the original design assumptions. Although the thermal and air quality concerns do not have to be generic to the VAV system type, the density of dampers, controls, and sensors in the Toshiba building is inadequate, and modification difficult or costly.

Surprisingly, Toshiba fails to use their own product lines of personal computers, unit air conditioners, and task lights for local functional and environmental quality. The shortage of personal computers is a serious concern of the employees, who feel that productivity is low due to waiting time. Some employees have purchased their own laptop computers and are using them without mainframe connections, and in inadequate visual and ergonomic settings. There is also a notable absence of Toshiba unit air conditioners to cope with localized window solar loads, and an absence of Toshiba task lights to allow dimming of the glaring overhead lights, and in turn more flexible desk layouts.

**SPOT MEASUREMENTS IN
THE TOSHIBA BUILDING**

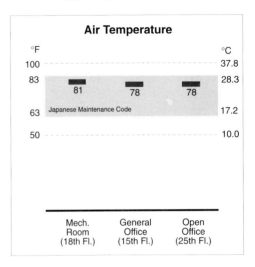

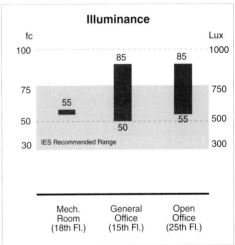

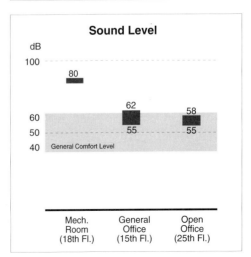

Figure 5.26 Spot measurements in the Toshiba building reinforce findings that light levels and glare were often beyond control.

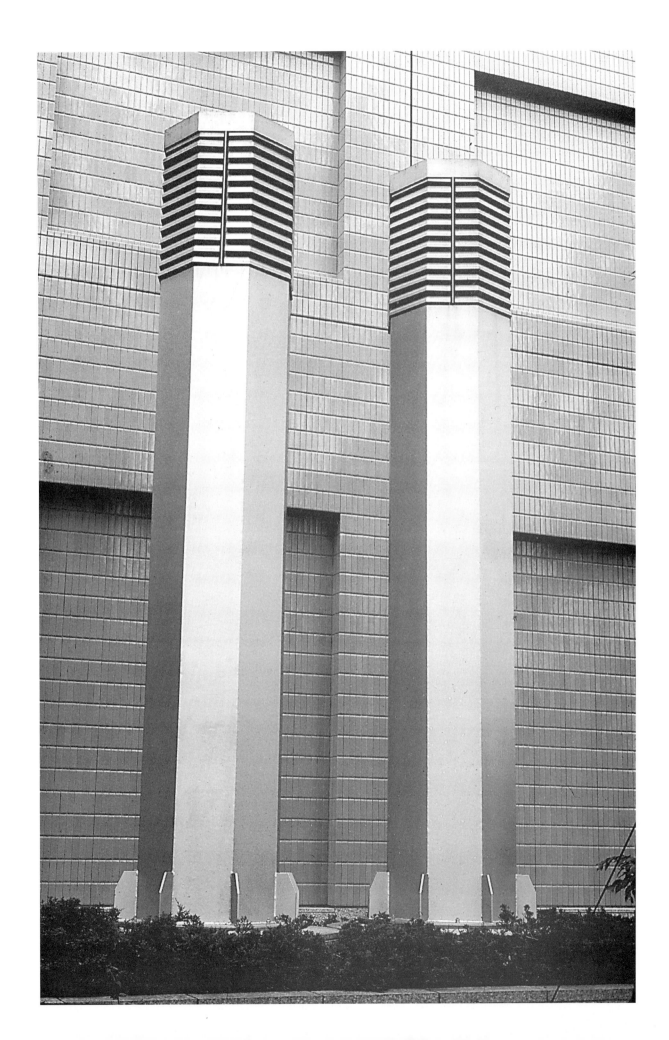

6

NTT Twins Regional Headquarters

Location:	Shinagawa, Tokyo
Completed:	1986
First Occupied:	October 1986
Occupants:	100% NTT employees
Population:	3,000 NTT employees
	• 70% union workers
	• 30 % executives
Uses:	Corporate office space and manufacturing, adjacent to computer facility
Hours of Operation:	7:00 a.m. - 8:00 p.m. (standard)
	Lights left on after hours
Design:	NTT
Construction:	Shinagawa
Construction Period:	March 1984 - September 1986
Site:	30,422 square meters
Building Footprint:	9,421 square meters
Height:	61 meters
Stories:	14 above ground
	2 underground
Structural Span:	3.6 meters x 18 meters
	3.6 meters x 2.4 meters
Total Floor Area:	128,292 square meters
Floor-to-Floor Height:	3.75 meters
Ceiling Height:	2.60 meters
Typical Office Floor:	3,520 square meters
Office Area:	1,000 square meters/wing
	100-130 persons/wing
	model (10-12 square meters/person)
Computer Setup:	Extensive, sophisticated local area network (LAN)
	180 office automation (OA) workstations for 3000 employees
Total Cost:	4 billion Yen
	(US$1= 250 Yen in 1986)

Profile

Following the erection of the Toshiba Headquarters building, other intelligent building projects began to appear in Tokyo. The 14-story twin towers of NTT Regional Headquarters is exemplary, housing a significant arm of Japan's largest corporation (300,000 employees) in a new central facility completed in 1986 in a corner of Shinagawa, near Tokyo Bay (figures 6.1 and 6.2).

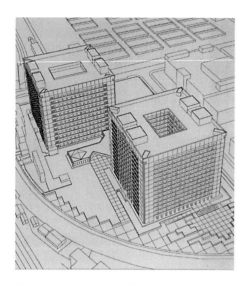

Figure 6.1 The NTT Twins Regional Headquarters comprises an office tower and a central computing tower. (sketch, NTT)

Tokyo's central facility for the National Telephone and Telegraph, by its very nature, demanded intelligence to manage the tremendous number of calls and billing data for the entire Tokyo region. One of the two towers is dedicated to the central computing facility, and is supported by an independent chiller plant building, a major chilled water storage system (using off-peak power), and a fiber-optic network for data transmission. (Figure 6.3 shows the site plan and floor plans of the NTT Twins.)

The second of the two towers is dedicated to the general and executive offices, with elegant lobbies and elevator cores, central dining, and outdoor spaces. A first floor demonstration area houses a model office environment for the promotion of NTT's in-house design and engineering services, and the eventual development of the Japanese workplace throughout NTT's facilities. Ten major innovations in the NTT Twins facility are discussed in this chapter, drawn from the building as a whole and the model office environment.

Figure 6.2 An approach to the office tower of the NTT Twins. (photo, NTT)

One of the most significant factors contributing to the success of this building is the building delivery process. Instead of a plaque honoring a single architectural figure, the NTT cornerstone shows etched photographs of over 100 individuals actively involved in the design, engineering, and construction of the regional headquarters building (see chapter 10, figure 10.12). This tribute is indicative of the team decisionmaking process Japan is famous for rather than a hierarchical and linear process. There is no question that this team process facilitated certain system innovations and critical integrations, as described in the following pages.

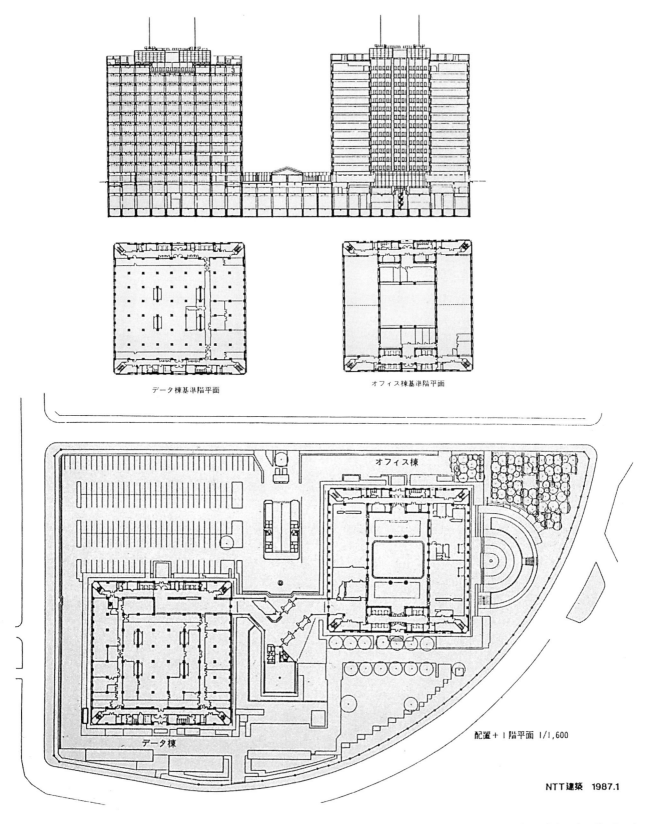

データ棟基準階平面　　　　　　　　オフィス棟基準階平面

オフィス棟

配置＋Ⅰ階平面 1/1,600

データ棟

NTT建築　1987.1

Figure 6.3 The NTT Twins building section (top), typical floor plans of the data and office wings (center), and site plan (bottom). (sketches, NTT)

Open Air Court and Reoriented Massing Improve Exposure to the Outdoors

Both old and new Japanese buildings consciously address nature's "environmental compass," in an effort to reduce thermal stress and enhance the occupant's outdoor contact.

The NTT office tower is a good example of this pervasive attitude toward responsive environmental design. Despite its square form, the office spaces face only north and south, with east and west facades dominated by servicing systems: mechanical, elevator, telecommunications, toilets, and stairs. The service spaces thus act as a buffer to the low, glaring sunlight from the east and west and to the strong winds. The office environments benefit from ideal northern and southern light, natural ventilation, and unshuttered views to the north and south. To further increase environmental contact for the occupants, an open air courtyard has been cut out of the center of the building, significantly increasing the perimeter exposure for all of the building occupants. The outdoor courtyard is beautifully finished with fountains and seating areas that serve as an extension to the lower floor cafeterias. All these features combine to ensure that NTT workers have quality views and access to fresh air at their desks, at the computers, in the lounge areas, and at lunch (figures 6.4 to 6.6).

The intelligent office — with its high level of office automation affecting the worker's visual, spatial, acoustic, thermal, and air quality environmental contact — should feature reduced building depths, appropriate orientations, and the introduction of fresh air and views through open green spaces for all employees.

Figure 6.4 Employees enjoy fresh air and the beautifully landscaped scenery of both the indoor and the outdoor courtyards from their office windows and at lunchtime. (photo, NTT)

Figure 6.5 A walkway leading to the building entry.

Figure 6.6 An interior open air courtyard adjacent to the cafeteria.

Operable Windows and Punctured Blinds Allow Individual Control of Light, Air, and Sound

The debate continues as to whether tomorrow's office buildings should provide operable windows for natural ventilation and outdoor access, and if so, how the reintroduction of operable windows affects the maximum height of the building, the maximum depth of office areas, and the configuration of today's mechanical system.

The design team for the NTT Twins maintains that this amenity is critical to worker satisfaction, resulting in electrically operated windows throughout the complex, facing both the street and the courtyard. At the push of a button, the occupants can slide their windows down a maximum of 12 inches, resulting in the intake or exhaust of air, depending on the window's orientation and the distance of the floor from ground (figure 6.7). To compensate for window heat loss or heat gain, independent non-ducted fan-coil units sit over these windows. A four-pipe system on the south manages both heating and cooling when greater solar stresses occur, and a two-pipe system manages heat loss on the north, each with an automatic shutoff control when windows are opened.

The window control is wired for readout at the EMCS (Energy Management Control System) station, though the window can be opened and closed only at the individual unit. Punctured venetian blinds can also be electrically lowered over the windows to reduce the brightness contrast or glare on computer screens, while still allowing air flow (figure 6.8). These punctured blinds may also contribute to improving the office acoustics, by breaking up sound reflection from the window.

In general, the individual NTT office worker has only timidly operated the shared windows and blinds, though in areas of thermal or visual stress they are consistently used.

Although only marginal air flow was measured in several locations, and erratic mechanical air flow distribution patterns were also noted, the addition of operable windows in intelligent office buildings should not be dismissed. Instead, an attempt at solving these system problems should be undertaken by today's design professionals. In a questionnaire distributed to NTT workers, the operable windows in the building were ranked very highly as an amenity, reinforcing previous findings in Germany that a scenic view, daylight, and access to fresh air are the most desired amenities of the high-tech office worker.

Figure 6.7 Electrically operated windows provide fresh air to workers, increasing air quality and overall worker satisfaction.

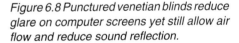

Figure 6.8 Punctured venetian blinds reduce glare on computer screens yet still allow air flow and reduce sound reflection.

Multiple Cores Combine the Efficiency of Central Systems and the Control of Distributed Mechanical Systems

Similar to the Toshiba building, the NTT Twins building incorporates multiple distributed cores at the perimeter wall on the east and west facades. These core areas contain elevators, fire stairs, break rooms, toilets, tea rooms, mechanical rooms, and telecommunication rooms.

The mechanical rooms house individual air handlers for independently conditioning four zones on each floor, with direct access to outside air through louvered windows on the facade. Hot water from the central heat recovery system and cold water from the off-peak cold water storage tank are brought through vertical shaft space in the distributed mechanical rooms to the individual air handlers, maximizing energy efficiency while enabling independent control.

The fire stairs are situated at the corners of the buildings, naturally lit to invite pedestrian circulation, and to enable safe passage without lighting energy usage or daytime emergency lighting. Close to the central elevator bank, the fire stairs remain open to the corridors to entice circulation, with automatic door closures activated in the event of a fire (figure 6.9).

The telecommunication rooms are oversized in anticipation of future needs. Presently, the rooms handle only vertical cabling and telephone patch panels, with all mainframes housed in the adjacent computer tower.

Although the horizontal runs from these distributed mechanical and telecommunication rooms are still excessively long, the zone control is improved over conventional single core central system buildings, and the access for maintenance and expansion is far superior (figures 6.10 to 6.12).

The introduction of continuous core areas along the east and west facades, seen in both the NTT and Toshiba buildings, effectively reduces the environmental stress on the occupied spaces (from low sun angles and wind), and enhances the size, proximity, and access to servicing systems. In the case of the NTT building, these perimeter core areas do not extend into the heart of the building, enabling the introduction of an open air court for views, light, and air. This court provides critical amenities to the office areas, employee break areas, smoking rooms, and ground floor cafeteria.

Figure 6.9 Open fire stairs encourage workers to circulate between floors. Automatic door closures provide fire safety.

NTT Shinagawa TWINS feeder line system

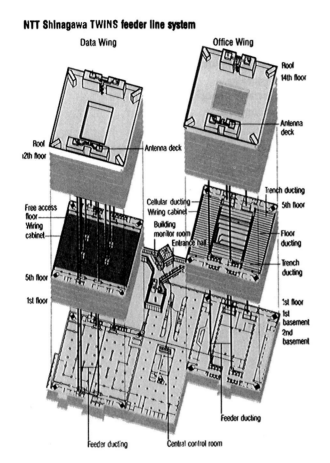

Figure 6.10 *Substantial distributed cores ensure adequate capacitance and access for the HVAC and telecommunications systems. (sketch, NTT)*

Wiring on each floor

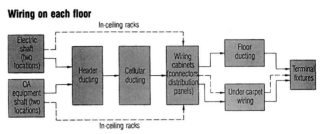

Figure 6.11 *In the main distribution routes, trenches are used to lay thick cables. Office area feeder wiring is handled through a cellular duct system. Telephone and data lines are connected to workstations by under-carpet wiring.(sketch, NTT)*

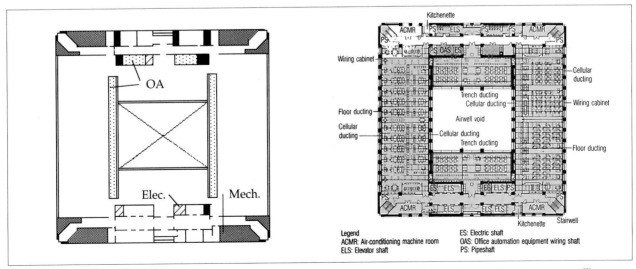

Figure 6.12 *Distributed cores increase the flexibility of office layout (left), allowing for two large columnless open office areas of approximately 1000 square meters each on the north and south sides (right). Office areas of 300 square meters along the east and west facades support either electronically equipped conference/training rooms or OA workstations. (right sketch, NTT)*

Resource Conservation Becomes an Intelligent Office Goal: Heat Recovery from Computer Tower to Heat Office Tower, Off-peak Chilled Water Storage, and Gray Water Recovery

The NTT Twins building designers recognized at the outset of the project that limited resources and excessive operational costs affect the long-term economics of the organization and, indeed, the city of Tokyo. The mechanical system design at the NTT Twins building takes significant advantage of internal load balancing, off-peak energy use, and gray water recovery to fully utilize all electrical, heat, and water resources.

A gray water reclamation system has been incorporated to recover water from the cooling towers as well as rain runoff, for secondary use in toilets and irrigation. Although not as extensive as the Toshiba gray water reclamation system with aerobic and anaerobic filtering, the NTT project continues the commitment to the management of limited resources through a full range of conservation measures. Each of these resource management systems has major space and configurational implications in the design of the building and contribute to the overall project massing and enclosure design (figures 6.13 and 6.14).

For all perimeter heating needs in the office tower, heat is recovered from the mainframe computers in the computer tower through double-bundle condensers. For cost effectively meeting the cooling demands of the office and computer towers, the third basement is filled with chilled water

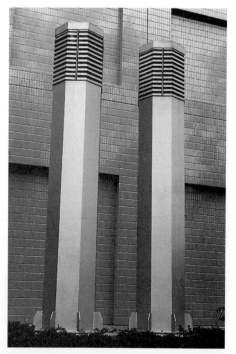

Figure 6.13 Air intake and exhaust towers become futuristic sculptures on the site.

Figure 6.14 As well as providing energy-efficient heat exchange, the NTT cooling towers provide enclosure to the landscaped areas. (photo, NTT)

storage tanks to allow off-peak electricity to be used for cold water production (figure 6.15). The tanks are multiple baffled to prevent the warmer return water from diluting the cooler stored water, thereby increasing the efficiency of the system. The recovered hot water from the computer tower and the chilled water from the off-peak storage tanks are then piped to the individual air handling units on each floor to meet heating and cooling loads. The chilled water storage tanks also provide shock absorption for the building in the event of an earthquake.

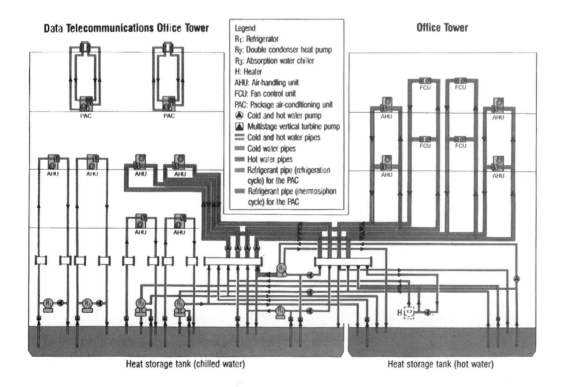

Figure 6.15 Within the air-conditioning system of the NTT Twins, the off-peak water storage tanks filling the basement provide energy-efficient thermal and peak-load management for the complex. (diagram, NTT)

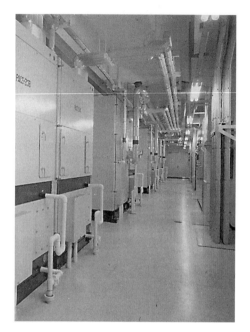

Figure 6.16 Thermosiphoning systems distribute liquefied refrigerants between indoor and outdoor heat exchangers contributing to energy conservation. (photo, NTT)

Thermosiphoning System Further Contributes to Energy Conservation

Seven of the distributed mechanical rooms in the NTT Twins building house experimental Mitsubishi thermosiphoning systems. Such systems distribute the liquefied refrigerants through natural thermosiphoning action between indoor and outdoor heat exchangers (figure 6.16). The evaporator is installed inside on the tenth floor computer center, and the condenser is mounted outdoors at a higher level with a minimum vertical distance of 4 meters and a maximum of 30 meters. The capacity of each thermosiphon unit is 1200 kcal/ hr. With full use made of economizer cooling without conventional compressors, significant energy savings are possible. To date, an 18% savings has been recorded, and NTT plans to increase the number of thermosiphon systems from seven to all 100 mechanical rooms. Dedicated mechanical refrigeration units back up and supplement the thermosiphoning systems.

The Solar Domestic Hot Water System, with Heat Dissipation Units for Cooling at Stagnation Temperatures, Offers Energy Conservation and System Longevity

Figure 6.17 Energy conservation measures include solar hot water needs; Dakin™ fan-coil units are used to prevent overheating, thereby increasing system longevity. (photo, NTT)

Most of the domestic hot water needs of the kitchen and cafeteria in the NTT Twins building are supplied by 270 hot water solar panels. The solar panels, 4 feet by 8 feet in length, are arranged in two rows of racks on the roof (figure 6.17).

Although the use of solar hot water systems is not in itself unprecedented, the Dakin™ heat dissipation units for cooling the panels at stagnation temperature are unique. These fan-coil units dissipate excess heat above set point temperatures to prevent overheating in the collectors.

Ceiling Unit Houses Lighting, Mechanical, Fire, and Emergency System Terminal Units Without Impairing Acoustic Integrity

One of the most serious concerns in the design of acoustic ceilings is the weakened noise reduction (NRC) ratings that result after lighting, mechanical, fire, and emergency systems are inserted into the ceiling plane.

The NTT Twins building uses a fully integrated and refined drop-in ceiling fixture for mechanical supply and return, ambient lighting, emergency lighting, public address, smoke detectors, and sprinkler heads (figure 6.18). Although integrated ceiling drop-ins are not novel, this system is well resolved aesthetically, acoustically (still ensuring a very high level of noise absorption by the ceiling system), and in terms of mechanical performance, by avoiding short-circuiting between supply and return (figure 6.19). However, the bare-bulb light fixtures predominantly shown in this drop-in unit, with ineffective reflectors and no daylight balance, definitely need improvement.

The advantages of an integrated drop-in fixture extend beyond the acoustic integrity of the ceiling and the improved performance of mechanical air distribution. The effective modification of office layouts and addition of OA equipment are most often dependent on the mechanical, electrical, and other servicing system density, accessibility, and integration with each other. This drop-in unit recognizes the spatial and functional adjacencies of the various systems, potentially enabling effective facilities management in relation to changing occupancy densities and activities, over time.

Figure 6.18 Mechanical, electrical, fire, and emergency systems are effectively integrated within the ceiling unit while still maintaining aesthetic and acoustic performance.

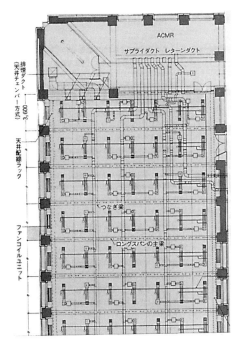

Figure 6.19 This detailed section of the ceiling plan illustrates a design that is well resolved aesthetically, acoustically, and in terms of mechanical performance. (sketch, NTT)

Figure 6.20 Under-carpet wiring extends from the window bench to service local connectivity needs.

Distributed Telecommunications Control Boxes are Housed in Window Benches to Facilitate Access and Localized Enhancements

The NTT Twins building was the first Japanese intelligent office to use the window bench area for housing the boards, connectors, and controls for data, telephone, and power. This outside wall distribution point offers the advantages of feeding cabling from two sides; shortening horizontal runs from each control box; and easing wire labeling and pulling. In addition, the window bench areas are easily accessible, easily ventable, and an effective use of space at NTT, where the fan-coil units are above the windows. A fiber backbone, 100 V electricity, and telephone cable are fed into the window wiring cabinet through three channels in the floor cellular duct. An optic cable connector, 100 V distribution panel, and a small PBX distribution panel are then fed to flat under-carpet wiring for localized connectivity needs (figure 6.20).

The concept of distributed window benches allows for quick modification of the existing office wiring, as well as easy installation of additional equipment and wiring (figure 6.21). Since one of the most critical conditions for the Office of the Future is well managed "connectivity" with an ever-changing menu of office automation equipment, the concept of window benches should be pursued, especially where perimeter heating and cooling loads are eliminated.

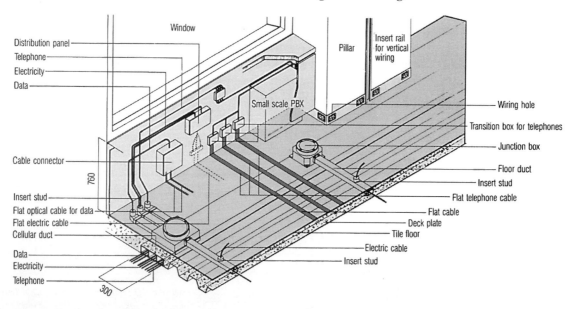

Figures 6.21 Effective use of space includes housing data, telephone, and power controls in window benches, which simplifies accessibility and modification. (diagram, NTT)

Innovations in the Model Office

As previously mentioned, there is a disparity between the general workstations in NTT and the model demonstration office. The majority of floors contain a high-density "typing pool" of desks with few spatial, acoustic, or lighting amenities. On the first floor, however, a model office has been established to demonstrate the possible future office environment and to market the design services of the NTT design/engineering division (figure 6.22). This model office area offers a number of additional design innovations that should be highlighted.

Figure 6.22 The model office area incorporates innovations such as more flexible office furniture systems, improved local environmental controls, and raised-floor cable management. The Kokuyo OA furniture system features raised adjustable arms for telephones and task lights, adjustable height and tilt worksurfaces for VDTs and keyboards, as well as roll-out file cabinets freeing extensive legroom. (photo, NTT)

Figure 6.23 Independent half-ton air conditioners installed under windows on the outside wall supply chilled or hot water to free-standing fan-coil units.

Figure 6.24 Fan-coil columns allow localized control of heating and cooling.

Independent Half-ton Air Conditioners in Window Benches Feed Chilled Water to Central Free-standing Fan-coil Units for Local Control

An attempt was made in the model office area to enable random layouts of the open office furniture systems by freeing the mechanical and lighting systems from a rigid ceiling grid and placing them into free-standing floor units or "columns."

In this case, independent half-ton air conditioners were installed under the windows on the outside wall (figure 6.23), and chilled or hot water is piped from these units through the floor to the free-standing fan-coil units (figure 6.24). These columns allow the workstation group to turn on and off the internal fans with manual switching, and to change the set point temperatures locally. The free-standing columns also house an uplighting system for ambient lighting needs in the office, while task lighting is provided by desk lamps with flexible positioning. All servicing systems were eliminated from the ceiling, resulting in an uninterrupted expanse for acoustic absorption and hidden spline finish.

Although the concept of free-standing environmental conditioning units for local control of heating, cooling, and lighting is excellent for open office planning, the NTT system still shows the problems associated with early demonstrations. The columns are bulky and inapproachable with furniture; the controls for hot and cold water are sometimes crossed (blowing hot rather than cold air); there is only displacement ventilation (an outward spiral) with no laminar flow at the desk; the high-intensity discharge (HID) lighting causes hot spots on the ceiling due to low ceiling heights; fresh air supplies are inadequate; and the multiple chillers are inefficient compared to central chillers.

These problems exist in other forms in the conventional, less flexible office environments. For this NTT innovation, alternatives and refinements can be developed, including integrating environmental conditioning units into the workstations themselves, along with ducted fresh air.

Raised Floor Tiles with a 45-mm Wiring Space and Flush Monuments Provide for Safe, Flexible Power Connections in the Evolving Office

In addition to the free-standing heating, cooling, and lighting columns, the model office area incorporates flush pop-up monuments for power and telephone throughout the model office (figure 6.25). Thus, power is supplied without the bulk and safety hazards of traditional monuments. The model office area also demonstrates a new system for above-floor cable management. A 45-cm square asbestos cement tile with integral feet at the four corners provides 45 millimeters of cable space to enable complete flexibility in workstation layout (figure 6.26). The tiles are set up on the concrete floor slab, sanded on site for leveling, and covered with carpet squares to finish the floor area.

Although both telephone and power are managed in the 45-mm space, data is carried over flat cable under the carpet, presenting all the traditional problems of bumps in the carpets and plastic ports sticking out of lifted carpet squares. Given estimates of the number of peripherals to be connected per workstation in the future, the 45-mm space will eventually present capacity problems. Nonetheless, the development of a thick tile for cable management with flush outlet boxes would provide major opportunities for the extensive existing open office workplace.

Figure 6.25 Flush pop-up monuments house power and telephone connections, eliminating the bulk and safety hazards of traditional monuments.

Figure 6.26 Raised floor tiles of asbestos enable additional data and power cabling over existing floors. The feet can be sanded on site for leveling, providing a solid walking surface. (photos, Kyodo Kizai Co.)

Problems and Prospects

Much like the Toshiba building, the major problem with the NTT Twins building is the quality of the workstation for the occupants, most clearly illustrated by the vast disparity between the model office and the other 2,000 workstations.

In sharp contrast to the model office area, the typical office areas are expansive, with undifferentiated desk areas, dull colors, a lack of storage area, and a lack of acoustic, thermal, or lighting control (figure 6.27). The bare-bulb light fixtures are poorly related to the office layout and have ineffective reflectors and no daylight balance, although they can be individually switched on and off by the occupants.

In addition, the desperate need for more computers cannot be met by the isolated office automation areas. These dedicated OA areas also demonstrate serious environmental problems of glare, noise, excessive density, inadequate storage, and poor user access (figures 6.28 and 6.29). The waiting time for computer access is too long and hampers overall productivity and communication between work efforts.

Figure 6.27 Individual workstations lack separation, are densely packed, and provide little or no acoustic, thermal, or lighting control.

The design of effective lighting systems and of effective furniture systems to resolve the problems of the individually intelligent workplace is a major market area in the Japanese intelligent office. The model office demonstrates major innovations in movable heating, cooling, lighting, and power systems, as well as demonstrating state-of-the-art ergonomic furniture systems.

Figure 6.28 The OA areas have serious problems of glare, noise, excessive density, inadequate storage, and poor user access.

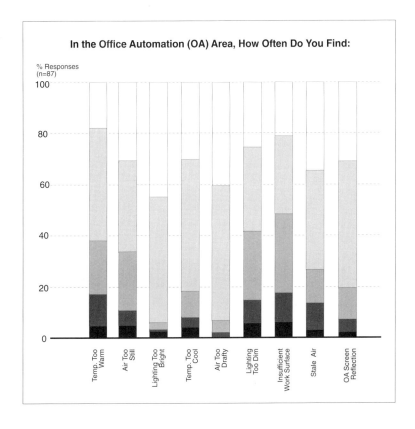

Figure 6.29 The OA areas are too small, too few, and often too warm.

7

ARK Mori Building

Location:	Akasaka, Tokyo
Completed:	1986
First Occupied:	March 1986
Owner:	Mori Building Co., Ltd.
Occupancy:	30% Foreign branches
	50% Financial institutions
Occupant Population:	6,500
Design & Supervision:	Mori Biru Architects and
	Engineers Co., Ltd.
Design:	Irie Miyake Architects & Engineers,
	Inuzuka Engineering Consultants
Construction:	Kajima Corp.,
	Toda Construction Co., Ltd., and
	Fujita Corp.
Construction Period:	November 1983 - March 1986

ARK Hills Complex

Total Site Area:	41,130 square meters
Total Construction	
Costs:	More than 70 billion Yen

ARK Mori Office Building

Ground Floor:	7,900 square meters
Typical Office Floor:	2,800 square meters
Total Floor Area:	181,800 square meters
	(1,960,000 square feet)
Stories:	37 above ground
	4 underground
Height:	153 meters
Floor-to-Floor Height:	3.8 meters
Ceiling Height:	2.6 meters
Structural Span:	6 m x 15 m
Construction Costs:	10 billion Yen
Hours of Operation:	24 hours
	(Main entrance: 7:30 a.m. - 10:00 p.m.)

Figure 7.1 The ARK Hills Complex integrates social space, living space, and working space in a "city within a city." (photo, Urban Renewal Association of Japan)

Figure 7.2 The trademark of the ARK Hills Complex is Fresnel lenses of the Himawari™.

Profile

Known to some as the city within the city of Tokyo, the ARK (Akasaka-Roppongi Knot) Hills Project comprises two million square feet of office space (ARK Mori Building), a 1,000 bed hotel (ANA Hotel), 500 apartments, a television station, and a concert hall, complemented by an array of shops and an urban plaza. Located in the center of Tokyo, it is the largest private urban development in Japan, made possible through the joint efforts of government and private organizations. The land purchase began in 1967 and took 15 years to complete. During that time, the master plan was continuously revised, resulting in the development of an innovative office complex with the direct support of hotels, shops, and apartments for area residents and newcomers (figure 7.1).

The ARK Mori Building in this complex, which is the focus of this study, is owned and managed by the Mori Building Company, which also operates 79 other office buildings in central Tokyo. This major speculative office building was designed for the foreign business community. Some of the world's most influential security companies and banks are among its tenants — Credit Suisse, the Bank of America, Deutsche Bank AG, and Salomon Brothers Asia Ltd. Since its opening in 1986, the Mori Building Company has provided intelligent telecommunication facilities for the advanced communication needs of the tenants, with direct links to major branch offices around the world.

The ARK Mori Building has a number of major innovations to contribute to the definition of the intelligent office, ranging from the advanced communication services, to fiber-optic daylighting (figure 7.2), to a mobile robot for environmental assessment. Figures 7.3 to 7.5 show an aerial view of the complex as well as a section and floor plan of the office building.

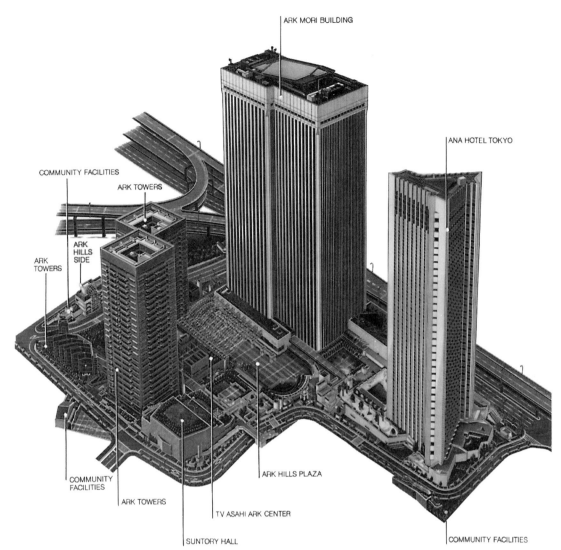

ARK MORI BUILDING

ANA HOTEL TOKYO

COMMUNITY FACILITIES

ARK TOWERS

ARK HILLS SIDE

ARK TOWERS

COMMUNITY FACILITIES

ARK TOWERS

COMMUNITY FACILITIES

ARK HILLS PLAZA

TV ASAHI ARK CENTER

SUNTORY HALL

Figure 7.3 The dominant building in the ARK Hills Complex (above) is the ARK Mori office building, with a double-square floor plan. The building rises 37 stories, with four below-grade floors. (sketch, Mori Biru Architects and Engineers Co., Ltd.)

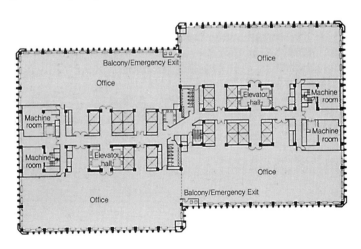

Figure 7.4 A floor plan of the ARK Mori Building. (sketch, Mori Biru Architects and Engineers Co., Ltd.)

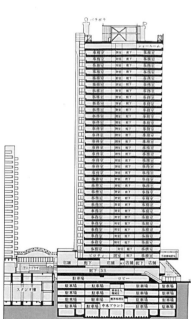

Figure 7.5 A section of the ARK Mori Building. (sketch, Mori Biru Architects and Engineers Co., Ltd)

Figures 7.6 & 7.7 The ARK Hills Complex provides a wide range of amenities from terraced plazas, shops, and restaurants, to concert halls and adult education. (lower photo, Urban Renewal Association of Japan)

"The Total Environment City": The Mixed-Use Complex of Facilities Enhances Socialization and Provides Intelligent Resources for a 24-Hour Community

As a result of an unprecedented and long-range public-private partnership for development, the ARK Hills project represents a major step toward the goal of bringing together human activities throughout the day and year. Avoiding the common problems of long commutes between residence and office, hotels and professional meeting areas, the ARK Hills project offers an integrated urban place to meet a range of needs for the building complex and its adjacent communities. The campus of buildings and functions are not under one roof, but instead surround "green lungs" of open-air urban plazas, filled with fountains, terraced gardens, and even bird sanctuaries (figures 7.6 to 7.8). The development incorporates a 37-floor office building, three residential towers for 500 families, a 900-room hotel, the ASAHI TV production and broadcasting studios, a 2,000-seat classical concert hall, and a plaza/shopping center with restaurants and entertainment.

With careful attention to the scale and activities in the neighboring areas, the ARK Hills Complex offers the resources of an "intelligent city" to the community, going beyond the idea of a self-contained intelligent building. The mix of functions provides a wide range of services and amenities to 6,500 tenants and more than 6,000 visitors daily. The ARK Hills management brings adult education programs, trade and technology shows, and live entertainment to the complex, for the benefit of the tenants and the surrounding community. The project design also enables a highly efficient use of resources with cogeneration and district heating, shared between the offices (that generate heat) and the residences (that need heat). The shops, restaurants, and cultural activities attract customers beyond the workday, from the hotel, apartment complex, and surrounding community, to providing 24-hour usage of all services, parking facilities, plazas, and gardens.

Striving to become the "total environment city-within-a-city," the ARK Hills project incorporates commercial, residential, and cultural activities into an open-air campus, to respond to a growing need for face-to-face socialization and continuing "education" in the information era.

Taikichiro Mori, Chairman and Managing Director of the Mori Building Co., Ltd., views the complex as much more than a conglomeration of multi-functional buildings:

"ARK Hills represents the birth of the 'intelligent city,' a concept that extends beyond the intelligent building.... We believe this space concept represents a major step forward toward the goal of reintegrating human activities split up as the result of industrialization, and of creating coordinated urban spaces that can meet a variety of human needs.

"ARK Hills has, within its grounds, a television station, an office building, a hotel, a concert hall, plaza, and other facilities. By networking these facilities, I would like to develop an educational environment in the broadest sense of the word. I hope that ARK Hills will become the cradle of 21st century civilization."

Figure 7.8 The interior and exterior social spaces are beautifully landscaped and detailed, drawing in 6,500 tenants and 6,000 visitors daily.

An Energy Management Center for the ARK Hills Complex, with a Robotic "Ambassador," Ensures Resource Conservation and Tenant Satisfaction

The efficient distribution and use of energy and water resources are keys to the everyday operation of not only the ARK Mori Building, but the entire ARK Hills Complex (figure 7.9). A centralized energy center in the ARK Mori Building provides state-of-the-art management of the energy systems, water resources, and facilities maintenance within the complex. Through the use of an on-site energy plant, cogeneration and district heating, central steam and chilled water provide for all of the thermal needs of the complex, with excess energy for adjacent neighborhoods. Given the divergent needs of residences and offices in various seasons and times of day, heat recovery can be effectively used, as well as 24-hour load management.

The ARK Mori Building is planned to provide local control and occupancy comfort through VAV zones of 600 square meters, containing approximately 30-35 workstations. Most significant, however, is the development of a mobile robot for use as an automatic environmental measuring device, to ensure that inadequacies in thermal, acoustic, air quality, and

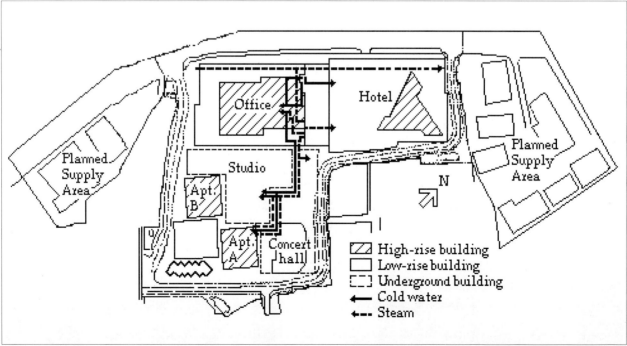

Figure 7.9 The centralized energy center in the basement of the ARK Mori Building is only one example of the advanced energy management effort in the ARK Hills project, in which cogeneration and district heating meet the needs of the diverse facilities.

lighting conditions are quickly recognized and solved (figure 7.10). The TAMS-21™ robot or mobile diagnostic unit can be circulated through the building on a monthly (or more frequent) cycle to measure local temperature, humidity, air speed, noise and light levels, as well as levels of oxygen, carbon monoxide, carbon dioxide, dust, and other particles. The data are logged, in accordance with the grid system of the building floor plan, and recorded on an internal floppy diskette in an Epson personal computer (figure 7.11). The data provide effective feedback to the control center for sensor and controller validation and for adjustment of the environmental systems.

This diagnostic unit, which can be effectively calibrated and maintained in the facilities center, provides a critical service for building management and its tenants. Most buildings have a marginal number of sensors, which are rarely calibrated at move-in, much less years later. Consequently, it is up to the tenants to report complaints of heat, draft, stale air, poor acoustics, or inadequate light — creating a confrontational management style.

Figure 7.10 The TAMS-21™ "robot" circulates throughout the ARK Hills facilities to check sensor/controller calibration and ensure occupant comfort.

The TAMS-21™, on the other hand, is an affordable and maintainable preventative diagnostic tool that offers critical input to the facilities managers and confidence to the ARK Hills tenants, acting as an ambassador for environmental quality between owner and tenant.

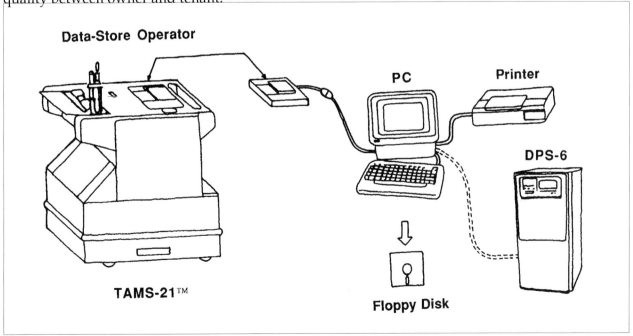

Figure 7.11 Data from the TAMS-21™ provide the control center with effective feedback on building environments. (sketch, Azizan Aziz)

Energy Systems are Built of High-performance Products, Chosen Through Competitive Evaluation

The products that comprise the heating, ventilation, and air conditioning systems for the ARK Hills project, as well as the power, lighting, electronics, and communications systems, were selected after careful study of component and subsystem performances in other buildings owned by the Mori Building Company (figure 7.12).

This was the result of Dr. Kei Mori's insistence that responsible design/building companies should develop physical plants that consist of highly selective, individual components having the best possible performance, which are then integrated into high-performance systems. Although comparative analyses of existing building HVAC components can be seen in Japan, the comparative study first of independent components, then of possible integrated systems incorporating these components, is an important step forward.

One example of this competitive design process is the development of the Sol-Air™ heat recovery heat-pump system by the La Foret Engineering Company, a research arm of the Mori Building Company. This Sol-Air™ heat recovery system uses black aluminum solar panels to absorb heat on winter days and to dissipate heat on summer nights. The solar gain/night loss system provides an energy-efficient thermal source for the screw-type heat pump, via a primary storage tank (of hot water in winter and ice in summer) and an auxiliary storage tank. The Himawari™ Building, in which this system is used, won an award for having the lowest electricity utilization rate in the region.

The competitive evaluations of products and assemblies led to the design of individual yet complementary mechanical solutions for each of the building types in the ARK Hills Complex, collectively using economies of load balancing and heat recovery. While the hotel and residences provide individual environmental control through fan-coil air conditioning units, the office building, television studio, and concert hall provide effective environmental control through single-duct systems and supporting fan-coil units for perimeter comfort and special use spaces.

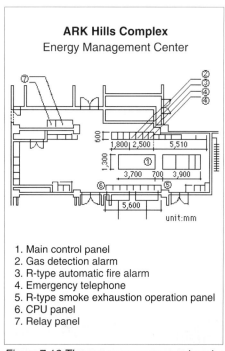

ARK Hills Complex
Energy Management Center

1. Main control panel
2. Gas detection alarm
3. R-type automatic fire alarm
4. Emergency telephone
5. R-type smoke exhaustion operation panel
6. CPU panel
7. Relay panel

Figure 7.12 The energy management center relies on the high-performance products and assemblies throughout the ARK Hills Complex to ensure energy effectiveness.

The in-depth study of the performance of existing HVAC components and systems led to the development of some long-needed innovations, including the TAMS-21™ mobile diagnostic unit described previously. The competitive selection and design of components and assemblies ensure building energy systems that can perform efficiently to keep stride with dwindling resources, and systems that can perform effectively to enable workplaces to keep stride with new technologies (figure 7.13).

Figure 7.13 The HVAC system products were competitively selected and carefully integrated in the central energy plant, a space so polished that it is a showcase of products and performance.

*Figure 7.14 From microwave to fiber
backbones to distributed power/data/voice
closets to the under-floor trench system, the
ARK Mori Building provides connectivity for
the most demanding of clients. (photo, Urban
Renewal Association of Japan)*

The Telecommunications Network Configuration Anticipates the Dynamic and Increasing Office Automation Needs of the International Banking and Investment Communities

The ARK Mori Complex is located in the prestigious Akasaka district of embassies and businesses, and was a natural site for attracting the most advanced international businesses, offices that need 24-hour linkage to data networks and stock exchanges around the world. The Mori Building Company clearly planned for the dynamic office environments that would be necessary, by incorporating shared tenant services, CATV (community antenna television), fiber-optic backbones, cable trenches, high-density mechanical diffusers and controls, and extra structural support for increased computer needs (figures 7.14 and 7.15). In Nobuyuki Sakamoto's article in *Japan Update*, he describes the demands that ARK Mori tenants place on the telecommunications and mechanical systems, "There can be no time difference for the ARK Mori Building, no rest for the air conditioning, the special circuits for the computers, or the lights. At about the time the New York Stock Exchange is closing, the Tokyo Stock Exchange opens." ("The Intelligent Revolution Comes to Japan," *Japan Update*, Winter 1988, page 12.)

The central telecommunications technology in the ARK Hills

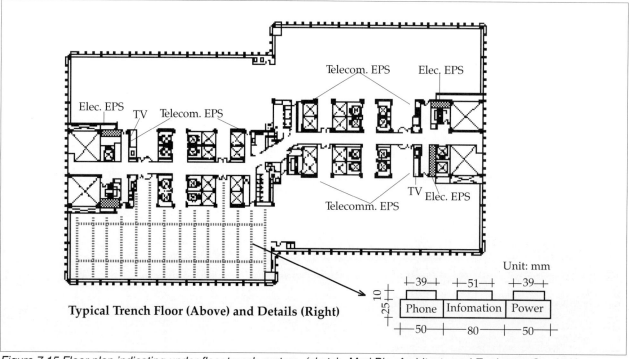

Figure 7.15 Floor plan indicating under-floor trench system. (sketch, Mori Biru Architects and Engineers Co., Ltd.)

Complex includes telephone networks that can be offered as shared tenant services; microwave service; and an extensive CATV service also shared by tenants (figure 7.16). The CATV supports both television and a sophisticated security system. The television service is a necessity, since the complex is in the shadow of Tokyo Tower, where broadcasts block out most other reception. The television service also provides the teleconferencing capability for the ARK Hills Complex, connecting any business with its main office for corporate meetings. The security system with closed-circuit TV is utilized for motion detection and fire and earthquake detection, and also enables distress calls from elderly residents. The system monitors send information to the central plant through closed-circuit TV, for automatic system modification, or management response and broadcasts.

Within the office complex, the developers of the office building provide the flexibility for tenants to add any service they want, similar to sophisticated shared tenant services in the United States. In addition to the fiber-optic backbone with four outlets per floor, there are two types of communications networks running through the floor trench ducts — 50 mm x 25 mm telephone and electric cables and 50 mm x 80 mm data cables — as well as provision for overflow cabling in the ceiling. In addition, each floor is equipped with two sets of circuits connected to a rooftop parabolic antenna for satellite communications. The trench floor ducts in the building are equipped with outlets at one-meter and three-meter intervals throughout every floor. This design enables tenant companies to locate their computers or telephone terminals literally wherever they wish. There are eight electrical/mechanical closets for each floor, with enough riser capacity to provide the necessary services to all office floors over time.

The tenants have the option of installing a second raised floor to accommodate increasing connectivity and thermal conditioning needs. Salomon Brothers Asia, Ltd., for example, installed a raised floor to support the massive number of terminals, printers, and other peripherals needed on a trading floor, and to increase the cooling capability for the floor. In anticipation of the high density of computers to be introduced by the international tenants, the ARK Mori Building has heavy-duty flooring, structurally reinforced to support up to 500 kilograms per square meter. This represents nearly twice the capacity of an ordinary structure in Japan. Planning for the ever-changing and increasing use of computers, telephones, and electrical needs, has enabled the ARK Hill Complex to attract and retain over sixteen international financial and securities institutions, the highest density of "intelligence-dependent" businesses in Tokyo.

Figure 7.16 A television studio and TV cable throughout the building provides an extensive CATV service to tenants, including teleconferencing between Tokyo offices.

Himawari™ Sunlight Collector Provides Natural Daylight to Deep Interior Spaces, and an Alternate Energy Source for the Future

As buildings have become taller and deeper in response to development pressures, workplaces and social spaces have begun to be further removed from the nurturing qualities of daylight. In response to this growing condition, Dr. Kei Mori began the development of the Himawari™ sunlight collector in the 1980s, for use in the most remote corners of architectural space (figure 7.17). The Himawari™ system uses fiberoptic light transmission devices to filter ultraviolet and infrared rays while transmitting daylight with a high color temperature. The Himawari™, or "sunflower," has wide-ranging applications in architecture, health care, agriculture, horticulture, space exploration, biotechnology, and hazardous environments.

The principles of the Himawari™ have been outlined by Stephen Mallery in *Architectural Lighting*:

"Light enters the collection system through a protective acrylic resin capsule. Inside the capsule, hexagon-shaped

Figure 7.17 The Himawari™ provides natural daylight deep into interior spaces through Fresnel lenses and fiber optics. (photo, Urban Renewal Association of Japan)

honeycomb-patterned Fresnel lenses capture incoming parallel light rays. These rays are focused onto the highly
polished input ends of fiber-optic cables. The capsule filters
out some ultraviolet light, but the prismatic qualities of the
Fresnel lenses filter out almost all of the remaining ultraviolet
and about 60% of the infrared rays." (October 1987, page 28.)

The result is a highly flexible system of daylight transmission
from a single-source collector to a myriad of relocatable
fixtures throughout a building via a fiber-optic network
(figure 7.18). The daylighting properties of the Himawari™
make it particularly suitable for the dark interiors of urban
office buildings and underground spaces (figure 7.19), for
museums that need illumination without discoloration or
heat stress, for growing food and flowers, and for environments treating depression, neuralgia, and rheumatism.

In the ARK Mori Complex, a rooftop Himawari™ collector
brings daylight to plants in the hotel lobby and parking
complex, as well as to chandeliers in lobby, conference, and
lounge spaces (figure 7.20). Xenon is integrated into the
system for use as a light source on cloudy days and at night.
A microprocessor-controlled tracking system keeps the lenses
trained on the sun throughout the day and seasons, with a
clock-controlled back-up mechanism for positioning the
Himawari™ when the sun is obscured. Even though eighty
installations of the Himawari™ are operating throughout
Japan, the long-term cost effectiveness of this natural light
source for offices will depend on more competitively priced
fiber-optic cabling (one half the total cost), as well as the
honest long-term accounting of the combined lighting, air-
conditioning, pollution, and health costs of continuing to

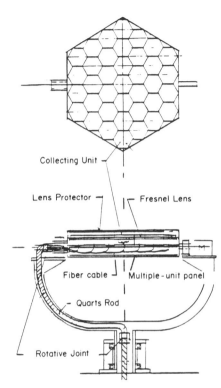

Figure 7.18 Basic design of the Himawari™
solar collector (from *Acta Astronautica*, Vol.
13, No. 2, ©1985 Pergamon Press).

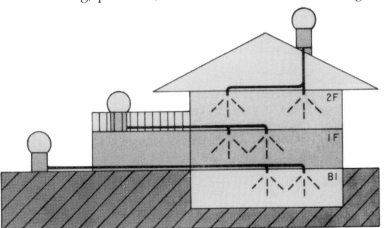

Figure 7.19 The Himawari™ can easily be installed on a roof or balcony,
and transmits light to any area within reach of the optical fiber cables (10m).
(sketch, La Foret Engineering and Information Service Co., Ltd.)

Figure 7.20 The Himawari™ uses fiber optics
to bring sunlight to the lobby and flowers to
the garage.

Figure 7.21 Though the image may be amusing, such environmental and physical therapies are important responses to the stresses of the electronic workplace.

Executive Refreshment Room Helps Reduce Stress in the Electronic Office

One other major innovation in the ARK Mori Building is the addition of an executive lounge or "refreshment" room to escape the stress and noise of the electronic office. Three components of this facility are most unique:

1) enclosed lounge chairs with options for private individual relaxation through gentle massage and enveloping music (figure 7.21);

2) an "environmental room" in which individuals can select various natural settings, such as mountains, forests, or beaches, and then relax in a lounge chair surrounded by the sights and sounds of the selected setting; and

3) a special shower room fitted with a shower head through which daylight is fed to give individuals a therapeutic light dose that stimulates circulation and promotes relaxation and well-being.

These experiments with environmental and physical therapy for the office worker are important steps toward the realization of the impact of technology on the workforce, and important responses to the increasing dislocation of office workers from natural environments and environmental control.

8

Umeda Center Building

Location:	Osaka, Japan
Completed:	1987
First Occupied:	March 1987
Occupants:	24 tenant companies and 14 shops
Uses:	Office space, showrooms, shops, event hall, and art gallery
Owner:	Takenaka Fudosan Co., Ltd.
Design, Construction:	Takenaka-Komuten Co., Ltd.
Design Period:	April 1983 - February 1987
Construction Period:	March 1985 - March 1987
Operated by:	Intelligent Service Umeda Co., Ltd. (ISU)
Site Area:	11,600 square meters
Building Footprint:	3,770 square meters
Total Floor Area:	80,100 square meters
Height:	135 meters
Stories:	32 above ground 2 underground
Floor-to-Floor Height:	3.7 meters
Ceiling Height:	2.6 meters
Typical Office Floor:	2,110 square meters
Total Cost:	24 billion Yen (US$1= 250 Yen, in 1987)

Figure 8.1 The Umeda Center Building is a
modern high-rise with high-tech details from
the urban plaza to the distributed mechanical
rooms. (photo, Takenaka-Komuten Co., Ltd.)

Figure 8.2 Landscaped courtyards integrate
details from the building into an open air
setting.

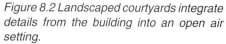

Profile

Situated in Osaka, Japan's second largest city, the Umeda
Center Building was completed in 1987 by the Takenaka-
Komuten construction company as a 32-story speculative
office building surrounded by low-rise, mixed-use facilities
(figures 8.1 and 8.2). Although the ABSIC team did not have
the opportunity to complete an in-depth study of this building,
two one-day walkthroughs, conducted without instrumentation and questionnaires, revealed several major innovations.

Similar to the Toshiba and NTT buildings, the Umeda Center
Building demonstrates team decisionmaking, an evolution-
ary design process in which the building is a learning showcase,
and a coordinated development of site, building, and detail.
Figures 8.3 to 8.5 show the site plan, a building section, and a
typical floor plan. The Umeda Center Building is unique in its
approach to individual control of heating and ventilation
systems, through a highly distributed HVAC system. An
unmanned window-washing system, a portable teleconferencing system, and a storehouse of office furnishing options
are additional innovations demonstrated in this building.

Takenaka's intelligent buildings department considers the
following major features as desirable for intelligent buildings:

"1. *Amenity* — The working environment must provide mental and physical comfort, including space for general purposes, common use, and
resting. Workstations should be attractively arranged. A multi-purpose
atrium is desirable for relaxation and casual meetings. Dining areas
should be attractive. The building should have public spaces with
greenery. Several break areas, equipped with vending machines and
comfortable furniture, should be dispersed throughout the building.
2. *Efficiency* — The efficiencies of office functions such as decisionmaking,
office work, and communications must be improved while reductions
in time spent, space, manpower, facilities, energy, and overall costs are
sought.
3. *Flexibility* — This is required for future organizational changes, for
upgrading existing equipment and accommodating new technologies.
4. *Convenience* — Both manageable office space and easily handled office
equipment are indispensable requirements for future offices. Improvements in the potential of individual functions and facilitation of the
effective use of these functions are required.
5. *Safety and Security* — The prevention of destruction, alteration of
information and data, and the unauthorized use of systems is needed.
The safety of human lives, properties, and buildings is essential.
6. *Reliability* — Abnormalities should be detected early to prevent trouble,
minimize potential harm, and promptly restore normal conditions.
7. *Ergonomics* — The arrangement and improvement of the working
environment should be carried out in conformance with the
psychological and anatomical characteristics of human beings."
(Takenaka-Komuten Co., Ltd.)

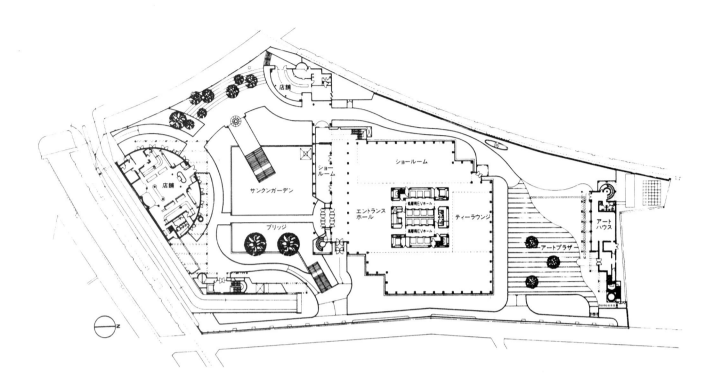

Figure 8.3 Site plan of the Umeda Center Building. (sketch, Takenaka-Komuten Co., Ltd .)

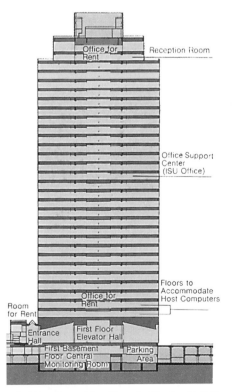

Figure 8.4 Section of the Umeda Center Building. (sketch, Takenaka-Komuten Co., Ltd.)

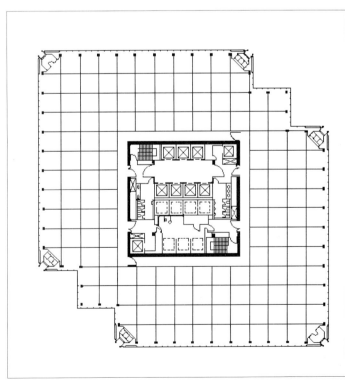

Figure 8.5 Typical floor plan.

Distributed Heating, Cooling, Ventilation, and Lighting Systems Allow Individuals to Control Their Environment at the Desk, and Tenants to be Billed Independently

The major innovation in the Umeda Center Building is the use of over 350 distributed electric air-to-air heat pumps to enable individual control of environmental conditions at the workstation. Conceptually generated to meet the varying needs of tenant occupancies, the building houses 128 distributed HVAC rooms, four per floor, at outside corners for fresh air intake (figure 8.6). Each HVAC room houses three heat pumps that provide heated or cooled air to a maximum of twelve workstations. The workstations are defined by invisible "cell bodies" of 3.2 meters square (10 feet by 10 feet), and each of the more than 4000 workstations is complete with independent environmental controls (figure 8.7).

Through the use of the 128 distributed heat pump rooms, located on the exterior wall of the articulated eight-corner facade, the typical central heating or cooling plant in buildings has been eliminated. Indeed, no central system or controls exist, only central metering of tenant energy uses. No vertical shaft space is needed for HVAC distribution ducts or pipes, and horizontal distribution distances are minimized with the four corner mechanical rooms. Most significant, however, are the independent controls provided within each cell body.

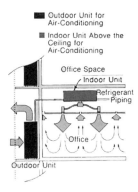

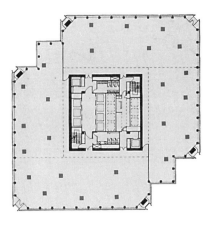

Figure 8.6 Four HVAC rooms per floor provide heated or cooled air to four individual zones (upper). Localized air conditioning units eliminate the need for a central heating or cooling plant (lower). (sketches, Takenaka-Komuten Co., Ltd.)

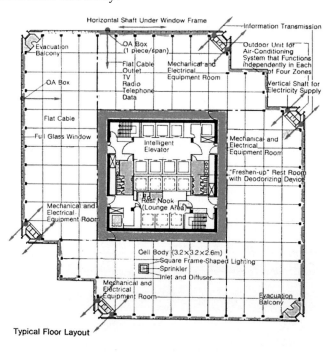

Figure 8.7 The "cell bodies" are served by distributed heat pumps (12 per floor), which feed hot or cold water to the 24 distributed fan-coil units in the ceiling plenum. (sketch, Takenaka-Komuten Co., Ltd.)

The cell body is invisible in terms of wall or desk position, but is outlined by the ceiling HVAC and lighting systems (figure 8.8), and serviced by the under-carpet flat cable for telecommunications. The square, frame-shaped lighting fixture elegantly houses air supply and return diffusers on opposite sides of the periphery (figures 8.9 and 8.10). The fixture surrounds acoustic ceiling tiles, with distributed insets for sprinklers, a suction smoke exhaust system, and speakers for public address (figure 8.11). The floor carpet tiles provide access to under-carpet flat cables for telecommunications, with the data and telephone controllers housed in window benches, as previously described in the NTT building.

Within the cell, each office worker can independently turn the lights on and off and turn the air on and off (to five air changes per hour, maximum). The small group of office workers in a heat pump zone (8 to 12 individuals) can collectively control the supply air temperature to meet local variations in climate, internal heat generation, or time of use. The on/off controls can be changed by dialing up a preset code on the telephone. The air temperature, air velocity, and lighting can be adjusted by selecting the desired conditions from a graphic display on the desktop computer screen (figures 8.12 and 8.13). The "environmental envelope" can remain invisible in an open office plan layout, or each cell can be closed in with walls to accommodate changing needs in privacy, layout, or function (figure 8.14).

Figure 8.8 HVAC/lighting fixtures delineate the perimeters of cell bodies.

Figure 8.10 The ceiling HVAC and lighting system is unobtrusively integrated into the office setting. (photo, Takenaka-Komuten Co., Ltd.)

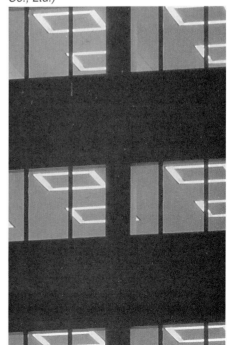

Figure 8.9 The key to individual control of temperature, light, and air is the "cell body," a 3.2 meter square space. (sketch, Takenaka-Komuten Co., Ltd.)

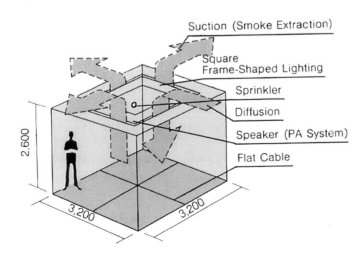

*Figure 8.11 The "cell body" is visually defined
by the light fixture, which houses supply and
return air, individually controllable task-
ambient lighting, and fire and smoke exhaust.*

*Figure 8.12 Desktop computers and telephones enable the individual
worker to set air on and off, lights on and off, as well as set temperatures
to the needs of the small work group.*

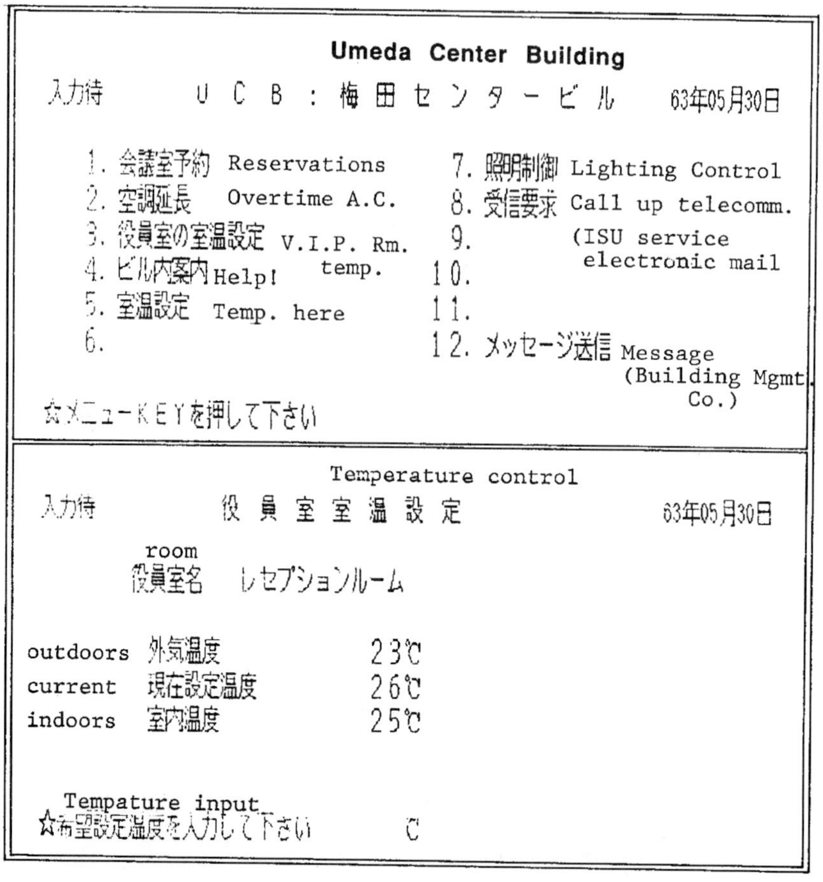

```
                    Umeda  Center  Building
入力待      U C B ： 梅 田 セ ン タ ー ビ ル      63年05月30日

   1. 会議室予約 Reservations     7. 照明制御 Lighting Control
   2. 空調延長   Overtime A.C.    8. 受信要求 Call up telecomm.
   3. 役員室の室温設定 V.I.P. Rm.  9.          (ISU service
   4. ビル内案内 Help!   temp.               electronic mail
   5. 室温設定   Temp. here     1 0.
   6.                         1 1.
                             1 2. メッセージ送信 Message
                                       (Building Mgmt.
                                                Co.)
 ☆メニューKEYを押して下さい

                        Temperature control
入力待        役 員 室 室 温 設 定         63年05月30日
            room
      役員室名   レセプションルーム


outdoors  外気温度            23℃
current   現在設定温度         26℃
indoors   室内温度           25℃


    Tempature input
 ☆希望設定温度を入力して下さい        ℃
```

*Figure 8.13 Workers can adjust temperature settings through a menu on a
desktop computer screen.*

Although supply air set-point temperature changes are communicated to the central plant, along with data from the distributed carbon dioxide and temperature sensors, only the individual or work group decides on comfortable temperatures, air, and light conditions. The central plant simply monitors excesses and economizes in shut-down periods. There is central control of pressurization and smoke extractors, and it took over a year to balance the system. Fresh air is limited to five air changes per hour. All these factors contribute to highly controlled thermal, visual, and air quality.

As a result, the Umeda Center Building can provide excellent environmental quality to the range of tenant layouts: high- and low-density areas, enclosed conference areas, heavily automated areas, and even a computer showroom with its massive heat generation. Lights remain off in many work areas, due to more than adequate daylight, and are off whenever individuals are out of the office. Occupant satisfaction with the workplace is very high, and the quality of the workstation furniture and layout is comparable with standards in the U.S.

Figure 8.14 Whether enclosed with walls or left as part of an open plan office, the cell body remains a distinct "environmental envelope."

Although the system provides excellent local environmental control and billing, some questions about the use of distributed mechanical plants and individual controls are still to be answered: Couldn't the system be designed to enable some economies of scale and load balancing through the use of a central chiller/boiler feeding a closed water loop to distributed water-to-air heat pumps, without sacrificing independent control? Can the system maintain effective pressurization in all user control conditions? Does the on/off air control ensure adequate fresh air at the minimum setting regardless of user density and activity? Were dimming controls for light and air too costly?

Despite these potentials for improvement, the provisions in the Umeda Center Building for individual control of light and air, and small group control of heat and air conditioning without central supervision, have led to excellent environmental quality and worker satisfaction.

Figure 8.15 The thick rubberized tiles enable a greatly increased internal cable network over the original approach of flat cables in existing offices. The thick carpet tile provides 6 to 8 cm of cable channel space. (photos, Kokuyo Corp.)

Thick Channelized Carpet Tiles Enable Undercarpet Cabling to be Installed in Offices Lacking Raised Floors or Trenches

The limited capability of the flat-wire system installed under carpet squares in the Umeda Center Building has to some extent been addressed through an innovative "fat carpet tile" manufactured by Kokuyo. This carpet square, 5 to 10 centimeters in thickness, is a built-up black rubber grid surfaced with carpet (figure 8.15). The rubber grid leaves multi-directional channels below to straddle greater quantities of cable for the increasingly automated office and showcase areas.

In one computer showroom in the Umeda Center Building, a 10-centimeter-thick carpet tile provides 6 to 8 cm of cable channel space. There are no seaming problems or unevenness in the showroom, even with extensive cabling underneath. A subtle manufactured ramp of the same thick tile material enables the floor surface to slope up 10 cm out of the elevator core without a step (figure 8.16). A range of flush outlets for power and data connections has also been developed for integration with the thick tile.

Although this product is an excellent development for offices with modest office technology, it cannot replace a raised floor system for the cabling quantity, flexibility, and access that are needed in highly automated offices. Indeed, it requires a carefully managed template on the existing floor slab to ensure appropriate cable configuration, prior to the laying of these thick, densely footed carpet tiles.

Similarly to the asbestos cement tiles in NTT, the thick rubber-based carpet tile is a very interesting development for existing office environments with modest cabling needs. In addition, it does not suffer from vibration or noise problems associated with many raised floor technologies.

Figure 8.16 A subtle manufactured ramp enables the floor surface to slope up 10 cm out of the elevator core without a step. (photo, Kokuyo Corp.)

Team Design Results in Highly Integrated and Harmonious Decisions for Site, Building, and Detail

Like most of the prominent intelligent buildings in Japan, the Umeda Center Building was designed by a *team* of professionals in design, engineering, construction, and facilities management. In opposition to the Western notion that "A camel is a horse designed by committee," this team decisionmaking process resulted in a building that is highly integrated and harmonious from site to building to detail.

The overall assembly of tall and short buildings, their massing and incorporated site planning, provide a series of outdoor places and experiences that are textured, planted, and detailed to be at one with the main building. Entries, pathways, canopies, benches, tables, even storage sheds and trashcans are detailed in the Umeda style, a level of resolution that can be achieved only through team design (figures 8.17 to 8.22). Independent long-term leases were sold to clients—Canon, Dunkin' Donuts, a night club — before design development, so they could "purchase" uniquely appropriate buildings within the complex.

In the building design, the selection of components, materials, and finishes is carried from the exterior facade through the lobby and into all the distributed service areas. Specialized interior functions, entertainment and conference areas, and even the distributed HVAC rooms are given means for expression on the facade. Indoor settings echo and spill over into the numerous and varied outdoor settings, which comprise 68% of the site, rather than into vacuous windswept plazas. This integration of indoor and outdoor places provides a serenity to office entry and circulation, pleasant views, and a choice of scenes for enjoying coffee, lunch, discussions, or relaxation in the fresh air.

The Umeda Center project demonstrates a concern for the entire office "experience" from the means of transport to the site, from entry, workgroup and office workstation, to break areas, meeting areas, lunch areas, and shops. This concern translates into a necessity for team decisionmaking by developers, clients, facilities managers, exterior and interior architects, landscape architects, engineers, and construction specialists. There is a growing body of proof that today's workforce — tied to computer screens and keyboards for a majority of the workday—benefits physiologically, psychologically, and sociologically from a fully resolved, detailed, and harmonious work environment with continuous design experiences.

Figure 8.17 The team decisionmaking process resulted in a building that is highly integrated and harmonious from site to building to detail. (photo, Takenaka-Komuten Co., Ltd.)

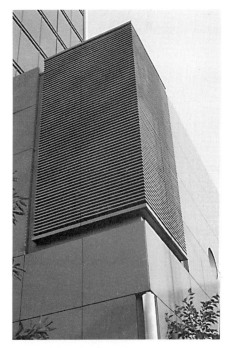

Figure 8.18 Building details extend to the design of fresh air intakes, which define the corners of the building.

Figure 8.20 The landscaped plazas provide "green lungs" for the cluster of shops, restaurants, and offices — refreshment areas for employees and visitors alike.

Figure 8.19 The ground floor cafe provides an elegant place to meet, with views of and access to the outdoors.

Figure 8.21 Even the maintenance shed is integrated into the design.

Figure 8.22 Details provide a harmonious transition from the indoor to the outdoor environment.

Unmanned Window-washing System Offers Manpower and Water Conservation as well as Consistently Clean Windows

The window-washing process at the Umeda Center Building is in direct contrast to that of many "high-tech" office buildings, where window washing is still left to mountain climbers with scaffolds and buckets. Instead, the Umeda Center Building demonstrates the use of robotics married to design rules, for keeping the all-glass facade sparkling.

Despite the articulated form of the Umeda Center Building, it is equipped with a unique unmanned window-washing system that operates from the four roof terraces (figures 8.23 to 8.25). A 14-ton water reservoir and pump is anchored to tracks around the circumference of the top roof, feeding jets of water to a suction vacuum system that hydrofoils its way down the facade, catching and recycling the water to minimize waste and drippage. The unmanned window-washing system is then lowered on a boom arm to the next of the four roofs, to wash the lower facades. A complete window-washing cycle occurs every few months.

The use of a window-washing robot ensures that the facade is regularly cleaned for maintenance and appearance, as well as for views and light, without risk to individuals. In addition to minimizing excessive long-term maintenance costs, the unique configuration of this system supports critical water conservation, by recycling the runoff from each window.

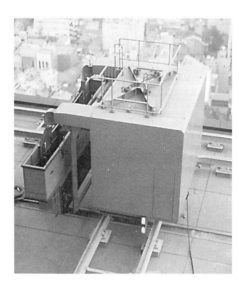

Figure 8.23 The unmanned window-washing system keeps the glass facade sparkling while conserving water.

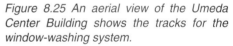

Figure 8.25 An aerial view of the Umeda Center Building shows the tracks for the window-washing system.

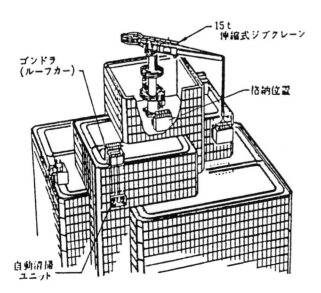

Figure 8.24 A schematic diagram of the system shows the action of the boom arm. (sketch, Takenaka-Komuten Co., Ltd.)

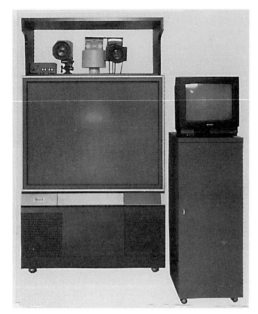

Figure 8.26 The portable teleconferencing system can be set up in any room with video, data, and voice connectors. (photo, Intelligent Service Umeda)

Figure 8.27 Portable teleconferencing facilities include video and audio output, movable microphones, electronic blackboard, and fax machine.

Portable Teleconferencing System Enables Communication between Groups without High Investment in Video Teleconferencing Facilities

Although the Umeda Center management intends to create a permanent teleconferencing room with rear screen projection and multiple screens, the existing teleconferencing assembly is unique in its portability and affordability.

The portable teleconferencing trolleys assembled for the Umeda Center enable any available conference room with fiber-optic connections to be turned into a teleconferencing facility (figure 8.26). A fiber-optic cable connected to the phone line brings video images to a TV on wheels with split-screen capability. Two cameras mounted on this trolley record both conversations and faces, with additional microphones that can move about the conference table and are hardwired into the trolley (figure 8.27). One control box allows for focusing audio and video monitors on certain individuals. The electronic blackboard enables copies to be made of the meetings charts, with the option to reduce four full boards of discussion onto one record sheet. A fax machine is set up alongside the room's telephone for instant transfer of these charts and other records to the remote teleconferencing room.

All of the components in this teleconferencing room are portable and relatively compact, enabling them to be set up in an executive office, a production or demonstration area, or a temporary conference area, with only the cable TV connection or port as a built-in necessity. The time and expense that can be saved through teleconferencing are well known, but up to now the costs of teleconferencing facilities have been prohibitive for use in conventional offices. Eventually, every phone or computer may have video recording and sending capability to enable individuals or groups to meet "face to face" a thousand miles apart. However, until that widespread capability is available, the creation of this portable package of critical equipment provides needed access to teleconferencing capability for the modern office.

Furniture and Option Store in the Umeda Center Building Accommodates Changing Tenant Needs

Many of the environmental and physical shortcomings in office environments result from office "churn," or the changeover of occupancies and functions. In the most successful offices, densities and furniture layouts change continuously, while the necessary mechanical, electrical, lighting, and acoustic modifications corresponding to these changes lag far behind.

The Umeda Center Building attempts to solve the most serious of the thermal and air quality problems that occur in office churn through the dispersion of the central mechanical plant and the introduction of individual control in cell bodies.

The resolution of spatial, lighting, and acoustic problems that occur in office churn, however, has been approached through an in-house option store, which offers such products as parabolic louvers for the frame-shaped light fixture to reduce glare; "thick carpet tiles" with channelized rubber bases for cable management; free-standing acoustic partitions; insert metal stud walls with two sheets of plasterboard and acoustic filler; and ergonomic furniture for spatial and physical comfort.

Many of these spatial and environmental control options can be seen throughout the building (figures 8.28 and 8.29). The Umeda "store" honors returns and trade-ins as office activities and occupancies change. Consequently, the typical mismatch between functional and physical settings that evolves in most conventional office buildings even over a six-month period is not often found in the Umeda Center Building. The thermal, air quality, visual, acoustic, and spatial accommodations supplied by the base building systems along with a well-stocked and informed building "store" are unique, in Japan and elsewhere.

Figure 8.28 The office tenants in the Umeda Center Building can select from a wide range of furnishing and interior options to fine tune the workplace to their needs. (photo, Takenaka-Komuten Co., Ltd.)

Figure 8.29 Workstation furnishings available through the Umeda Center store are compatible with base building systems. (photo, Takenaka-Komuten Co., Ltd.)

9

Glimpses of Invention

As with any research effort, time does not stop for book publication. This is especially true in the case of Japan, where investment and innovation continue at a very rapid pace. The four buildings studied in this book remain four of the most significant advanced workplaces in Japan — each has received the Intelligent Building of the Year award, an award cosponsored by the Japanese Ministry of Construction and the *Nihon Keiza: Shinbun* newspaper. Even so, a number of new projects have built on these successes and have forged further into the future of building design (figure 9.1). Advances from corporations, firms, and individuals range from vapor crystal ice storage systems, intelligent mail robots, intelligent ID cards, individual workstation air conditioning systems, to completely modular office buildings assembled robotically. Each of these endeavors demonstrates a reliance on learning from the efforts of others and investing heavily in future generations. In contrast to common rumors, Japanese innovators freely show their latest developments, listening to criticisms carefully. They see each building and each invention as another stage of development — development evolving so quickly that protectionism is unnecessary.

Without the benefit of the interdisciplinary field team and the two-day evaluation period, we cannot discuss these innovative projects at a level of detail equal to that of the previous chapters. However, offering glimpses of these inventions should at least inspire other studies of these advanced workplaces and concepts. On the following pages, three building projects are discussed — NEC's new head office building in Tokyo, the IBM building in Hakozaki, and the TRON house — and

Intelligent Office Building Projects to Study

IBM Japan, Hakozaki Office (1989)
Makuhari Techno Garden (1990)
NEC Headquarters, Tokyo (1990)
Gotenyama Hills, Tokyo (1990)
Crystal Tower, Osaka (1991)
NTT Gotanda Building
Hi-Touch Research Park, Kansai (1990)

**Players to Watch for
Intelligent Office Developments**

The Big Six:
Ohbayashi Construction Company
Shimizu Construction Company
Takenaka-Komuten Construction Company
Kumagai-Gumi Construction Company
Kajima Construction Company
Taisei Construction Company
and:
Mitsui Construction Company
Mori Development Company
NTT Design and Engineering
Nihon Sekkei Design and Engineering
Ken Sakamura, TRON

Intelligent Products and Joint Venture Partners

Toshiba
NEC
Hitachi
Fujitsu
Matsushita

Figure 9.1 Japanese progress toward the Office of the Future is manifested in a number of intelligent office building projects, dominated by a handful of construction companies.

two workplace innovations — the aromatherapy concept currently being tested by Shimizu, and wearable computers under development by NEC.

NEC New Head Office Building, Tokyo

NEC's 43-story high-rise introduces an innovative "wind avenue" 14 stories up to provide views of the sky and fresh air for the open-air atrium and 13 floors below (figures 9.2 and 9.3). This large three-story cutout, 50 meters above the ground, reduces the violent wind load common to the broad face of a high-rise, and brings in natural light and sky views through strategically positioned mirrors. Indeed, one experiences a feeling of only sky overhead in the atrium, with no building in view due to the mirrors. The rain- and sun-sheltered wind avenue also permits the large atrium serving the lower floors to be open-air for natural ventilation in summer, and glass-enclosed for comfort without conditioning in winter (figure 9.4). Steel fire shutters over the windows in the atrium enable the glass areas to be large and not fire-rated. The 55-meter-high atrium provides a spacious focus for the employees of NEC as well as a source of light and view for the interior offices.

Towering 180 meters into the Tokyo skyline, the NEC headquarters office demonstrates a number of the features of the Japanese intelligent office. It

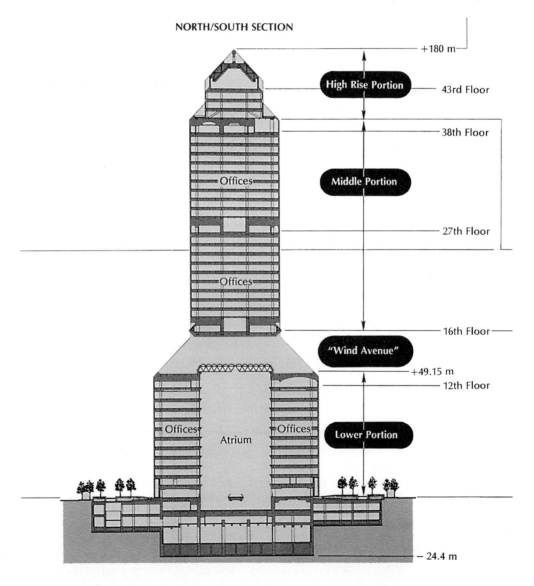

Figure 9.2 The NEC New Head Office Building features a wind avenue at the thirteenth story to provide views and fresh air. (sketch, NEC)

Figure 9.3 The "wind avenue" in the NEC building reduces violent wind load common to high-rises. (photo, NEC)

Figure 9.4 The atrium of the NEC building has access to fresh air and natural light from the "wind avenue" above.

is an earthquake resistant, cross-braced structure with a wide base and tapered top. Lush public park settings surrounding the building (over 66% of the site). Long north/south faces enable workplaces to be daylit without excessive glare, while the east and west facades are dominated by mechanical and elevator systems. The advanced energy management system that controls floor zone temperatures, ventilation, lighting, and security can be reviewed and modified at individual touch-screen control panels found in the elevator lobby of each floor (figure 9.5). The corporate teleconferencing facility goes one step beyond the Toshiba board room to provide data terminals for each seat, connected to the worldwide data network (figure 9.6). Finally, each worker has

Figure 9.5 The elevator lobby on each floor of the NEC building features touch-screen controls for energy management.

Figure 9.6 Each seat in the boardroom of the NEC building is provided with a terminal connected to the worldwide data network. (photo, NEC)

an individual telephone workstation called the "Super Alladin System," which provides a wide range of office automation services such as electronic mailing and filing, an electronic system for telephone directories, telephone messages, automatic dialing, and other services to ensure efficient telephone communication (figure 9.7). Building on advances such as the Minitel™ system in France and the individual screens for every seat on Japan Air Lines, the Alladin system merges data and voice capabilities into a single piece of desktop equipment.

Figure 9.7 The "Super Alladin System," an individual telephone workstation, provides a wide range of services, from telephone messages to electronic mailing and filing. (photo, NEC)

IBM Japan: Hakozaki

Since the mid 1980s, land prices and building lease prices in Tokyo have skyrocketed and vacancy has plummeted to less than 0.3% (figure 9.8). As a result, growing companies must seek innovative ways to centralize disparate divisions and to enable expansion. IBM in Tokyo tackled this problem with a two-fold solution: by embracing a new approach to office planning called the "free address, or group address, system" and by moving 20 miles from the central business district in Tokyo to Hakozaki, in order to consolidate the region's distributed offices (figure 9.9). Prior to the move, goals were established to minimize occupancy cost, increase productivity, improve asset management, provide quality space and amenities, increase employee satisfaction, and support business growth in information technology.

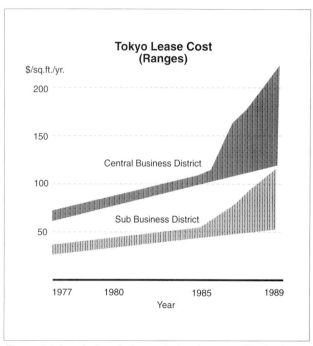

Figure 9.8 Land prices in the central and surrounding business districts in Tokyo have seen a sharp increase since the mid 1980s (Nakatsu 1990).

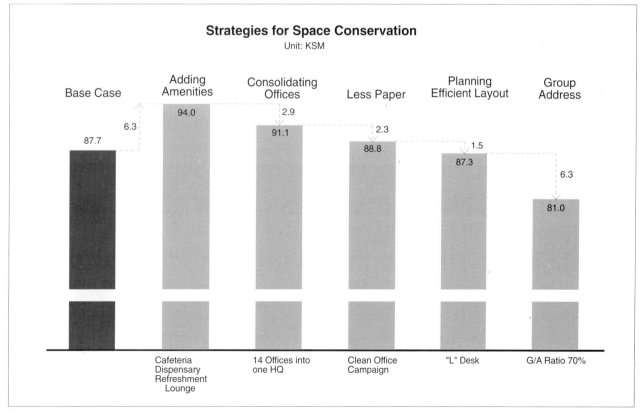

Figure 9.9 IBM Japan has developed a strategy for maximizing space utilization through a number of options, including consolidation, layout, and group address workstations (Nakatsu 1990).

The Hakozaki building was leased by IBM to house 5600 people on 25 floors, with over 60% of the employees from sales and marketing. In preparation for the move, office studies revealed that less than 50% of the IBM regional workforce (comprised of sales representatives, management consultants, and account auditors) are in the building at any one time, with less than 30% actually at their desk. In addition, IBM encourages its sales force to spend a majority of the time out of the office in face-to-face contact with the customers.

Since the ultimate in space efficiency is not the small office but the shared office, IBM decided to provide seats for only 60% of the total population, leave them unassigned, and develop a new addressing concept (figures 9.10 and 9.11). Forty workstations can now serve 60 people, with 50% larger work areas, and double the work surface as compared to single workstations. Each morning, workers move their rolling file from their cupboard to an available workstation in their workgroup. There, they sign in on the computer and identify their desk location on the touch-screen. Their

personal telephone number and data files are automatically assigned (figure 9.12).

Earlier examples of the "free address or non-territorial office," such as the Shimizu office in Tokyo and the Digital office in Helsinki, provided each individual with a movable file, a cordless telephone, and a laptop computer. In Hakozaki, IBM provides a full service telephone and PC at each workstation, and relies on electronic addressing to personalize the equipment. With the largest LAN network in the world and over 40 token rings, the electronic network provides for free addressing of information and software on a global basis. Each workgroup houses workstations for the department and line managers as well as for the group secretary and support staff.

In an early IBM internal review, the response to the free address system was over 50% favorable— less than 25% unfavorable— (figure 9.13), with special enthusiasm for the increased worksurface and the ability to spontaneously set up group meetings in an empty workstation without booking a meeting room. The system has proven flexible for coping with staff modifications and growth.

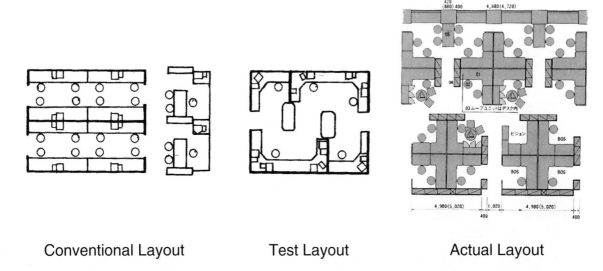

Conventional Layout   Test Layout   Actual Layout

Figure 9.10 IBM Japan developed a new group address system, whereby workstations were provided for only 60% of the total building population. (left and middle sketches, Samantha Ciotti; right sketch, IBM Japan, Ltd.)

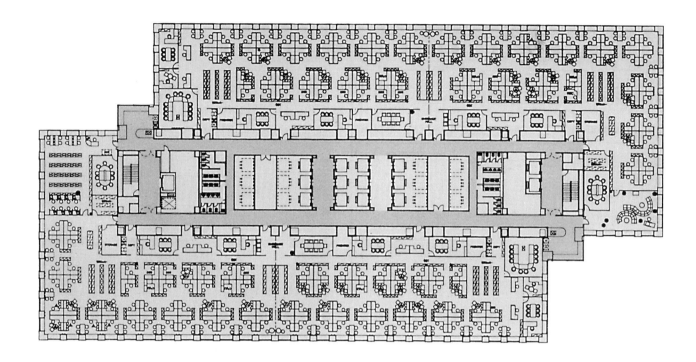

Figure 9.11 Floor plan of the IBM building, indicating the group address workstations. (sketch, IBM Japan, Ltd.)

Figure 9.12 In the group address system, when office workers sign on the computer and identify their desk location, their personal telephone numbers and data files are automatically updated. (photo, IBM Japan, Ltd.)

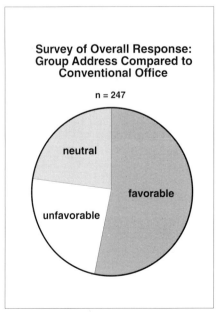

Figure 9.13 Over 50% of the office workers favored the group-address system over the conventional office (Nakatsu 1990).

There are a number of other innovations in the IBM Hakozaki that warrant exploration. Strengths such as those present in the Toshiba headquarters are clearly evident: north-south facing offices for daylight and thermal management; expanded and accessible central core facilities spanning east to west; and large column-free floorspace in the office area.

Completely distributed through-wall air-to-air heat pumps were installed below each window, building on earlier advances in the Shin-Nikko building designed by Nihon Sekkei (figure 9.14). These pumps provide individually controlled cooling and heating as well as additional fresh air. The individual all-electric units labeled ASPAC (air source prefabricated air conditioner system by PMAC) are combined with the centrally supplied VAV system (for core conditioning) to ensure thermal comfort in the highly electronic workplace. These innovative through-wall heat pump units have been used in a variety of configurations in new intelligent offices. In the Gotenyama Hills and Shin-Nikko buildings, the heat pumps are combined with distributed air handlers for core conditioning (one air handler per floor in

Gotenyama Hills, six per floor in the Shin-Nikko building). In other projects, distributed heat pumps placed in the ceiling or floor, with ducted fresh air intake and exhaust at the envelope, offer the opportunity for completely local conditioning — independent of a central system.

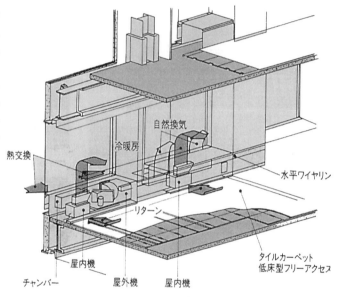

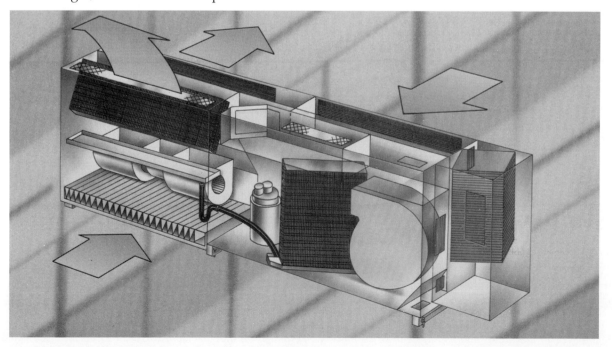

Figure 9.14 Distributed through-wall air-to-air heat pumps (above) are located along the perimeter wall of the IBM building (top right), providing individually controlled cooling and heating, as well as fresh air. (upper sketch, IBM Japan, Ltd.; lower sketch, Nippon P-MAC Co., Ltd.)

Finally, concern for worker relaxation and urban contribution continues, with sites mostly dedicated to park areas, including a publicly accessible waterfront and a traditional Japanese garden and tea house (figures 9.15 and 9.16). Such amenities reflect the success of earlier intelligent office projects such as Toshiba, ARK Hills, and Umeda, where extensive landscaping with direct employee access was the norm.

Figure 9.15 A landscaped waterfront on the site of the IBM building. (photo, IBM Japan, Ltd.)

Figure 9.16 A traditional Japanese garden and a teahouse are some of the landscape features that contribute to worker relaxation. (photo, IBM Japan, Ltd.)

TRON House

The TRON house, located in Tokyo, is an experimental prototype of the future house, the functions of which are governed by the Real Time Operating System Nucleus (TRON). The TRON, a new computer operating system that integrates innovative hardware and over 1,000 microprocessors, is the brainchild of Dr. Ken Sakamura, a University of Tokyo professor who is the maverick inventor and entrepreneurial force behind the TRON house. In a two-year, six-million-dollar effort, Dr. Sakamura has created the TRON house in collaboration with eighteen firms, has created the TRON operating system with eight major companies, and has begun the masterplanning of TRON city, which networks residences, offices, transportation facilities, and public facilities. The concepts demonstrated in the TRON house have clear implications for both office and urban design.

The major goal of the TRON project is to create a highly functional distributed system to enhance livability, through connecting a large number of computer objects, and to create new concepts for building intelligence (walls, chairs, ceilings, floors, furniture, HVAC, lighting, and communications). This is achieved through a TRON architecture (TRON VLSI CPU), an operating system (ITRON and B,C and MTRON), and a general purpose bus system (Tobus). Despite its massive number of sensors, actuators, and controllers, the house is designed as a traditional, peaceful, and functional Japanese home, using natural materials and natural surroundings (figures 9.17 to 9.19). But behind this beautiful setting lies a test bed for an impressive range of computerized capabilities, some of which are described below.

For climate and comfort, a weather station with interior and exterior sensors keeps track of temperature, humidity, wind direction, air pressure, carbon dioxide concentration, rain, interior air supply velocity, and occupancy conditions. Computer software with occupant input governs numerous decisions: to open windows

Figure 9.17 The TRON house is indicative of the kind of entrepreneurial force behind Japanese innovation. (photo, TRON Intelligent House)

Figure 9.18 Despite the large number of intelligent products and systems in the TRON house, the design is sensitive to traditional Japanese design.

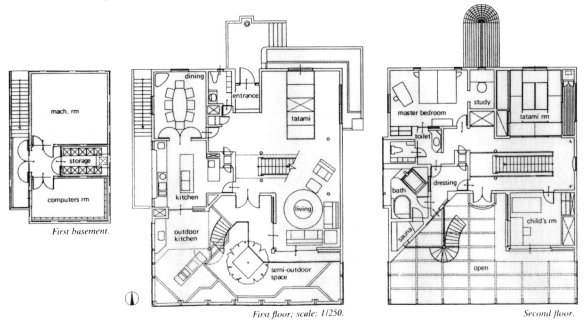

Figure 9.19 The floor plans of the TRON house reflect the integration of traditional Japanese architecture with contemporary design. (sketch, TRON Intelligent House)

Figure 9.20 Operable windows and skylights in the TRON house are computer controlled with occupant input, thereby maximizing energy conservation and comfort. (photo, TRON Intelligent House)

and skylights in order to maximize energy conservation and comfort (figure 9.20); to turn light-sensitive glass opaque for privacy and shading; to turn on air conditioning only when outside air is too hot or in case of rain; to control a water spray evaporative cooling system on the roof; to turn on fans to assist natural ventilation; and to control the radiant heating in floors and radiant cooling in ceilings to ensure even temperature distribution.

For kitchen management, a computerized recipe book suggests meals and provides recipes, and a laser disc video demonstrates preparation. The multimedia functionality of the BTRON operating system sets temperatures and times for the oven according to the recipe, and even dispenses the right dose of spices. A mobile dishwasher can be taken to the table, and automatic faucets at the kitchen sink eliminate the need to have free hands (figure 9.21). Shopping lists are maintained and accessible by telephone, for shopping on the way home from the office. The telephone can also start food preparation, and turn on and off ovens as well as other household appliances. Dr. Sakamura's ambition is to create a controller and operating infrastructure with core standardization to ac-

Figure 9.21 The kitchen in the TRON house features automatic faucets and computers to do chores ranging from operating appliances to maintaining shopping lists. (photo, TRON Intelligent House)

commodate a wide range of new appliances from different manufacturers, as they are developed.

Bathroom computerization performs urinalysis and monitors body temperature, cardiovascular activity, and body weight. The bathtub (with temperature and water level control) can be filled on a timer or through a phone call.

Home entertainment facilities are computer linked to the security system and to human presence. As the occupants move through the house, speakers and televisions turn off and on in the appropriate rooms. Telephone, video, audio, and utility sub-systems are linked. The multi-function telephone contains a digital PBX to access telephone, inter-com, and computer communication. The video system broadcasts images from interior cameras and from television. The audio system broadcasts sounds from internal and external sources. A movable bar is equipped with electricity and data connections, a hot plate, as well as hot and cold water, and can be accessed through a one plug jack from a preset outlet in each room.

An automatic storage system places objects to be stored into containers and moves them through a dumbwaiter to the basement warehouse. The container contents are photographed, and an inventory list can be displayed on the TV screen. Automatic plant-watering supports hydroponic growing techniques and the experimental use of artificial "aquasoil," assisted by solenoid water-level sensors. Computerized fire safety and security systems use infrared and internal heat sensors. Electric lights are programmed at different levels for each room, with choices for variations in mood. For energy savings, lights go on as needed while the occupants circulate, and the computer controls the opening and closing of curtains.

From operating systems to intelligent sensor/controllers to keyboards (figures 9.22 and 9.23), Dr. Sakamura's TRON project demonstrates an integrated approach for accommodating the rapid growth in new personal electronics toward a completely new computer-assisted architecture.

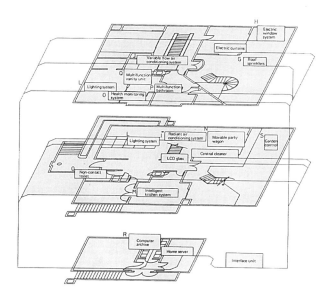

Figure 9.22 The TRON house features a host of integrated intelligent products. (sketch, TRON Intelligent House)

Figure 9.23 Dr. Sakamura's projects even include the design of a keyboard that reflects the anthropometrics of the human hand. (photo, TRON Intelligent House)

Shimizu — Aromatherapeutic Design

Building on early explorations in varying temperature, light, color, and sound to improve worker comfort and satisfaction, Shimizu has extended this effort one step further — to the introduction of fragrances. Shimizu has found that certain aromas at certain concentrations reduce stress, improve relaxation, refresh workers, and set positive moods (figure 9.24). Statistics show that the introduction of fragrances increased keypunching effectiveness and improved effectiveness in meetings (figure 9.25). These studies have resulted in the development of the Aromatherapeutic Environmental Fragrancing System. In this system, a computerized unit introduces fragrances such as lavender, chamomile, lemon, and cypress into the air conditioning ducts (figure 9.26). In a mixed-use building project that combines offices, hotels, and recreational/cultural facilities, the system was found to significantly enhance efficiency and reduce stress among office workers. Keypunch operators, who were monitored eight hours a day for one month, reduced their errors by 53% when exposed to a lemon aroma (figure 9.27). According to Junici Yagi, Vice President of Shimizu's Boston subsidiary S. Technology Center America, the operators reported that they enjoyed the fragrance. "Even when the scent was below conscious levels," Mr. Yagi commented, "they reported feeling better than they did without it."

Meeting Room Study:
Survey Results of Meeting Efficiency
n = 270

Type of Fragrance	No Smoking Allowed	Smoking Allowed
Lavender Series	●	⬤
Jasmine Series	●	⬤
Lemon Series	●	⬤

● meeting efficiency unaffected *   ⬤ meeting efficiency increased

* Although statistically significant results were not obtained, 21%, 52%, and 59% of the survey respondents did indicate an increase in their efficiency when lavender, jasmine, and lemon, respectively, were used.

Figure 9.25 Fragrances were found to increase meeting efficiency (Shimizu Construction Co. 1990).

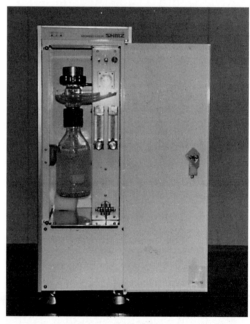

Figure 9.26 The Aromatherapeutic Environmental Fragrancing System is a computerized unit that introduces fragrances into the air conditioning ducts. (Shimizu Construction Co.)

Fragrance Group	Principal Effect
Jujube, Lavender, Chamomile, etc.	Reduce stress
Chamomile, Bergamot, Lavender, etc.	Relax
Basil, Peppermint, Clove, etc.	Refresh
Lemon, Japanese Cypress, Basil, etc.	Set positive mood

Figure 9.24 Studies have shown that certain fragrance groups produce positive effects on test subjects (Shimizu Construction Co. 1990).

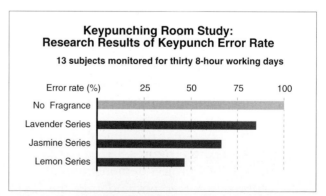

Figure 9.27 Keypunching errors were reduced by more than 50% when the operators were exposed to a lemon aroma (Shimizu Construction Co. 1990).

NEC — Wearable Computers

In addition to building an innovative headquarters building, NEC has extended its explorations in mobility and communication through the further miniaturization of electronic equipment. NEC's research group has put together an amazing exhibition of possible wearable computers for the future office worker, with wide-ranging applications (figures 9.27 to 9.30). In the medical profession, paramedics might wear armband computers that can read vital signs at the site, access the patient's history, and transfer data to the receiving hospital. In the traveling office, the worker may wear a keyboard belt and a shoulder harness CRT to free hands between work sessions — excellent for construction site supervisors. Computer belts, purses, watches, and necklaces provide workers new opportunities to extend their place of work, and even to select their place of work in relaxing and beautiful surroundings, with full telecommunication capability. According to NEC, the computer of the future may well be seen as a "piece of clothing," unobtrusive or elegant, out of the way yet easily accessible.

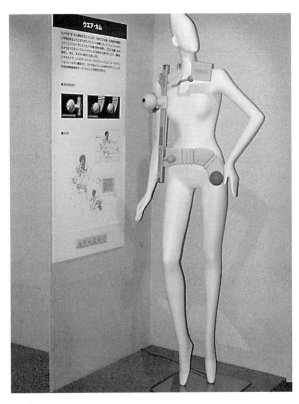

Figures 9.28 to 9.30   NEC is expanding possibilities in electronic communication through development of "wearable computers."

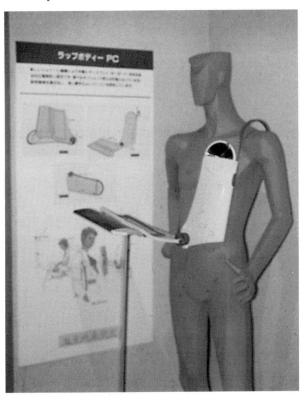

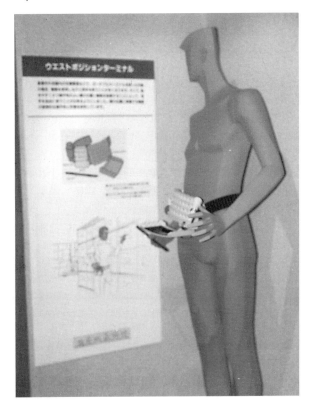

Conclusion

These glimpses of Japanese innovations and innovators reinforce the discussion in chapter 4 of Japan's rapid approach to the Office of the Future. This approach continues to be typified by an interactive demonstration process with competitive products, a team decisionmaking process from the outset, distributed and highly accessible servicing systems, a rapidly improving quality of life, a continued commitment to resource management, and the introduction of robotics, computerization and miniaturization into construction, maintenance, and operation.

Iterative demonstration and team decisionmaking processes are clearly driving the IBM and NEC projects. Government and industry continue to provide substantial financial incentives and team intelligence towards research, development, and iterative demonstration of advanced building concepts.

Advances in distributed and highly accessible servicing systems as well as a continued commitment to resource management are evidenced in each of the recent projects profiled. In an effort to save energy and manpower, as well as enhance facility management, Japan has been developing some of the most sophisticated information and communications facilities and the most sophisticated maintenance and control capabilities to be seen in office buildings.

The Japanese interest in the introduction of robotics and electronics into building construction, maintenance, and operation has led to the development of a range of new advanced electronics, merging computer intelligence with miniaturization. The growth and development in electronics have rushed into the workplace, not only improving facilities management but enabling better communication, improving space shortages, and enhancing worker productivity. There are clear signs that these amenities of today will become necessities of tomorrow. The NEC wearable computers and the Tron embedded sensor/controllers are examples of the exciting new Japanese developments in robotics and electronics.

Toward rapidly improving the quality of life in the workplace, there has been a major focus on improving environmental quality and individual control of thermal, visual, acoustic, spatial, and air quality — evidenced in the TRON, IBM, and Shimizu efforts. This environmental planning extends from the interior spaces to spacious landscaped sites, accessible to the individual worker and the public. The government actively promotes and financially supports moves to create new "garden" centers of commerce outside Tokyo, addressing the limited space and soaring costs of city property. TRON city and Tsukuba Science City are examples of these new landscaped centers under development for living, working, and socializing. With room to breathe, these new cities should have the mixed-use planning and pedestrian vibrancy of Tokyo, with the fresh air and landscaped beauty of the country.

These characteristics all accelerate the progression toward increasingly advanced intelligent buildings. Mr. A. Kitamura, of the Intelligent Buildings and Cities Group at NTT, describes the trend in intelligent buildings as follows, "Having emerged as an architectural form responding to qualitative changes in offices in the age of advanced information technology, intelligent buildings are entering a new network age." The Japanese are indeed involved in an internal race to produce the most advanced intelligent buildings.

Chapter References

Nakatsu, Motosugu, "Office Innovation at Hakozaki IBM Japan," IBM Asia Pacific, photocopy, August 1990.

Shimizu Construction Company, "Aromatherapeutic Environmental Fragrancing System," photocopy, August 1990.

Additional Major References

Barron, Janet J., "Will TRON Succeed?" *Byte*, April 1989, p. 301.

Building Report: IBM Hakozaki Office, Tokyo: IBM Japan, Ltd., 1989.

Cohen, Charles L., "Update: TRON Moves In — To Real-Time Control," *Electronics*, January 1989, p. 168.

Dambrot, Stuart M., "Open Systems, Oriental Style," *Datamation*, August 1, 1989, pp. 3-4.

deCourcy Hinds, Michael, "Finding New Ways to Make Smell Sell," *The New York Times*, July 23, 1988, p. 16.

"First TRON Microprocessor Gets Japan into the 32-bit Fray," *Electronics*, January 21, 1988, pp. 31-32.

Gillin, Paul, "Mixing High Tech and High Rises," *Computerworld*, August 13, 1990, pp. 25-26.

Hi-Touch Research Parks Cooperative Association, "Hi-Touch Research Parks — Research Parks in Japan (10)," *JETRO*, March 1991, pp. 6-9.

Hirata, Shinichi, "System Engineers and Office Amenity," *NAND, Quarterly Magazine of Facility Planning for Yutori*, July 1991, pp. 30-33.

Jerome, Marty, "TRON's Global Net," *PC-Computing*, December 1989, pp. 175-176.

Kallan, Carla, "Focus on Fragrance," *USAir Magazine*, October 1990, pp. 114-119.

Kitamura, Atsushi, "The Implications of Intelligent Buildings," *NAND, Quarterly Magazine of Facility Planning for Yutori*, July 1991, pp. 18-19.

Lecht, Charles P., "There's No Place Like TRON City," *Computerworld*, May 29, 1989, p. 19.

NEC's New Head Office Building, NEC brochure, undated.

Poe, Robert, "Japan's TRON Tactics," *Datamation*, October 1, 1987, p. 21, 24.

Rubin, Arthur, *Intelligent Building Technology in Japan*, NISTIR-4546, Washington, DC: U.S. Department of Commerce, April 1991.

Sakamura, Ken, "The TRON Project," *Microprocessors and Microsystems*, October 1987, pp. 493-502.

Sakamura, Ken, and James J. Farrell, *TRON Project* (brochure), 1990.

Sakamura, Ken, and Richard Sprague, "The TRON Project," *Byte*, April 1989, pp. 292-301.

"TRON Takes Hold," *Scientific American*, June 1988, p. 114.

"TRON-concept Intelligent House," *The Japan Architect*, April 1990, pp. 37-40.

Valigra, Lori, "TRON Inventor Decries Growing U.S. Fear of Japan Infiltration," *Computerworld*, May 22, 1989, p. 99.

Watanabe, Teresa, "House of Controversy," *Los Angeles Times*, July 2, 1990, sec. D, p. 1.

"The Wizard of TRON," *The Economist*, February 27, 1988, pp. 73-74.

Part III

Part III presents the major findings of the international case studies of advanced buildings, and includes an evolving list of major design changes in the Office of the Future.

10

Major Design Changes for the Office of the Future

The Japanese building studies have contributed to an evolving list of major design changes in the Office of the Future. The growth and change in this list will be evident in future ABSIC publications focusing on building studies in Germany, the U.K., and North America.

The field studies of the Toshiba, NTT Twins, ARK Mori, and Umeda Center buildings, along with the supporting literature referenced, have contributed significantly to the understanding of issues impacting the design of the Office of the Future. The combination of these studies and earlier work by ABSIC with the National Academy of Science Committee on Electronically Enhanced Office Buildings has produced an evolving list of building design and management changes needed in tomorrow's offices.

This list is driven by the fundamentals described in chapter 1:

- ensuring physical and environmental performance qualities for the individual;
- ensuring systems integration for performance; and
- ensuring changes in the building delivery process for systems integration and total building performance.

With knowledge of the expanding range of new technologies facing the workplace, ABSIC has distinguished twelve new design directions, profiled in the following pages. These design directions are already in evidence in innovative buildings in various countries, and provide opportunities for developing new products and processes, and integrating them into the design of tomorrow's workplace.

Distributed over Central Servicing Systems

In Japan and in Germany, significant development has been made in distributed heating, ventilating, and air conditioning systems for servicing multiple work zones with independent controls. Multiple, distributed telecommunications networks also have undergone development. The multiple systems enable independent metering, independent time of use, and greater control in the face of constantly varying loads; and, if the distributed systems are modular and repetitive, very reliable maintenance. Although the emphasis has been on distributed prime movers, the opportunities for linking highly efficient central systems with decentralized equipment for local distribution and control are significant.

In Japan, multiple-zone HVAC was evident in all the buildings studied. In the Umeda Center, NTT Twins, and Toshiba buildings, highly accessible distributed mechanical rooms were introduced throughout the building (see figure 10.1). The Toshiba Headquarters even demonstrated competitive manufacturers within the distributed HVAC rooms (servicing four to six floors), for a comparative assessment of systems and future project optimization. The Toshiba building also incorporates two specially conditioned mainframe rooms per floor, to enable a large concentration of noisy and hot computer equipment to be thermally and acoustically isolated, while remaining accessible within the work area.

The "cell body" system in the Umeda Center Building demonstrated the most refined multizone system, with 12 heat pumps per floor, enabling small clusters of workstations to have independent control of air temperature and air speed.

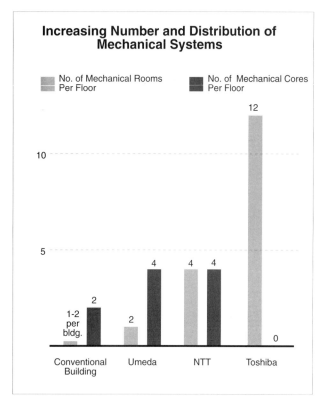

Figure 10.1 *The advanced offices in Japan demonstrate a significant shift away from the single mechanical HVAC room per building — to as many as 128 rooms.*

Distributed Cores over Central Cores for Vertical Distribution of Services

Even with central HVAC and telecommunications systems, there is a movement in the U.K., Germany, and Japan toward multiple vertical cores to support accessible and efficient distribution of environmental conditioning, power, and data (see figure 10.2). These cores are oversized and strategically placed to service manageable work groups without excessive horizontal runs. In some cases, the multiple cores have been moved to the building perimeter to facilitate access and growth, and to free up usable floor space, such as in Lloyd's of London.

The Toshiba Headquarters incorporates two distributed cores for HVAC, four distributed cores for power, four for telephone, four for data, and two for distributed mainframe rooms. These core spaces, as well as the fire stairs, elevators, toilets,

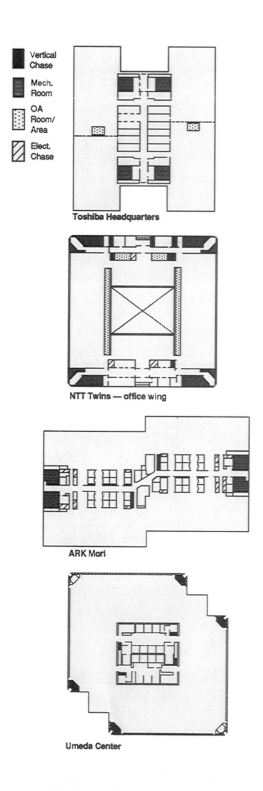

Figure 10.2 *Rather than a single core or two vertical distribution chases, many of the advanced offices invest in four, six, eight, or more vertical chases, well distributed across the floor plate to minimize horizontal runs and maximize local control.*

and kitchenettes, line the shared circulation areas, with easy access and maintenance through continuous "cupboard walls." Indeed, the core area stretches from the east to the west facade, with all office areas facing predominantly north and south.

The NTT Twins building also demonstrates extensive vertical core area. In this case, the vertical cores and servicing rooms fill the east and west facades to provide for easy access and growth as well as fresh air supply (again ensuring that offices face only north and south). In the Umeda Center Building, vertical cores have been reduced to a minimum through the introduction of highly distributed mechanical rooms on the outside wall, eliminating ducted air or piped water systems between floors. The Umeda Center Building also demonstrates fully distributed inter-office telecommunications networks.

Open Horizontal Distribution Plenums: Floors over Ceilings

Given the immense quantity of existing office area, ceiling distribution systems of HVAC and telecommunications will always maintain a significant market. However, in the advanced workplace, there is a growing emphasis on raised floor technologies for the horizontal distribution of cables and of conditioned air. There are some misconceptions about the costs of raised floors having to reflect higher floor-to-floor heights. In fact, the effective integration of raised floors with mechanical systems can actually reduce the amount of horizontal plenum space needed (see figure 10.3). Not only does raised floor distribution provide ease of access, growth, and change (of both cable and HVAC), but also good performance of floor air supply systems in relation to many ceiling "down-draft systems" (minimizing

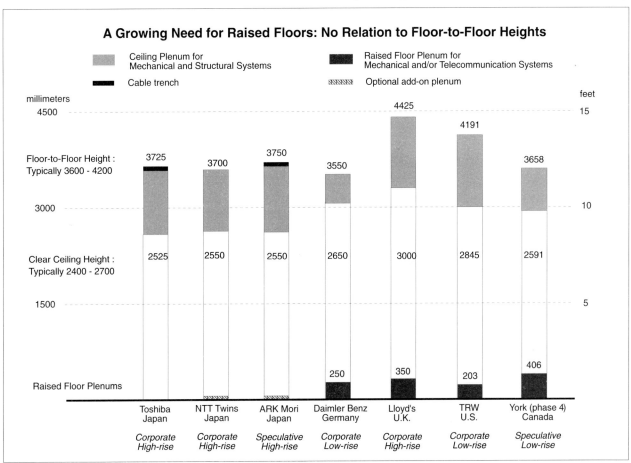

Figure 10.3 Raised floors do not demand higher floor heights, especially if HVAC is incorporated under the floor. Much of the floor-to-floor height in conventional buildings is driven by poor mechanical and structural integration (Chiu 1991).

short-circuiting and pollution migration). Raised floor distribution also simplifies the final connection of power, data, and air directly to the desk and worker, to more effectively support today's constant churn and layout changes.

The second variable in relation to the horizontal distribution of HVAC and telecommunications from the building cores is the final connection to the workstation. A number of advanced buildings demonstrate innovation in this area, ranging from pre-chased wall systems for direct connection to floor or ceiling plenums, to pre-chased furniture systems for direct connection to floor plenums. A critical subset of this direction is the modularity of the floor and ceiling system as well as the density of ports (light, heat, telecommunications, power) for connection with the interior wall and furniture systems.

The Japanese buildings studied did not demonstrate outstanding solutions to horizontal distribution. Relying heavily on cast-in-place trench systems or under-carpet flat cable, changes in the horizontal distribution of cables are cumbersome and already poorly matched to the electronic density or re-layout of workstations. Despite the adequate size of well-marked trenches, extensive cabling is slung over the ceiling and across the floor, with "tombstone" outlets often within circulation areas. HVAC distribution is confined to the ceiling, typically in a rigid grid limiting changes in technology or workgroup configurations.

On the other hand, both the NTT Twins and Umeda Center buildings demonstrated innovative solutions for dealing with modest horizontal cable distribution in *existing* office environments. Both buildings demonstrated the use of "thick carpet tiles," tiles built up of rubber or cement, with multiple feet for stability, and 2 to 4 centimeters of open plenum for laying cables in any direction. These thick tiles were combined with perimeter distribution (patch) panels, located under the windows since very little perimeter heating and cooling is required in Japan. Elegant flush power outlet boxes were developed for the NTT model

offices, eliminating tripping hazards and providing adequate connection to vertical chases in the workstation furniture.

In reference to these first three design directions for the Office of the Future, it should be emphasized that the team approach in Japanese design enables strong three-dimensional skeletons or servicing trees to be established prior to interior floor planning. These servicing trees allow appropriate decisionmaking about type, configuration, size, density, and access to HVAC, cabling, fire, structure, and elevators. In addition, the full design team can more effectively address other cultural, climatic, and safety issues impacting whole-building decisionmaking at the project's outset — such as facing offices only north and south and designing for earthquake prone areas.

"Fresh Air" Architecture

There are many aspects of the human requirement for environmental contact, ranging from the need for fresh air, sunshine, and view, to the need for a sense of time, season, and place. With the introduction of central heating and cooling, however, the office workforce has been removed further and further from the outside environment, in some cases entering a building at 8:00 a.m. and not emerging to see the light of day for ten or more hours. Focus on the environmental needs of building occupants has diminished to such an extent that building-related illnesses and dissatisfactions have been directly tied to poor environmental contact.

Despite the flexibility of large open plan offices, the cost-saving abuses of the concept have led to unbearable work environments with no outside contact and inadequate mechanical and environmental control. The failures are as much physiological as psychological, resulting in a shift in some countries toward increased environmental contact, increased system/environmental interfaces and control, as well as more contact with natural finishes, daylight, and outside air.

Indeed, there is a rapid movement away from building floor plates the size of football fields (that must be totally mechanically conditioned), toward highly articulated buildings with the potential for natural ventilation and daylighting, especially in Germany and Sweden.

Several efforts toward increasing the quality of environmental contact were common to all the buildings studied in Japan. In each of the projects, buildings were clustered to create outdoor landscaped areas for walking, sitting, and eating, in lieu of indoor recreational "malls." Each building deeded a significant percentage of ground space and financial investment to create these outdoor landscaped areas (gardens, not paved plazas) as an integral part of the entry sequence, lunch and coffee areas, and work-break garden areas (see figure 10.4). Operable (unlocked) doors provide easy access from several parts of the building to the open-air greenspaces, at ground level and on rooftops. The landscaped areas and courtyards displayed all of the attention to detail and meaning to be found in the traditional Japanese garden.

Smoking was forbidden throughout the office areas in the buildings studied, with dedicated, well-ventilated smoking rooms on each floor. A number of other features revealed Japan's environmental biases: north and south office exposures for effective views and shade; open-air landscaping for filtration and oxygen production; and experimentation with operable windows; and grey water usage for protection of limited water resources while ensuring the beauty of the gardens.

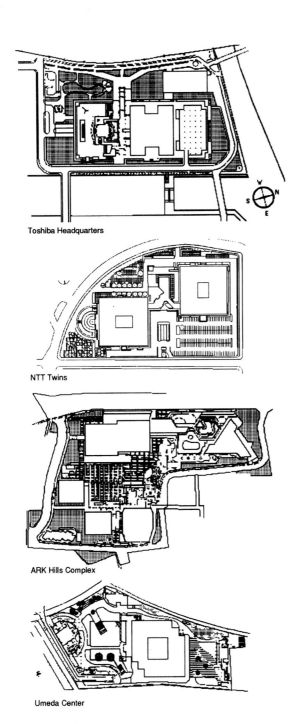

Toshiba Headquarters

NTT Twins

ARK Hills Complex

Umeda Center

Figure 10.4 There is a growing interest in mixed-use planning with extensively landscaped outdoor areas, rather than interior malls or megaplexes, to entice workers out into the fresh air.

More Effective Thermal Balancing Between Envelope and Multiple Interior Zones

There is an odd misconception that the greatly increased interior heat gain in today's automated office has displaced perimeter heating demands. In fact, the growing internal heat loads have only increased the disparity between interior and perimeter loads, demanding a more refined response to both conditions. Indeed, entirely new concepts are needed to deal with thermal balancing in an office where one work group may have extensive heat-generating equipment, another minimal equipment, and a third serious losses from envelope locations. To compound the problem, the location of these work groups could change on a monthly basis. As a result, the Office of the Future demands developments in load balancing technologies, toward reducing load variations and developing adaptable, multi-zoned mechanical systems, with local sensors and controls.

The load balancing concepts in use in Germany, Japan, and the U.K. include air flow windows routing return air through the envelope; multiple heat pumps fed by closed water loops, enabling waste heat from one system to be a source for the next system; and flywheel construction in which fans pre-chill or heat vast areas of exposed capacitance (typically concrete) with off-peak energy or borrowed energy from other parts of the building.

Through the use of north/south orientations for the workspace, and east/west orientations for mechanical and servicing rooms, the Japanese office buildings minimize excess cooling loads from low-angle sunshine entering east and west facades. Heating loads are kept to a minimum through well-insulated facades and a naturally benign climate. Thermosiphoning cooling methods are being developed by NTT, relying on natural propensities for cool air to descend for reducing electrical distribution loads.

More significant, however, is the Japanese attention to day/night and seasonal load balancing. The NTT Twins building has a massive off-peak water storage system for cool water storage at lower electric prices. The Toshiba Headquarters and ARK Mori Building demonstrate strategic peak power shaving strategies through energy management software. These efforts, in addition to the massive gray water system in Toshiba, demonstrate the Japanese continued commitment to resource conservation — be it fuel, power, water, or air.

More Effective Balancing of Daylight and Artificial Light

The desire for increased environmental contact, to reduce worker's stress from long hours in front of computer screens, has heightened the need for effective daylight/artificial light balancing. Totally new lighting concepts are needed, combining low ambient light levels (from daylight and artificial light sources) with task light levels determined locally by the time of day and the activity. Lighting system innovations include continuous dimming fixtures, individually switched (on/off) fixtures, easily relocatable tether or pigtail fixtures, and shielded fixtures in which neither the image of the bulb nor the lens is reflected on the worksurface or the computer screen.

With overhead artificial lighting at reduced levels (or off), the management of daylight glare and brightness contrast becomes even more critical, demanding a host of new products and integrations. A number of innovations have been developed in various countries, such as diffusing glass, prismatic glass, light shelves, diffusing blinds, self-shading inwardly-sloping glass, and exterior shading devices.

In general, the Japanese workplace does not demonstrate innovation in artificial or daylight design and management. Many offices still rely on a fixed grid of bare-bulb fluorescent fixtures, controlled by a single light switch. Very modest efforts have been introduced in the NTT general offices with work group on/off controls and diffusing venetian blinds, both managed by the group leader. The NTT model offices, however, demonstrate early efforts to combine HID (high-intensity discharge) uplighting for ambient light needs and task lights for the desk. The Umeda Center Building demonstrates individual on/off controls of the overhead lights in each 3.2-meter-square "cell body," managed through telephone dial-up or computer menu change.

The significant Japanese contribution to most artificial light/daylight balancing is their continued commitment to manageable north and south orientations for all offices, eliminating the glare and brightness contrast caused by low-angle sun penetration through east and west facades.

Introduction of Movable, Tether, or Pigtail Services for Heat, Conditioned Air, Light, Power, and Data

The concept of fixed-grid, fixed-density systems for HVAC, data, and lighting has proved problematic in advanced offices due to the rapid changes in occupancy activity, location, and density. There are also indications that the fixed-grid, fixed-density systems are more expensive in first costs (unnecessary investment) and operating costs than flexible-grid, flexible-density concepts, such as tether or pigtail services. Tether services can provide conditioned air, light, or data connections for the individual workplace from a series of distributed controllers with tether or star connections. This allows for "port" location changes given the length of the tether and the ceiling or floor modularity. Alternatively, a pigtail (expandable ring) system allows for the introduction of additional ports (e.g., lights, power, or HVAC controllers), at any location within the existing chain. Both the tether and pigtail systems provide for continuous changes in workstation location and overall density, as well as changes in type and quantity of electronic equipment.

Although examples for easily moving HVAC, lighting, and data connections in floor and ceiling plenum spaces were evident in innovative buildings in North America, Germany, and the U.K., this does not appear to be a current design focus in Japan.

Introduction of Individual Environmental Controls for Temperature, Air, Light, and Sound

Today's advanced office has a growing need for more local environmental control, due to the significant variations in activities and equipment found between workstations. Specifically, the local control of conditioned air and task/ambient light has become very important, to cope with the rapid introduction of office automation equipment.

A number of international projects have introduced individual control of temperature (both air temperature and radiant temperature), of conditioned air (direction and speed and outside air content), of ambient and task light (on/off and dimming), and of background sound (in the case of the Johnson Controls Personal Environments™ system). Although further study is needed, this individualized control has neither sabotaged the central system nor increased the total energy demand. Instead, the individualized control has helped in relieving the thermal and visual stresses in the automated office, as well as more effectively dealing with individual differences in setting comfort.

The Umeda Center Building by the Takenaka-Komuten construction company in Osaka, Japan, is one of a handful of truly far-reaching projects in regard to individual controls. Through the introduction of multiple HVAC systems with direct access to outside air, and independently wired lighting controls, the 3.2-meter-square "cell body" workspace (whether open or enclosed) can be independently managed by the occupant (see figure 10.5). The individual worker can easily control lights (on/off), air supply (on/off), and even air temperature. Admittedly, temperature is controlled on a larger grid, approximately 20 meters square, to be negotiated between five or six workstations. Individual control is provided by either telephone or computer dial-up, and cannot be overridden by central management. Indeed, the building's central computer only *monitors* indi-

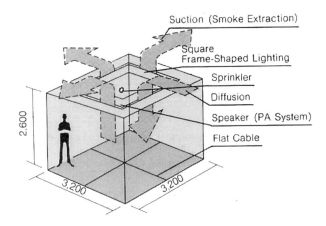

Figure 10.5 Each "cell body" in the Umeda Center Building can be managed independently. (sketch, Takenaka-Komuten Co., Ltd.)

vidual actions, for a better understanding of variations in individual needs toward system optimization in future building projects. As a result of these individual control options in the Umeda Center Building, complete acoustic isolation of individual offices or densely shared computer facilities can be pursued as needed in the open office plan, with assurance of adequate thermal, air, and visual environmental quality.

Many office buildings in Japan, however, are still beleaguered with inadequate noise and pollution isolation as well as light and heat control, especially around office automation clusters.

Introduction of New Individual and Group Workstation Concepts

The introduction of the landscaped office in the 1960s created a worldwide commitment to the economies and "community" of the open plan office. However, the abuses and inadequacies of the concept (excessive vastness, spatial confusion, difficult wayfinding, noise, thermal and air qual-

ity anomalies, lack of daylight and view for many) have contributed to an alternative movement in office planning. Worker reactions to the inadequacies in the open office plan have led to a stronger desire for personal control over environmental conditions (see figure 10.6). The design of the open plan office may not function to promote effective working relationships. Social psychologists have speculated that work groups of over 20 people will not form a strong community, and that work groups of over seven people cannot relate to a collective agenda at the same time (see figure 10.7). In some advanced buildings, these findings have led to smaller, more articulated open office areas housing 20 or so workstations, with greater proximity to daylight and view as well as shared services. Other alternatives can be seen:

- the concept of small closed offices (caves) for personalization and permanent possessions, and collective workstation areas for group projects (coves), such as the R&D centers of Steelcase and Apple Computer (Becker 1990);

- the concept of workstation on wheels where permanent possessions are housed within a mobile unit to be wheeled to the most appropriate location for a specific project (to a workgroup area, to a quiet zone, to a computer or CAAD workstation, to a window) such as at the Digital Marketing Headquarters in Finland;

- the concept of unassigned (free address) workstations and shared workstations in manageably sized work areas servicing large sales forces that spend a majority of the time on the road;

- the acceptability of home offices and on-the-road offices for a significant percentage of the work week (sometimes accompanied by enforced hours in the office, from 10:00 a.m. to 2:00 p.m., for example);

- and the re-emergence of closed offices as the only acceptable workplace for the "gold collar" worker (Levin 1988).

This reconsideration of the vast, efficient open

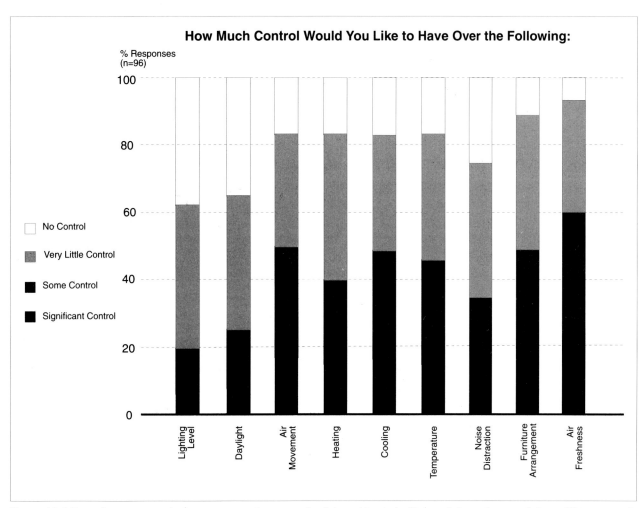

How Much Control Would You Like to Have Over the Following:

% Responses
(n=96)

Legend:
- No Control
- Very Little Control
- Some Control
- Significant Control

X-axis categories: Lighting Level, Daylight, Air Movement, Heating, Cooling, Temperature, Noise Distraction, Furniture Arrangement, Air Freshness

Figure 10.6 Even Japanese workers are expressing a growing interest in controlling certain environmental conditions — such as air movement, air freshness, and cooling — to deal with the changing conditions of the advanced office. (This chart is based on questionnaire responses in the Toshiba Building.)

office has also influenced building massing in a number of new projects. Vertically extruded "high-rise" offices, in which interfloor communication is restricted to the elevator and garage, are being re-evaluated. Instead, the creation of social centers and service/support centers has appeared, surrounding open stairs and atria. There is also a re-emergence of traditional campus or village planning with lower rise walk-up buildings, mixed use planning, heavily landscaped areas, and shared services and amenities.

One final aspect in the evolution of new workstation concepts is the furniture design itself. Beyond the individual environmental controls previously described, a series of individual spatial controls and fittings now enable the workstation of the future to be tailored to the individual's physique, psyche, and work style. These "necessary amenities" include ergonomic chairs; adjustable supports for screens, paper copy, and keyboards; variable-height work surfaces; innovative storage systems; variable-height acoustic enclosures; and new, integrated electronics and cable management.

The recent pallor that has been shed on the "open office concept" has not yet extended to Japan. In some respects, this is because the Japanese have abused the concept less, maintaining views and

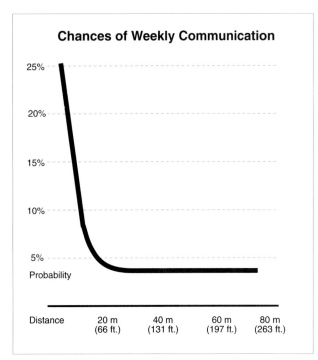

Figure 10.7 Distances contribute significantly to the level of communication between office workers, suggesting that effective working groups are quite small (*Officing* 1988).

Figure 10.8 Modern furniture developments in Japan address new developments in desktop technology and their ergonomic effects on the occupants, with adjustable work surfaces, adjustable pivot arm supports, and other innovations.

daylight for every worker, and avoiding excessive building depths and compartmentalization. To deal with the social inadequacies of the large open office, the Japanese have introduced a greatly increased number and variety of shared areas throughout the building, as described in the following section.

To date, the Japanese office has not demonstrated major innovation in workstation furniture. However, this lag behind the Western world is quickly disappearing. The model offices in the NTT Twins building, equipped with modern workstation furniture by Kokuyo, display such features as adjustable two-tier worksurfaces; hollow-frame cable management; and phones, task lights, and VDTs on adjustable pivot arms (see figure 10.8).

Shared Facilities and Services for Changing Uses and Changing Technologies

Besides the spatial layout modifications intended to improve communication and productivity in the advanced office, there are also changes in the type and number of shared facilities and services. Although the concept of shared tenant services (typically referring to telephone switches) has fallen into disfavor, other shared services and facilities are rapidly growing (see figure 10.9). These include fax services; copy and production facilities; coffee areas and eating facilities; conference facilities with audiovisual equipment management; shared main frames, or shared rooms and servicing for individual's mainframes and processors ("black box parks"); postal and mailing facilities; office automation display and purchasing centers (hardware and software); furniture rental facilities and installation services; and accessible landscaped areas for meeting, eating, and relaxing. These shared facilities and services provide economies of scale that starter high-tech companies cannot afford alone, as well as providing knowledge about changing office automation options and expediting advancements.

Each of the Japanese office buildings studied demonstrates a major commitment to increased shared facilities for the educational and social benefit of their employees. At ground level, the major investment in outdoor landscaped areas and courtyards is immediately evident, along with restaurants, cafeterias, shops, and tea service. In addition, small conference rooms and open meeting areas are distributed throughout the building, with nearby tea rooms, lounges, and smoking areas. Open fire stairs have become standard, to enhance interdepartmental communication and minimize elevator use, with a corresponding development in a range of automatic fire closure systems (see figure 10.10). Lobbies and elevator core areas are elegantly finished to provide addi-

Developments in Shared Services in the Modern Office

1. Postal and fax services
2. Copy and production services
3. Public relations and newsletter services

4. Coffee areas/ cafes
5. Vending machine areas/ food carts
6. Cafeterias and restaurants
7. Party and take-home food services

8. Garden and park areas
9. Terraces
10. Atria

11. Health clubs
12. Medical suites /doctors

13. Conference facilities
14. Portable conferencing equipment

15. Computer/OA training
16. OA display centers (hardware and software)
17. Shared mainframes
18. Shared servicing for OA equipment

Figure 10.9   The range of shared facilities and resources offered in buildings is growing to attract starter high-tech companies, to improve organizational capability, and to support individual well-being.

Figure 10.10 Stairs are emerging as a focal point for intergroup communication. In the NTT mid-rise generously daylit stairs are open to the office floors, with automatic fire closures for emergency use.

tional meeting areas. In both the Toshiba and Umeda Center buildings, a conference center is provided with computer-assisted registrations to ensure appropriate size, equipment, and services on the designated meeting day. A portable "teleconferencing" package is even available with cable TV, microphones, telephone, fax, and electronic blackboards to enable groups in two cities to stage meetings. The electronic boardroom in the Toshiba building was the most advanced telecommunication center seen, with worldwide connections for satellite TV, videodisc, computer, slide, film, transparency, and even document page presentations.

The weaknesses in Japanese shared services centered around the office automation (computer) clusters and printing/fax areas. The overall inadequacy of these shared services in number, location, and environmental quality (heat, light, noise, air) was seen in almost all of the new Japanese offices.

Introducing Architecture and Software for Team Management: The Building Management Trio

At least three individuals — the facilities manager, the personnel manager, and the technology manager — make decisions about the flux and change in the modern office, often with inadequate collaboration (see figure 10.11). The constant alterations of technology and of the space that houses it, along with the rapid redistribution of the workforce in high-tech offices, demand a far more refined system for making spatial decisions. Moving workstations (personnel managers' territory) and adding office equipment (technology managers' territory) impact not only the design of the spatial layout but the data and power network, the air conditioning, and the lighting (facility managers' territory). Yet these three players often have vastly different positions in the organization and maintain separate inventories, specifications, and maintenance schedules.

The social, economic, and technical consequences of office churn should be considered by the man-

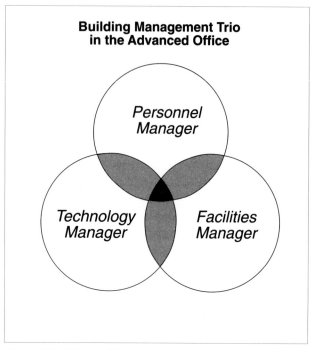

Figure 10.11 Toward improving workplace performance and satisfaction, the vision of people, facilities, and technology forming a set must be reflected with a management team of personnel, facilities, and technology managers.

agement trio collectively. To support decision-making, computer-aided facilities management (CAFM) packages should be developed to maintain information on a building's hardware, cable networks, environmental control systems, and architectural systems (structure, envelope, vertical chases, horizontal plenums, workstation components). This information should allow for access, modification, reconfiguration, or relocation of people, settings, and technologies — while indicating any thresholds or limits to change. The CAFM and the expertise in the management trio (now working as a team) will enable decisions that consider the cost, disruption, and workability of a change, prior to its enactment.

The "equal peers" or team structures in Japanese businesses are well suited to collective decision-making about new office layout and automation (see figure 10.12). Without question, all those affected by major purchases or decisions are consulted to contribute to those decisions. Even without the formal structuring of CAFM software packages, adequately responsible decisions can be made without serious side effects (such as thermal, acoustic, spatial, structural, and power inadequacies). However, the introduction of formal decisionmaking structures and software for team management of office automation and churn should be set in place while the density of new electronic equipment in the Japanese workplace is still low.

Introducing Architecture and Software for Interactive Learning: Expert Systems for Occupants, Facilities Managers, and Building Designers

One of the greatest challenges for individual control over environmental systems is the impact it has on the overall performance (including energy and cost effectiveness) of the building as a whole.

A number of advanced buildings now demonstrate the design and operational strategies that can evolve from interactive learning between managers, designers, and occupants of buildings (Hartkopf et al. 1990).

In the case of the Lloyd's of London Headquarters, input as to occupant air settings allows for the modification of central air temperatures. Input about daytime temperature fluctuations (with changes in occupancy density) led to the development of a night ventilation system using the building mass as a flywheel. In Germany, the Colonia building demonstrates a unique dialogue between facility management and occupant management, concerning the operable windows. Whenever the central air conditioning system is cooling, a light turns on in the office area to suggest that closing the window will allow the system to work more

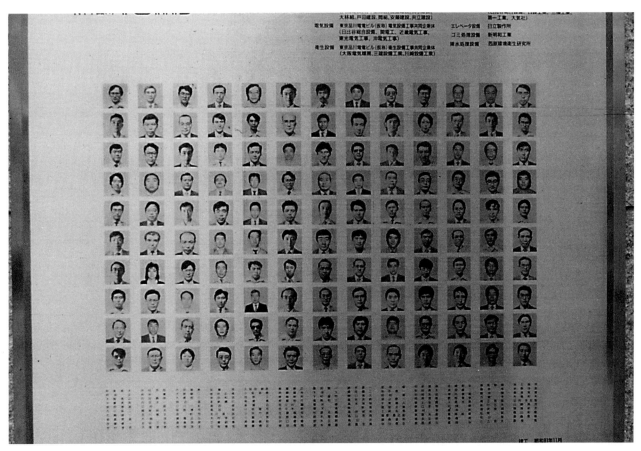

Figure 10.12 The NTT cornerstone listing 130 designers is the most striking representation of team design, a sharp contrast to the typical single name.

efficiently. When the chiller is off, the occupants are encouraged to open and shut windows depending on their local comfort needs. In the United States, the Smart House project demonstrates another concept for interactive learning, with the use of automatic power factor controllers triggered by "communication" between appliance and outlet.

In their advanced office building projects, the Japanese have heavily invested in programs to iteratively optimize resources. Reducing total energy use, shaving peak power demands, maintaining system efficiency, and minimizing water usage are all goals of facility management. The college-educated facilities management group — supported by extensive, well-calibrated, and well-maintained monitoring equipment — continuously evaluates and tunes the building systems. Optimization and improvements result from an ongoing process of comparison and competitive assessments between building subsystems, between tenant spaces, and between buildings projects. The results of these assessments are then applied to subsequent, further refined building projects.

In Japan, a unique investment in interactive learning can be seen in the ARK Mori building, in the form of a mobile environmental diagnostic system. This mini "robot" has a range of calibrated sensors to enable the facilities managers to evaluate the thermal, humidity, acoustic, and air quality conditions in any occupied space. The mobile diagnostic unit provides long-range input into the overall performance of buildings in the ARK Hills Complex, as well as enabling quick response to occupancy and facilities concerns. In the Umeda Center Building, the individual control of lights, air temperature settings, and air on/off conditions is monitored (not controlled) centrally to facilitate the development of improved system concepts (such as a central water loop feed to the individual heat pumps for energy effectiveness). A host of "smart" building technologies and expert software will enable occupants to communicate more clearly with central systems, facilities managers, and eventually with building designers.

Toward Defining Major Changes for the Office of the Future

Clearly, this list of twelve major design changes is evolving. Developments in technology as well as in work responsibilities and relationships are constantly expanding, and the ability of buildings to accommodate these changes is continually being challenged. Interdisciplinary field evaluations of advanced office buildings around the world are critical to developing our understanding of tomorrow's workplace.

In addition to studying the rapid changes in Japan, Germany, the U.K., and North America, ABSIC is planning future studies of advances in France, Sweden, and Singapore. This list of twelve major changes has already proved inadequate in breadth to deal with a number of trends that can be seen in very recent building studies, including a renewed emphasis on resource management (energy, water, air); rapid developments in workstation furniture (independent of work group concept development); and new developments in building robotics and in situ diagnostics. A major mission of the Center for Building Performance and Diagnostics at Carnegie Mellon University is to expand the understanding of the impact of new technologies on the workplace, toward enhancing worker satisfaction, communication, and overall productivity.

References

Chapter References

(Becker 1990)
Becker F., *The Total Workplace: Facilities Management and the Elastic Organization*, New York: Van Nostrand Reinhold, 1990.

(Chiu 1991)
Chiu, Mao-Lin, *Office Investment Decisionmaking and Building Performance*, Ph.D. thesis, Department of Architecture, Carnegie Mellon University, Pittsburgh, PA, May 1991.

(Hartkopf et al. 1990)
Hartkopf, V., Loftness, V., Mill, P.A.D., Siegel, M., "Architecture and Software for Interactive Learning About Total Building Performance," presented at the 3rd International Buffalo CAD Symposium, Buffalo, NY, March 23-25, 1990.

(Levin 1988)
Levin, D., "Smart Machines, Smart Workers — 'Gold Collar' Force Vital to Automation," *New York Times*, October 17, 1988.

(*Officing* 1988)
Officing: Bringing Amenity and Intelligence to Knowledge Work, Osaka, Japan: Matsushita Electric Works and CRSS, 1988.

Additional Major References

ABSIC, *German Building Studies*, research report presented at the February 14, 1989, meeting of the Advanced Building Systems Integration Consortium, Pittsburgh, PA.

ABSIC, *Japanese Building Studies*, research report presented at the October 4, 1988, meeting of the Advanced Building Systems Integration Consortium, Pittsburgh, PA.

ABSIC, *North American Building Studies I*, research report presented at the May 30, 1990, meeting of the Advanced Building Systems Integration Consortium, Pittsburgh, PA.

ABSIC, *North American Building Studies II*, research report presented at the March 6, 1991, meeting of the Advanced Building Systems Integration Consortium, Pittsburgh, PA.

ABSIC, *U.K. Building Studies*, research report presented at the July 20, 1989, meeting of the Advanced Building Systems Integration Consortium, Milwaukee, WI.

Brill, M., with Margulis, S., Konar, E., and BOSTI, in association with Westinghouse Furniture Systems, *Using Office Design to Increase Productivity*, Vol. 1. Buffalo: Workplace Design and Productivity, Inc., 1985.

Cohen, E., and A. Cohen, *Planning The Electronic Office*, New York: McGraw-Hill Book Company, 1984.

Davis, G., F. Becker, F. Duffy, and W. Sims, *ORBIT-2™ Overview Report*, Norwalk: Harbinger Group, 1985.

Development Opportunities for Integrated Building Management Systems, Amersham: ProPlan, 1990.

Duffy, F., and A. Henney, *The Changing City*, London: Architecture Planning Design (DEGW), 1988.

Hartkopf, V., "The Office of the Future: Intelligence in Office Design," presented at the International Building Symposium, University of Karlsruhe, Germany, October 14, 1989.

High-Technology Workplaces, ed. Pierre Goumain, New York: Van Nostrand Reinhold, 1989.

IBMS-Manufacturer/Supplier Analysis, Amersham: ProPlan (undated).

Intelligent Building Definition Guideline, First Edition, ed. Richard Geissler, Intelligent Building Institute, Washington, DC, 1987.

The Intelligent Building Sourcebook, ed. J. Bernaden and R. Neubauer (Johnson Controls, Inc.), Lilburn, GA: Fairmont Press, 1988.

Intelligent Buildings, ed. B. Atkin, New York: Halstead Press, 1988.

Intelligent Controls in Buildings: The UK Market 1989-94, Amersham: ProPlan, 1990.

Loftness, V., "Trends in Intelligent Buildings," presented at Future Build 2000: The Globalization of Intelligent Buildings, sponsored by the Intelligent Buildings Institute, New York, NY, October 30-31, 1990.

National Academy of Sciences, Building Research Board, *Electronically Enhanced Office Buildings*, a joint report by the Committee on Technologically Advanced Buildings and The Committee on High Technology Systems for Buildings, Washington, DC: National Research Council, 1988.

NOPA, *Results of Survey on Office Environments in Japan*, Tokyo, Japan: New Office Promotion Association, 1988.

Pulgram, W., and R. Stonis, *Designing The Automated Office: A Guide for Architects, Interior Designers, Space Planners, and Facility Managers*, ed. Stephen Kliment and Susan Davis, New York: Whitney Library of Design, 1984.

Rubin, A., *Revised Interim Design Guidelines for Automated Offices*, NBSIR 86-3430, Washington, DC: U.S. Department of Commerce, National Bureau of Standards, 1986.

Rubin, A., "Office Design Measurements for Productivity — A Research Overview," NBSIR 87-3688, Washington, DC: U.S. Department of Commerce, National Bureau of Standards, 1987.

Schwanke, D., *Smart Buildings and Technology-Enhanced Real Estate*, Vol. I and II, Washington, DC: Urban Land Institute (ULI), 1985.

Steele, Fritz, *Making and Managing High-quality Workplaces: An Organizational Ecology*, New York: Teachers College Press, 1986.

Sundstrom, E., and M. G. Sundstrom, *Work Places: The Psychology of the Physical Environment in Offices and Factories*, ed. Daniel Stokols and Irwin Altman, Cambridge: Cambridge University Press, 1986.

Appendices

Appendix A

Checklist for Identifying Component and Systems Innovations

1 ENVELOPE SYSTEM Innovations

1.1 EXTERIOR WALL

Generic Components	Circle Standard Specifications	Identify Whether Non-Standard Material, Component, System Integration, or Performance *(Identify manufacturers and trade names of materials and components)*
Form/Slope & Orientation Internal Surface material and Finish		
Curtain Wall Bearing Wall		
Exterior Material	• Granite/Stone • Steel • Wood • Aluminum • Concrete • Glass • Plastic	
Surface Finish	• Anodized • Organic coating (fluorocarbon, polyester, acrylic) • Paint	
Composite Material	• Thermal barrier • Rigidity/structural • Vapor barrier • Acoustic barrier • Electric field barrier • Rain management	
Internal Surface Material and Finish Form/ Slope & Orientation Module Size & Shape Module Manufacturing (on-site, factory, poured-in-place)		

Connections within envelope	• Clips, ties • Caulks, sealants

Connections with Other Systems	• Structure, earthquake, hurricane resistance • Mechanical: HVAC • Fire management • Washing, maintenance • Interior systems • Systems telecommunications

1.2 EXTERIOR WINDOW/ GLAZING

Generic Components	Circle Standard Specifications	Identify Whether Non-Standard Material, Component, System Integration, or Performance *(Identify manufacturers and trade names of materials and components)*
Size, Shape, & Orientation		
Material	• Glass (annealed, heat strengthened, tempered) • Acrylic/ plastic • Fiberglass • Ceramic • Marble • Single/ monolithic • Double/ insulated • Triple/ insulated	
Coating/ Finish/ Color Static Specifications	• Reflectivity • Transmission • Absorption • Emission • Dynamics	
Composite	• Dimension • Vacuum • Air • Gas • Fiberglass • Independent film • Liquid	

Frame Connections & Plan (elevation & section)	• Caulks & sealants • Spacer technology • Framing technology: thermal breaks
Component	• Structural integrity • Heat loss/gain • Air infiltration • Ventilation • Water management • Electric field barrier • Acoustic properties
Control	• Sunshading (exterior, interior, integral) • Light management • Night insulation • Acoustic layer • Privacy
Dynamic Specifications (day, season, year)	• Sun • Light • Heat • Sound • Air
Access, Maintenance, & Cleaning	
Aesthetics	• Color, texture, ornament, appearance rating • Staining, discoloration • Corrosion • Cracking, delamination, mechanical stress
Systems Integration	• Daylight concepts management, control • Artificial lighting interface • Mechanical system, load balancing, waste heat usage • Data security, data transmission • Interior systems, modularity wall interface • Structural connection

1.3 ROOF

Generic Components	**Circle Standard Specifications**	**Identify Whether Non-Standard Material, Component, System Integration, or Performance** *(Identify manufacturers and trade names of materials and components)*
Material	• Granite/Stone • Steel • Wood • Aluminum	

	• Concrete • Glass • Plastic • Rubber
Composite Material	• Structural properties • Thermal barrier • Air/ vapor barrier • Acoustic barrier • Electric field barrier • Rain barrier
Form/ Slope & Orientation Internal Surface Material & Finish	
Module Size & Shape Module Manufacturing Connections within Envelope	• On-site, factory, poured-in-place • Clips, ties • Caulks, sealants • Rain management system • Access & maintenance
Systems Interfaces	• Structural frame, rooftop capacity • Mechanical systems/penthouses/intakes & exhausts • Telecommunications/downlinks/penthouses • Skylights, beam daylighting, fiber-optic lighting

1.4 SUBGRADE

Generic Components	Circle Standard Specifications	Identify Whether Non-Standard Material, Component, System Integration, or Performance *(Identify manufacturers and trade names of materials and components)*
Material	• Granite/Stone • Steel • Aluminum • Concrete (type) • Wood	
Surface Finish	• Anodized • Organic coating (fluorocarbon, polyester, acrylic, butyl) • Paint	
Composite Material	• Structural properties • Thermal barrier • Air/ vapor barrier • Acoustic/vibration barrier • Moisture/water barrier • Ventilation properties	

Form/ Slope & Orientation
Internal Surface Material & Finish

Module Size & Shape
Module Manufacturing
Connections within Envelope   • Clips, ties
                                             • Caulks, sealants

1.5 NOTABLE OVERALL PERFORMANCE OF ENVELOPE SYSTEM

	Poor				Excellent
Spatial	1	2	3	4	5
Acoustic	1	2	3	4	5
Air Quality	1	2	3	4	5
Thermal	1	2	3	4	5
Visual	1	2	3	4	5
Building Integrity	1	2	3	4	5

1.6 NOTABLE SYSTEMS INTEGRATION

Envelope & Structural   • Internalized structure vs. thermal bridging

Envelope & HVAC   • Air flow windows

Envelope & Lighting   • Light shelf ducts

Envelope & Power/Telec.   • Spandrel distribution of telecommunications

Envelope & Security

Envelope & Vert. Transp.

Envelope & Interior Ceiling   • Daylight distribution methods

Envelope & Interior Floor

Envelope & Interior Wall

Envelope & Interior Furnishings

2 STRUCTURAL SYSTEM Innovations

2.1 GENERAL SYSTEM

Generic Components	Circle Standard Specifications	Identify Whether Non-Standard Material, Component, System Integration, or Performance *(Identify manufacturers and trade names of materials and components)*
Type	• Frame • Tensile • Diaphragm • Inflated	
Material	• Granite/Stone • Masonry • Steel • Wood • Aluminum • Concrete • Plastic	
Surface Finish	• Anodized • Organic coating • (fluorocarbon, polyester, acrylic) • Paint	
Composite Material	• Thermal barrier • Air/vapor barrier • Acoustic /vibration properties	
Module Size & Shape	• Interface with interior systems/modules • Bay sizes • Floor-to-floor height • Depth of structural elements	
Module Manufacturing (On-site, factory, poured-in-place)		
Connections within Structure (elevation & section)	• Anchor, ties • Caulks, sealants	
Connections with Other Systems	• Envelope (thermal, visual, water management) • HVAC (support, distribution, modularity) • Interior subdivision, furnishing • Telecommunications (support, distribution, module) • Expandability	

Aesthetics	• Color, texture, ornament
	• Appearence rating
	• Accelerated staining
	• Discoloration
	• Corrosion
	• Cracking
	• Delamination

2.2 NOTABLE OVERALL PERFORMANCE OF STRUCTURAL SYSTEM

	Poor			Excellent	
Spatial	1	2	3	4	5
Acoustic	1	2	3	4	5
Air Quality	1	2	3	4	5
Thermal	1	2	3	4	5
Visual	1	2	3	4	5
Building Integrity	1	2	3	4	5

2.3 NOTABLE SYSTEM INTEGRATION

Structure & Ext. Wall/Roof	• Structure as Facade
Structure & Windows	• Overhangs for Shading
Structure & HVAC	• Use of Structure for HVAC Distribution
Structure & Lighting	• Lightshelves
Structure & Power/Telecom.	• Use of Structure for Cabling Distribution
Structure & Security	
Structure & Vertical Trans.	• Core & Structure
Structure & Interior Ceiling	• Truss Ceiling/Floors for Horizontal Distribution
Structure & Interior Floor	
Structure & Interior Wall	
Structure & Interior Furnishings	

3 INTERIOR SYSTEM

3.1 CEILING

Generic Components	Circle Standard Specifications	Identify Whether Non-Standard Material, Component, System Integration, or Performance (*Identify manufacturers and trade names of materials and components*)
Surface Material	• Fiberglass • Plastic • Vinyl • Gypsum/Plaster • Wood • Metal • Fabric	
Surface Properties	• Hard / soft • Stiff / flexible • Pattern ornament • Textured / smooth • Punctured / closed • Color - reflectivity • Aesthetics rating • Air quality / outgassing	
Composite Material	• Material type • Size, depth • Edge detail • NRC and STC ratings • Air quality / outgassing • Rigidity / structural	
Support	• Distance from ceiling/slab • Distance from floor slab • Grid — exposed/concealed • Grid dimensions • Steel/aluminum/plastic • Connection, glue	
Size & Shape	• Flush • Hung parallel • Hung perpendicular • Parabolic • Curved • Height variation • Module size, flexibility • Material variation	

Access, Maintenance, & Cleaning

Aesthetics	• Staining and discoloration • Chipping, cracking, and delamination • Dust build up • Rusting • Sagging
Cabling Connections	• Adequate structural support • Integrated trays • Access • Power, voice, data, video • Expansion
Mechanical Supply	• Grid dimension (between supplies) • Square, round, linear; (size) • Integrated aesthetics, materials of supply/return • Integrated with lighting, cabling, fire, public address • Duct plenum dimension • Access • Ceiling assistance in air distribution and air filtration • Ceiling assistance for radiant heat • Local control, independent wiring/controls
Lighting Connections	• Fixed grid dimension (between lights) • Fixture size, shape • Recessed, surface mount, suspended, track/downlighting • Integrated acoustics and aesthetics in lens covers • Ceiling support for light distribution • Uplighting & ceiling interface • Sunlighting & daylighting interface • Brightness contrast/glare management • Local control • Access
Other Connections	• Masking sound • Fire/smoke detection • Sprinklers • Signage/way finding
Systems Integration	• Structure (including seismic) • Interior walls • Envelope

3.2 FLOOR

Generic Components	Circle Standard Specifications	Identify Whether Non-Standard Material, Component, System Integration, or Performance (*Identify manufacturers and trade names of materials and components*)
Type	• Structural floor / slab • Trench, underfloor ducting • Cellular deek • Poke through • Raised, access floor • Integrated to floor / ceiling	
Surface Material	• Carpet • Carpet tiles • Plastic, vinyl, linoleum • Wood • Masonry, finished concrete • Paint • Maintenance • Air quality concerns, outgassing	
Composite Material	• Structural property, stability, & load support • Thermal property, resistance, & MRT	
Size & Shape Connections & Plan	• Module dimension • Even / level appearance • Safety (tripping concerns) • Caulks & sealants • Flexibility, replaceability	
Access, Maintenance, & Cleaning		
Aesthetics	• Color, texture, ornament • Staining, discoloration • Corrosion • Cracking, delamination	
Acoustics	• Surface & composite absorptivity • NRC rating • Static control • Vibration control	
Lighting	• Color • Reflectivity, ambient light quality • Gloss, specular reflection • Matte • Pattern, brightness, contrast, distraction	

PLEC Connections (Power, light, electronics, communication)	• Underfloor cable management: data, voice, video, power • Plenum dimension • Cable access — maintenance & expansion • Outlet design, access & expansion • Safety & security • Aesthetics
HVAC Connections	• Grid dimension (between supplies) • Square, round linear (size) • Duct plenum dimension • Integrated aesthetics / materials of supply/return • Assistance in air distribution, filtration • Assistance for radiant heat • Local control • Access
Interior Furnishings Walls Connections	• Modular match • Structural support • Structural connections • Adaptability
Other Connections	• Enclosure • Structure • Lighting • Signage • Masking sound

3.3 FIXED INTERIOR WALL

Generic Components	**Circle Standard Specifications**	**Identify Whether Non-Standard Material, Component, System Integration, or Performance** *(Identify manufacturers and trade names of materials and components)*
Surface Material	• Acrylic/ plastic • Fiberglass • Ceramic, glass • Gypsum, plaster • Marble • Fabric • Wood • Steel	

Composite Material Type:	
Thermal Quality	• Radiant heating, MRT balancing • Air distribution management
Air Quality	• Air filtering • Outgassing, shielding
Visual Quality	• Color & finish, reflectivity • Reflectivity and ambient light quality from task/ambient systems • Lighting system interface/integration • Gloss/matte: specular reflection • Integration of task or ambient lighting • Management of excess heat from equipment • Sun & daylight management • Borrowed light management, connection to ceiling, envelope, walls • Flexible task lighting with separate ambient
Acoustic Quality	• Composite material • Sound attenuation between spaces • Surface & composite absorption • NRC & STC ratings • Management of excess noise from equipment • Vibration control, structural stability
Size & Shape	• Module dimension • Spatial geometries, flex • Connections, caulks & sealants • Evenness, structural stability • Flexibility, modularity, replaceability • Height variation
Integrated Storage Space/System	• Capacity, size • Surface/impact on acoustic absorption • Light reflectivity • Ergonomics • Handling of equipment: noise, heat, air quality concerns • Plug-in amenities
Access, Maintenance, & Cleaning	
Aesthetics	• Color, texture, ornament • Staining/discoloration • Corrosion • Cracking, delamination • Maintenance and cleaning

Systems Integration: Interior Walls & PLEC (Power, light, electronics, communication)	• Cable management: data, voice, video, power • Cable access — maintenance & expansion • Safety & security • Aesthetics • Uplifting
Interior Walls & Mechanical	• Wall assistance in air distribution; HVAC air filtration • Radiant heating • Local control devices for the HVAC supply
Interior Walls & Structure	• Modular match • Structural support • Structural connections
Interior Walls & Enclosure (as well as fixed walls)	• Modular match • Seal • Finish
Interior Walls & Floors	• Modular match • Seal, connection • HVAC, PLEC connections, changeability
Interior Walls & Other	• Signage • Masking sound
Occupant Controls	• Visual privacy • Acoustic privacy • Sunlight • Air distribution • MRT

3.4 FURNISHINGS (EXCLUDING FIXED FLOORS, FIXED WALLS, ENVELOPE)

Generic Components	Circle Standard Specifications	Identify Whether Non-Standard Material, Component, System Integration, or Performance (*Identify manufacturers and trade names of materials and components*)

3.4.1 Movable Wall Surface/Panels

Size of panel/unit	• Connection • Expandability	
Surface & composite materials/integrity	• Acrylic/plastic • Fiberglass • Ceramic • Marble	

	• Fabric • Wood • Steel • Glass
Systems Integration: Interior Walls & PLEC (Power, light, electronics, communication)	• Cable management: data, voice, video, power • Cable access — maintenance & expansion • Safety & security • Aesthetics • Uplifting
Interior Panels & Mechanical	• Wall assistance in air distribution; HVAC air filtration • Radiant heating • Local control devices for the HVAC supply
Interior Panels & Structure	• Modular match • Structural support • Structural connections
Interior Panels & Enclosure (as well as fixed walls)	• Modular match • Seal • Finish
Interior Panels and Floors	• Modular match • Seal, connection • HVAC, PLEC connections, changeability
Interior Panels & Other	• Signage • Masking sound
Occupant Controls	• Visual privacy • Acoustic privacy • Sunlight • Air distribution • MRT

3.4.2 Worksurface

Spatial	• Height adjustability • Keyboard & screen positions • Size & shape • Multiple surfaces/supports • Connection
Material	• Acrylic/plastic • Fiberglass • Ceramic • Marble

	• Fabric • Wood • Steel • Glass
Thermal Quality	• Conductivity
Visual Quality	• Finish (matte/gloss), color, brightness, contrast
Acoustic Quality	• Reflectivity; vibration control; static control
Air Quality	• Control, shielding
PLEC management in worksurface	• Power, voice, data, video

3.4.3 Storage

	• Capacity, size • Surface impact on acoustic absorption, light reflectivity • Ergonomics • Handling of equipment: equipment noise, heat or air quality concerns • Modular amenities, drop-ins

3.4.4 Chairs

	• Stability - 3, 4, 5 legs • Ergonomics: adjustable seat height/tilt back position, small back support • Reduced thermal, conductivity

3.4.5 Office Equipment

	• Flexibility & modularity • Mobility • Ergonomic resolution • Acoustical resolution • Task lighting resolution • Air quality resolution • Thermal resolution

3.4.6 Overall Furniture Concerns

Air Quality	• Use of PVC • Formaldehyde presence • Toxic outgassing • Man-made mineral fibers

Integrity/Aesthetic	• Color, texture, ornament • Staining, discoloration • Corrosion • Cracking, delamination • Ease of access • Maintenance & cleaning
Thermal Quality	• Management of mechanical grid air flow patterns (no short circuiting) • Management of MRT imbalance • Management of excess heat from equipment

Acoustic Quality	• Overall sound absorption, NRC rating
	• Attenuation between closed spaces STC rating
	• Intelligibility between workstations in open
	  space (A.V.)
	• Occupant control of enclosure
	• Background sound levels; capability
	  of white/pink noise generation
	• Management of excess noise from equipment

Visual Quality	• Overall light absorption/reflectivity
	• Management of light grid distribution patterns
	  (elimination of shadows)
	• Provision of task light & management of
	  brightness contrast
	• Provision of ambient light (e.g., HID) without
	  hot spots
	• Management of electronic interference from
	  fluorescent lights

Spatial Quality	• Management of new technology
	  spatial needs: worksurface, access,
	  connection

3.5 AMENITIES

Generic Components	**Circle Standard Specifications**	**Identify Whether Non-Standard Material, Component, System Integration, or Performance** *(Identify manufacturers and trade names of materials and components)*
Conference Room	• Internal communication • External communication • Full visual display equipment (slides, video, computer overhead)	

Teleconference
Meeting Areas

Atrium
Reception
Lounge

Cafeterias
Vending Machine Areas
Coffee Areas

Restrooms
Smoking Areas
Storage Areas

Health Club
Medical Suite/Doctor

Technology Training
Equipment Showroom, Store

3.6 NOTABLE OVERALL PERFORMANCE OF INTERIOR SYSTEM

	Poor				Excellent
• Spatial Quality	1	2	3	4	5
• Acoustic Quality	1	2	3	4	5
• Air Quality	1	2	3	4	5
• Thermal Quality	1	2	3	4	5
• Visual Quality	1	2	3	4	5
• Building Integrity	1	2	3	4	5

3.7 NOTABLE SYSTEMS INTEGRATION

Interior & Structure

Interior & HVAC

Interior & Lighting

Interior & Power/Telecommunications

Interior & Enclosure

4 MECHANICAL SYSTEMS

4.1 HVAC

Generic Components	Circle Standard Specifications	Identify Whether Non-Standard Material, Component, System Integration, or Performance (*Identify manufacturers and trade names of materials and components*)

4.1.1 Fuel Sources

| | • Gas
• Oil
• Solar
• Waste
• Electric grid
• Electric, district, or local generation
• Other | |

4.1.2 Service Generators

Boilers/ Furnace	• Hot water • Low-pressure steam • High-pressure steam • Fire tube • Water tube • Cast-iron • Steel • Gravity warm air • Forced warm air • Central or distributed; # per sq. ft., or per population density	
Compressors & Chillers	• Refrigeration • Electric drive • Absorption units • Reverse thermosiphon • Central or distributed; # per sq. ft., or per population density	
Central Air-conditioning	• Cooling tower motor • Air-cooled condensor motor • Condenser pumps • Room air conditioners • Through-the-wall units • Economizer cycle	
Ventilation/Fresh Air	• Minimum settings • Economizer • CO_2/pollution sensors/controllers • Intake/exhaust configuration • Distributed systems	

Pumps *(# units, connected HP)*	• Chilled-water pumps • Condensor water pumps • Boiler feed pumps • Hot-water pumps for space heating • Recirculating pumps for domestic hot water

4.1.3 Service Conduits

All-Air-HVAC Systems *(# of a.h.u., total HP, cfm/ahu)*	• Single-zone • Terminal reheat (hot water, electric, steam) • Variable Air Volume • Induction • Dual duct • Multi-zone units • Unitary heat pumps • Sq. ft. vertical plenum/total sq. ft. • Depth horiz. plenum/slab-to-slab height
Water-Air Systems *(# units, connecteed HP)*	• Two-pipe fan-coil • Three-pipe fan-coil • Four-pipe fan-coil • Unitary heat pumps
Configuration/Distance Interface/Expansion Material/Ornament Access	

4.1.4 Service Terminals

(# units, connected HP, cfm/fan unit) Fans*(Supply & exhaust)*	• Backward-curved multivane fans • Forward-curved multivane fans • Axial fans • Propeller fans
Perimeter Units	• Fin-tube radiators • Cast-iron radiators • Radiant heating coils • Hot-water piping • Supply and return ducts • Outside air dampers
Local Distribution	• Ceiling, floor, wall, or furniture • Density diffusers, per sq. ft., per population • Air flow • Diffuser shape, configuration • Material, ornament

- Access
- Interface/Expansion
- Relocation capability

4.1.5 Systems Integration

- Structure
- Interior ceiling
- Interior floor
- Interior partitioning
- Lighting
- Enclosure (MRT management, perimeter/core balancing)

4.2 ENERGY MANAGEMENT CONTROL SYSTEM (EMCS)

Generic Components	Circle Standard Specifications	Identify Whether Non-Standard Material, Component, System Integration, or Performance *(Identify manufacturers and trade names of materials and components)*
Central Management	• Manual • Automatic • Location • Grouped controls and displays • Major functions • Indicators and controls • Schema "as wired"/"as installed" • Emergency telephone with separate line (not via PBX or switchboard) • Tests conducted • Scheduled maintenance • Performance/evaluation annually • Performance/evaluation semi-annually	
Resource Management Systems	• Off-peak cooling • Thermal storage (water, ice, other) • Peak power sharing • System shut-down/set back • Individual sensors • Programmable sensors • Density/type of sensors (temp, CO_2 particulates, humidity)	
Local Management Systems/Controls	• Location • Automatic/Manual • Density	

- Individual HVAC systems
- Radiant panel
- Terminal temperature control
- Terminal air control

UTILITY - ENERGY DATA

ELECTRICITY
- KWH/ month/ per service (i.e., lighting, air conditioning, hot water, office equipment)
- Peak demand/ month
- Connected load
- KWH/ sq. meter/ year

OIL
- BTU/ gallon
- Gallons/ month
- BTU/ sq. meter/ year

GAS
- BTU/ Cuft
- Cuft/ month
- BTU/Cuft/ month

OBTAIN
- Electric rate schedule
- Fuel; oil and gas rate schedule

To Determine
- HVAC — if VAV , how are fans controlled?
- Vaned inlet, multispeed motor, frequency controller, other
- Heat recovery — sources, applications
- Vibration control in building for instrumentation
- Wet & dry waste management
- Water-saving devices
- Energy storage - ice - chilled water - latent heat

Climate Forecasting
- Max high/ month
- Ave. high/ month
- Ave. temperature/ month
- Average low/ month
- Average max/ month
- Wind velocity - direction/ intensity
- Solar radiation global/ month (direct, diffuse, cloud cover, sunshine)
- Design wet bulb and dry bulb

Occupancy Density
- Workers
- Visitors

EMCS
- Is there energy optimization?
- Is indoor - outdoor air quality monitored & controlled?

4.3 PLUMBING

Generic Components	Circle Standard Specifications	Identify Whether Non-Standard Material, Component, System Integration, or Performance *(Identify manufacturers and trade names of materials and components)*
Configuration	• Size volume • Form, configuration • Planning module • Expansion capability • Material, ornament	
Method of DHW Generation & Storage	• Oil, gas, electricity, coal for DHW • Tankless heater on space-heating boiler • Tank heater on space-heating boiler • Tank insulation thickness	
Service Conduits/Piping	• Thickness, volume • Configuration, distance • Interface, expansion • Material, ornament • Access	
Fixtures in Service Terminals (kitchens, toilets, other)	• Planning module • Number, size, capacity • Form, ergonomics • Material, ornament • Integration with interior walls, ceiling • Interface/Expansion • Relocation capability • Access and maintenance	
Conservation	• Grey water system • Water conservation strategies • Secondary use of stored water (off peak, fire...)	

4.4 FIRE SAFETY

Generic Components	Circle Standard Specifications	Identify Whether Non-Standard Material, Component, System Integration, or Performance *(Identify manufacturers and trade names of materials and components)*
Service Generators	• Wet • Dry • Delayed action • Halon 1301 • Manual pull stations • Pre-action sprinklers	
Planning Module	• Size, capacity • Zoning • Raised floors • Closets • Ceiling - hidden • Exposed • Access, maintenace	
Sensor/Controllers	• Optical/photoelectric • Smoke • Heat/temperature • Ionization • Flame • HVAC modifications • Local shut off/delay • Halon discharge controllers • Pre-alarms • Time-delays • Leakage "tattletales," water monitoring • Cross zone alarms	
Integration	• Structure • Interior ceiling • Mechanical/HVAC • Lighting • Interior partitioning	
Automatic Systems	• Central computer • HVAC • Automatic startup fans • Automatic control fire damper • Air conditioner shutdown • Blocking air ventilation/positive &	

	negative pressurization
	• Control access computer
	• Life safety control system
	• Manual and automatic alarm systems
	• Separate fire-related circuits
	• Data log identification
	• Computer room doors opening
	• Easy restart of all systems
Disaster Resistance	• Equipment shutdown
	• Power shut off "Panic" button
	• Halogen gas
	• Alarms annunciate at control center
	• Fire dampers
	• Emergency lighting
	• Life safety systems
	• Manual (pull stations)
	• Automatic alarms
	• Location & status graphic display
	• Automatic fire doors
	• Programmable time delay

4.5 HVAC NOTABLE OVERALL PERFORMANCE

	Poor				Excellent
Spatial Quality	1	2	3	4	5
Acoustic Quality	1	2	3	4	5
Air Quality	1	2	3	4	5
Thermal Quality	1	2	3	4	5
Visual Quality	1	2	3	4	5
Building Integrity	1	2	3	4	5

4.6 NOTABLE SYSTEMS INTEGRATION

HVAC & Envelope	• Air flow window
HVAC & Lighting	• Light shelf ducts
HVAC & Power/Telec.	• Shared plenum/grid management
HVAC & Vert.Transp.	• Shared core planning; high accessibility
HVAC & Structure	• Use of structure for HVAC
HVAC & Interior.	• Personal environmental controls, workstation harness

5 PLEC (POWER , LIGHTING, ELECTRONICS & COMMUNICATION) SYSTEMS, TRANSPORT & SECURITY SYSTEMS

5.1 SERVICE GENERATOR

Generic Components	Circle Standard Specifications	Identify Whether Non-Standard Material, Component, System Integration, or Performance *(Identify manufacturers and trade names of materials and components)*

5.1.1 Central Power Type

	• Utility power — single- or multiple-grid supply • Self-contained generation • Cogeneration • Emergency standby power • Uninterrupted power supply (UPS) • Clean power vs. general power separation	
Size (KVA)	• Standard building load • Over sized (automation growth)	
Capacity Planning Module	• 110 V/120 V • 208 V/277 V/480 V • 50 Hz/60 Hz • 400 Hz	
Additional Backup	• Emergency standby • Diverse utility feeds • Uninterruptible power system • Motor generator • Automatic power transfer • Power conditioning to terminals	
Location/Distribution	• Basement utility room • Roof • Bullet middle floors	

5.1.2 Central Data/Video

Internal Communications Systems	• Voice mail system • Electronic mail • Videotex • Internal FAX • Communicating copiers • Internal videoconferencing	

Computer System	• Mainframe/multiprocessors • Super-computer (Cray, etc.) • Minis/networks & gateways • Micros/networks & gateways
External Communications Systems (ECS)	• Microwave • Satellite • Access to packet-switched network • Elect. tandem network (ETNs) • Facsimile, Teletype, Telex • Videoconferencing • Teleconferencing • Teleport • RF systems • CATV • Transparent internal gateways to ECS
Shared Tenant Systems	• Full building supported • Bullet partial building shared • Realcom (IBM) • Contel • TelCom Plus • AmeriStm (Lincoln Properties) • Martnet (Trammell Crow)

5.1.3 Central Telephone

Type	• Central office based (CENTREX) • Private branch exchange (PBX) • Key systems • Digital service from central office (ISDN)
Telephone Service Entrance Size and Facilities	• 1-1 number of telephones • Less than 1-1 (internal switch) • % of telephone anticipated • Direct Inward Dialing (DID) • Fiber-optic building service • Central office trunking over T-1 • Spans to PBX • Multiplexers in building
Main Telephone Room Location Size	• Close to riser distribution • Convenient to service entrance • To house existing equipment • Planned expansion • Environmentally controlled

5.2 SERVICE CONDUITS (INTERNAL SIGNAL: WIRING & CABLING)

Generic Components	Circle Standard Specifications	Identify Whether Non-Standard Material, Component, System Integration, or Performance *(Identify manufacturers and trade names of materials and components)*

5.2.1 Power, Data, & Voice

Vertical Distribution	• Sufficient density • Empty riser space for expansion/new • Cabling • Distributed risers, number & location • In conduits and riser ducts separate from power conductors • Separated and/or shielded from sources	
Network Topology	• Star • Bus • Ring • Hybrid	
Premise Wiring Scheme	• AT&T PDS • IBM • DEC	
Networking	• Local area networks • LAN compatible computer equipment • LAN variety of vendor equipment • Internal systems linked with external ones, such as telephone, microwave, satellite	
Wiring Closets	• Walk-in-shallow • Walk-in-deep • Size • Location • Expandability/flexibility • Battery room • Method of access to floor, conduit, deck • Power requirements • Services (layout) • Service list (voice, data, security) • Fire stops • Wall-mounted • 3 feet deep, access to risers • Separated from sources • Shielded from sources • Patch panels for data systems	

	• Secure • Bullet access to power • Patch panels • Space for multiplexers • Ventilated/power available
Wiring Type	• Twisted-pair (24 gauge) • Coaxial cable (including Twinax) • Fiber-optic • Dark fiber-optic cable (future use) • Shielded/ unshielded • Plenum/nonplenum • Number of conductors • Multimedia cable • Infrared devices • RF
Connectors/Wiring Blocks	• Single/multiple • Method of connection of wires • Furniture limitations • Orientation • Labeling convention • Termination method
Drop Cable	• Length limitation • Label convention • Connection to device • Shielded/unshielded • Gauge/ size • Plenum/nonplenum • Transition from wall/floor to drop cable • Transition from drop cable to device
	• Under-carpet cable (hot wire) • Number of conductors • Transition from closet • Transition to devices

5.2.2 Power, Data, & Voice
Horizontal Distribution

General Types	• Grid density • Raised access floor • Flat cable distribution • Integrated or cellular floors • Floor duct system • Poke-through • Ceiling distribution - hidden • Exposed cable trays

Horizontal Modifications	• Flexible conduits • Modular removable connectors
Workstation Connection	• Workstation distribution • Power poles • Raceways • Movable walls/partition distribution
Network Topology	• Bus (e.g., Apple-Talk) • Ring (e.g., IBM-token ring) • Star (e.g., VAX-Ethernet) • Hybrid • Power voltage/cycle availability at workstation

Access to Horizontal Distribution	• Composition of floor
	• Sizes & locations of trenches/ cells
	• Stringers/or not
	• Height above slab
	• Pedestal design
	• Conduit layout
	• Access to underfloor
	  - access box - configuration (box or tombstone)
	  - connection to cabling
	  - fire rating/ fire stops
	• Smoke detector requirement
	• Underfloor distribution from closet
	  - GMD system/ point to point
	  - wire manegement - pathways, etc.
	  - labeling
	  - Sealing of floor slab

Raised Floor	• Clear space (inches) • Floor material/module • Pedestal construction • Grounding • Access box/tombstone • Connection to cabling • Fire rating/fire stops • Smoke detector requirement • Grid underfloor distribution from closet • System/point-to-point • Wire management - pathways • Labeling • Treatment of floor slab
Cellular Deck	• Manufacturer • Depth & number of cells • Fire rating/fire stops • Size & location of trench(es) • Access at closet/trench

	• Access at office • Access box - configuration & materials • Connection to cabling
Conduit/Poke-through	• Conduit layout • Grid distribution • System/point-to-point • Wire management - pathways, etc. • Labeling
Overhead Distribution	• Power poles offices access • Wall and column chases • Grid distribution • Wire management - pathways, etc. • Labeling
Flat Wire/Flat Cable	• Number of conductors • Transition from closet/distribution point • Transition to devices
Wire Management Systems	• Diagnostic instrumentation • Cable identification, wire management software • Outlet identification, wire management software • Wire identification • Outlet capability identification • Wire removal/replacement strategy • Wiring and telecommunications integration in wireways • Other wire management software
Planning Module	• Standard building power for all devices • Separate feeders and branch circuits for automation equipment • Receptacles identified • On-going monitoring of plugged devices into special circuits • Power conditioning available
Reconfiguration	• Floors • 3-D • Integrated system digital network (ISDN) • Core distribution • Punch down block
Horizontal Distribution/ Integration with Other Systems	• Data, power & telephone distribution • Data & power distribution • Data & telephone distribution • Cable raceways with raised floor construction • Cable raceways with ceiling system construction • Cable raceways with furniture system construction

- Cable raceways with HVAC duct/pipe distribution
- Cable raceways with lighting
- Cable raceways & fire management

5.3 POWER, DATA & VOICE SERVICE TERMINALS

Generic Components	Circle Standard Specifications	Identify Whether Non-Standard Material, Component, System Integration, or Performance *(Identify manufacturers and trade names of materials and components)*

5.3.1 Data and Voice Connectors

	• Floor mounted • Wall mounted • Workstation mounted • Single • Duplex or more • Labeling • Length of "drop" cable • Method of termination	
Connected Transmission Speed	• Low • Medium • High	
Connector Type	• Voice/data • Voice/data/video • Fiber-optic spine • Satellite • Microwave	
Outlets	• Type and number of outlets • Integration of outlets into floors, walls, furniture • Labeling of capacity, smart outlets • Modularity, integration with telephone, data, video outlets • Aesthetics, integrity • Safety, security (flush, tombstones, pop-up...)	
Integration of Outlets with Other Systems	• With furniture • With floor • With walls (movable or fixed) • With ceiling • With HVAC • With lights	

5.3.2 Appliances

- Number and density (# per person)
- Types (# and density, connected power requirements)
- (Desk lamps, fans, clocks, ionizers, radios...)

5.3.3 Telephone Types

- Dummy
- Intelligent
- Standard POTS (2500 set)
- Feature phones (AT&T, NTI, ROLM, Siemens, NEC)

5.3.4 Computers and Peripherals

Major Computer Types	• Stand-alone micro (e.g., MACs, other PCs) • Micro with network • Workstations • Mini-computer (e.g., VAX) • Mainframe (e.g., IBM, HP) • Supercomputer (e.g., CRAY)
Major Computer Functions	• Word processing • Printing • Electronic mail • Database • Statistical • Accounting, financial • Graphic/CAD • Modeling • Simulation • Publishing • Archival storage
Other Data Peripherals (list)	• Line printers • Laser printers (Desktop, IBM 3800, etc.) • Plotters • Multiplexer • Network control equipment • Other
Integration of Computer Peripherals and Appliances	• With furniture • With walls • With ceilings • With HVAC Module • With lighting capability

5.4 VIDEO SERVICES

- Teleconferencing control facilities (describe setup)
- Portable teleconferencing (describe package)
- Cable type
- Cable vertical distribution
- Cable horizontal distribution
- Terminal units, type
- Integration w/ power, voice & data

5.5 DYNAMICS/CONTROLS

- Power demand and capacity, outlet location, terminal unit location & number, energy management
- Telephone (outlet location & number, terminal unit type and number, cost management), power demand
- Data (outlet location and number, terminal unit type and number, data management, power demand)
- Overload/surge management
- Emergency operation

5.6 MIS/TELECOMMUNICATIONS DELIVERY PROCESS

During Building Project

- Attendance in general planning meetings
- Integral part of building team
- Scheduling
- Programming and construction drawing review & approval
- Budgeting
- Right of veto
- Integration

During Building Operation

- General building user interface
- Wire manager
- Informed of all moves/adds/changes in MIS/telecomm
- Service order issuance

Other Functions

- Disaster planning
- Capacity planning input to building
- Program/occupancy planning
- Technology forecasting in building planning

5.7 NOTABLE OVERALL PERFORMANCE OF POWER, ELECTRONICS, COMMUNICATIONS

	Poor				Excellent
Spatial Quality	1	2	3	4	5
Acoustic Quality	1	2	3	4	5
Air Quality	1	2	3	4	5
Thermal Quality	1	2	3	4	5
Visual Quality	1	2	3	4	5
Building Integrity	1	2	3	4	5

5.8 NOTABLE SYSTEMS INTEGRATION

- PEC & Structure

- PEC & Interior

- PEC & HVAC

- PEC & Lighting

- PEC & Enclosure

5.9 LIGHTING

Generic Components	Circle Standard Specifications	Identify Whether Non-Standard Material, Component, System Integration, or Performance (*Identify manufacturers and trade names of materials and components*)
Service	• Power capacity • Control flexibility, expansion	
Fixtures	• Task lighting (table, pole, floor, ceiling) • Ambient (down, up, indirect, daylight) • Task/ambient lighting • Reflector, Troffer effectiveness	
Fixture Type	• Recessed coffers • Down lights • Track lights • Uplighting, free-standing • Coffer, recessed lighting • Flush lens • Parabolic louver	

Planning Module	• Grid dimensions, densities per sq. ft. or population • Ease of expansion, subtraction • Ease of relocatability, tether/pigtail
Lamp Type	• Cool white fluorescent • Deluxe cool white fluorescent • Warm white fluorescent • High intensity discharge (HID) • Incandescent • A — General service lamp • G — Decorative lamp • S — Decorative lamp • PAR — Lamp used for directional purposes • R — PAR lamp w/t wide beam spread • T — Tungsten-halogen lamp • Deluxe mercury • Phosphor-coated metal halide • High-pressure sodium • Low-pressure sodium • Ballasts • Daylight simulating
Central Management/Control	• Relay - microprocessor • Electric signals/radio frequencies • Lamp change • Voltage amplitude control • Front-end current limiter • Solid-state ballasts
Local Management/Control	• Automatic shutoff, dimming w/time, daylight • Manual/independent switching • Programmable
Automatic/Manual Controls	• Manual • Dimmers • Timer activated • Thermal/heat activated • Motion activated • Sound activated • Photoelectric activated
Fixture Efficacy	• Lumens/watt • Watts/sq. ft. • Reflector efficiency • Bulb efficiency • Lens efficiency • Ceiling/room/furniture configuration efficiency • Surrounding color, reflectivity & efficiency • Control strategy effectiveness/energy conservation

Visual Quality/Performance	• Appropriate light levels • Light distribution • Glaze control - direct & reflected • Brightness contrast control • Daylight interface • Color rendition • Fiber optic
Spatial Control	• Multiple switching • Tether • Pigtail • Perimeter/core separation • Number of zones & ease of modification
Other Performance Concerns/Opportunities	• Acoustic/noise generation - ballast maintenance • Data/noise interference • Acoustic reflection/absorption quality of lenses/fixtures • Thermal/heat generation • Heat recovery/heat minimization techniques • Radiant energy concerns • Outgassing/air quality concerns
Integrity	• Degradation of visual quality, control • Degradation of energy effectiveness • Degradation of appearance, discoloration, staining, dirt accumulation, cracking

5.10 NOTABLE OVERALL PERFORMANCE OF LIGHTING

	Poor				Excellent
Spatial Quality	1	2	3	4	5
Acoustic Quality	1	2	3	4	5
Air Quality	1	2	3	4	5
Thermal Quality	1	2	3	4	5
Visual Quality	1	2	3	4	5
Building Integrity	1	2	3	4	5

5.11 NOTABLE SYSTEM INTEGRATION

• Lighting and Structure

• Lighting and HVAC

• Lighting and Interior

- Lighting and Enclosure

- Lighting and PEC

5.12 NOTABLE VERTICAL TRANSPORTATION

Generic Components	Circle Standard Specifications	Identify Whether Non-Standard Material, Component, System Integration, or Performance *(Identify manufacturers and trade names of materials and components)*
Configuration	• Elevator • Escalator • Moving sidewalk • Mini-tram (goods, people)	
Elevator Type *(operation hrs., connected HP)*	• Single deck • Double deck • Hydraulic system • Cable system • Gear/gearless	
Speed	• Low-medium • High	
Location	• Central core • Distributed, multiple cores • External to building • Staggered cores • Lower lobby floors • Sky lobby	
Control/Management	• Local, manual or automatic • Central, manual or automatic • Optimization criteria (ride time, ride frequency, ride capacity) • Speed, satisfaction • Comfort, HVAC, lighting quality • Aesthetics • Cost/space effectiveness • Energy effectiveness • Fire management	
Emergency Systems	• Power • Air, ventilation • Light • Phone, safety	

| Integration with Other Systems | • HVAC, spatial effectiveness
• Vertical shafts PLEC
• Access, growth potential
• Pollution migration control
• Pressurization control | |

5.13 SECURITY SYSTEM

Generic Components	Circle Standard Specifications	Identify Whether Non-Standard Material, Component, System Integration, or Performance *(Identify manufacturers and trade names of materials and components)*
Physical Security	• Lock • Digital password • Card access (magnetic) • Card access (proximity) • Closed-circuit television • Camera eye/motion detectors • Voice-activated system	
Employee Identification	• Picture ID • General ID • Guard • Surveillance • Fingerprint/photograph system	
Employee Access Permission	• Access to building • Access to floors/elevators • Access to specific rooms • Access to computer files • Access to parking • Access to food services • Other	
Information Security	• Communication scrambling device • Secure telephone system • Non-radiating cable system • Cryptographic devices • IT room security • Cable safeguards	
Surveillance Type	• Patrols • Motion detectors • Camera (low light, infrared, standard)	

Intruder Alarm	• Surveillance • Manual "panic" switch • Barriers/gates • Mantraps/prevention system
Security & Building Subsystems	• Enclosure, windows & doors - physical security • Enclosure windows - data security • Interior, workstation enclosures & furniture - physical security

Appendix B
Occupancy Assessments — Toshiba Headquarters and NTT Twins Regional Headquarters

The occupancy analysis portion of the study included expert walkthroughs and plan reviews, focused interviews with a range of occupants, and a questionnaire (see below) distributed to approximately 100 occupants of each building. The questionnaire responses were statistically analyzed, as indicated in figures 5.22, 6.29, and 10.6. There are a few general observations that are important to clarify the cultural context of Japanese office work, which is different in certain respects from that of North America.

1) There are relatively few female office workers. In the NTT sample there were only 3%, while in Toshiba there were 20% females. The Japanese structure office work quite differently, and few positions equate with a secretarial position. A large proportion of the staff consider themselves general office workers.

2) People tend to stay with the same firm for long periods. Of those surveyed, 83% had worked with NTT for over ten years and 66% for twenty or more years. Perhaps for this reason, individuals seem to feel a sense of commitment and responsibility to look after the company's interest, whether it be switching lights off when not in use or taking care of building finishes.

3) A majority of those surveyed had come to these two, much-heralded new buildings from much older buildings, which had considerably lower levels of amenity and servicing. These people initially felt their physical office environments much improved. However, in both buildings and in other discussions we had in Japan, there are signs of changing expectations among Japanese office workers.

4) Even though high proportions of workers in both organizations work long hours, both buildings are run on 10-12 hour schedules of air handling, heating, and cooling. Although there are procedures for requesting extended hours of service, workers in both cases complained of the environmental conditions when working outside the standard operating hours. While building operators appear to be more highly trained than in North America, Japanese workers traditionally are given less control over layout and environmental options.

The six-page questionnaire distributed in the NTT Twins and Toshiba buildings enabled the field team to compare occupancy assessments with expert assessments of various innovations.

Ref. Code: _____
(Floor/zone)

OFFICE ENVIRONMENT STUDY
Impact of Advanced Technology Study
Center for Building Performance and Diagnostics
Carnegie Mellon University
Pittsburgh, Pennsylvania, USA

The Toshiba building has been identified as an innovative intelligent building. It has been selected for study as part of an international research program into the relationship between innovative design of intelligent office buildings and the comfort and well-being of office employees.

We would be grateful if you would answer the following questions about the office in which you work. Please circle the appropriate response to each question, unless another instruction is given. Your individual answers will be treated in confidence, and will not be seen by Toshiba management. When you have completed the questionnaire, put it into the attached envelope. It will be collected in a day or two.

1. How long have you worked for Toshiba? _____ years

2. When did you start working in this building?
   (Please indicate with numbers)   Month _____ Year 19____

3. What was the approximate age of the office building in which you previously worked?
   1   This is my first office building
   2   Less than five years old
   3   Five to ten years old
   4   More than ten years old

4. How would you describe the work you do? (Circle number)
   1   Secretarial
   2   Clerical
   3   Technical
   4   Professional
   5   Managerial

5. What is your gender? (Circle number)
   1   Female
   2   Male

6. What is your age? (Circle number)
   1   under 21 years
   2   21 to 30 years
   3   31 to 40 years
   4   41 to 50 years
   5   51 to 60 years
   6   61 to 65 years
   7   over 65 years

7. What is the highest level of education you have attained? (Circle number)
    1   Completed high school
    2   Completed two-year course in junior college
    3   Completed four-year course in university
    4   Master's, doctorate or professional degree
    5   Other (specify)

8. Where is your desk located?
    1   Near exterior windows
    2   Middle of the office space
    3   Near interior core of the building

9. How many hours per week do you normally work in your personal workspace during the following periods?
    January-April _____   May-August _____   September-December _____

10. What is the nature of your work in terms of the amount of physical activity you have to do in a typical work day?   (Please estimate percentage of total typical day)

	%
Sitting, no noticeable activity, e.g., reading	_____
Sitting, but using hands and arms, e.g., WP, OA	_____
Standing at rest, e.g., in a queue	_____
Light physical activity, e.g., photocopying	_____
Moving around in the office	_____
Moderate physical activity, e,g., fetching & carrying heavy files, exercises	_____
Being out of your office in another part of the building	_____
Being out of this building	_____

11. How often do you work with a word processor, laptop or other computer terminal at these locations? (Circle number corresponding to each of your answers)

	Daily	Several times/week	Less than once a week	Rarely	Never
At your desk	1	2	3	4	5
Elsewhere in your section	1	2	3	4	5
Elsewhere on your floor	1	2	3	4	5
Elsewhere in this building	1	2	3	4	5
In another building	1	2	3	4	5

12. Generally at this time of year how would you rate the following characteristics around your desk? (Circle number corresponding to each of your answers)

	Very poor	Poor	Adequate	Good	Very good
Air movement	1	2	3	4	5
Air freshness	1	2	3	4	5
Temperature	1	2	3	4	5
Humidity	1	2	3	4	5
Daylight	1	2	3	4	5
Lighting level	1	2	3	4	5

13. For your particular work, how appropriate do you find the following?
    (Circle number corresponding to each of your answers)

	Very Inappropriate	Somewhat Inappropriate	Somewhat Appropriate	Very Appropriate
Your main desk...............................	1	2	3	4
The number of electrical outlets...............	1	2	3	4
Your chair.......................................	1	2	3	4
The location of electrical outlets...............	1	2	3	4
The furniture arrangement.......................	1	2	3	4
The location of electrical cords................	1	2	3	4
The size of your individual work space...	1	2	3	4
Location of OA equipment.......................	1	2	3	4
Capacity and location of copier................	1	2	3	4
Capacity and location of FAX...................	1	2	3	4

14. Considering the conditions around your particular desk, how often do you find:
    (Circle number corresponding to each of your answers)

	Never	Seldom	Sometimes	Frequently	Always
The temperature is too warm....................	1	2	3	4	5
The air is too still.............................	1	2	3	4	5
The lighting is too bright.......................	1	2	3	4	5
Work storage is insufficient	1	2	3	4	5
Temperature is too cool..........................	1	2	3	4	5
Air is too drafty................................	1	2	3	4	5
The lighting is too dim..........................	1	2	3	4	5
The air is too humid.............................	1	2	3	4	5
Work surfaces are insufficient	1	2	3	4	5
Temperature shifts...............................	1	2	3	4	5
Air is stale.....................................	1	2	3	4	5
Total floor space for your work section is too small...........................	1	2	3	4	5
The air is too dry...............................	1	2	3	4	5
Daylight is too bright...........................	1	2	3	4	5

15. Considering the conditions around the OA, how often do you find:
    (Circle number corresponding to each of your answers)

	Never	Seldom	Sometimes	Frequently	Always
The temperature is too warm....................	1	2	3	4	5
The air is too still.............................	1	2	3	4	5
The lighting is too bright.......................	1	2	3	4	5
Temperature is too cool..........................	1	2	3	4	5
Air is too drafty................................	1	2	3	4	5
The lighting is too dim..........................	1	2	3	4	5
Work surfaces are insufficient	1	2	3	4	5
Air is stale.....................................	1	2	3	4	5
Reflections on OA screen........................	1	2	3	4	5

16. How often are you bothered by the following aspects of your particular desk location?
    (Circle number corresponding to each of your answers)

	Never bothered by	Seldom bothered by	Sometimes bothered by	Frequently bothered by	Always bothered by
People talking...................................	1	2	3	4	5
People nearby talking on the phone........	1	2	3	4	5
The lighting.....................................	1	2	3	4	5
People walking by..............................	1	2	3	4	5
The heating.....................................	1	2	3	4	5
The noise of printers...........................	1	2	3	4	5
Telephones ringing.............................	1	2	3	4	5
The noise of office equipment..................	1	2	3	4	5
The ventilation.................................	1	2	3	4	5
Being watched by other people when you are working......................	1	2	3	4	5
People smoking.................................	1	2	3	4	5

17. At this time of year, how often do you feel each of the following <u>distracts</u> you from your work either at your desk or at the OA? (Circle number corresponding to each of your answers)

	Several times daily	Daily	Several times/wk.	Less than once a wk.	Rarely at this time	Never at this time	Depends on weather
Feeling too warm................	1	2	3	4	5	6	7
Feeling too cool....................	1	2	3	4	5	6	7
Too little fresh air................	1	2	3	4	5	6	7
Too little air movement......	1	2	3	4	5	6	7

18. Please indicate the extent to which you agree or disagree with each of the statements about this Toshiba building overall.   (Circle number corresponding to each of your answers)

This building:	Agree strongly	Agree slightly	Disagree slightly	Disagree strongly
Usually has comfortable temperatures....	1	2	3	4
Has unpleasant smells...............................	1	2	3	4
Is pleasant to be in	1	2	3	4
Has plenty of facilities for staff................	1	2	3	4
Is unhealthy to be in	1	2	3	4
Is well designed...	1	2	3	4
Is well lit..	1	2	3	4
Is usually stuffy..	1	2	3	4
Is a building I'm proud of..........................	1	2	3	4
Is well ventilated.................	1	2	3	4
Makes it easy for staff to find their way...	1	2	3	4
Makes it easy for visitors to find their way...	1	2	3	4

19. We are also interested in the extent to which *you would like to be able to* adjust or change the conditions of *your work area.* How much control *would you like to have* over the following?
(Circle number corresponding to each of your answers)

	No control	Very little control	Some control	Significant control
Lighting level..............	1	2	3	4
Daylight..	1	2	3	4
Air movement...................................	1	2	3	4
Heating...	1	2	3	4
Cooling...	1	2	3	4
Temperature.....................................	1	2	3	4
Noise distractions............................	1	2	3	4
Furniture arrangement....................	1	2	3	4
Air freshness....................................	1	2	3	4

20. Please indicate the extent to which you agree or disagree with the statements below:
(Circle number corresponding to each of your answers)

	Agree strongly	Agree slightly	Disagree slightly	Disagree strongly
All things considered, I am very satisfied with my work space...........	1	2	3	4
The design of my work space helps me work efficiently.............................	1	2	3	4
I'm proud to show people my office........	1	2	3	4
The layout of the group space facilitates my work.............................	1	2	3	4
I have the right furniture for my job........	1	2	3	4
The OA workspaces are well designed...	1	2	3	4

21. How frequently do you experience the following health complaints?
(Circle number corresponding to each of your answers)

	Almost daily	Several times/wk.	Several times/mo.	Sometimes	Never
Eye strain..	1	2	3	4	5
Lower back pain..............................	1	2	3	4	5
General tiredness............................	1	2	3	4	5
Blurring vision................................	1	2	3	4	5
Sore neck..	1	2	3	4	5
Irritability......................................	1	2	3	4	5
Headaches.......................................	1	2	3	4	5
Sore shoulders................................	1	2	3	4	5
Sleeplessness..................................	1	2	3	4	5
Eye irritations................................	1	2	3	4	5
General feelings of stress................	1	2	3	4	5
Coughs..	1	2	3	4	5
Nose and throat irritations..............	1	2	3	4	5

22. To what extent, if any, do you feel your work has caused these health problems?
    (Circle number)
    1. The health problems are unrelated to work (skip to question 24)
    2. Work contributes to the health problems along with other factors
    3. Work is the primary cause

23. For which of these health problems has work been a contributing factor?
    (Circle all numbers that apply)
    1. Eye strain
    2. Lower back pain
    3. General tiredness
    4. Blurring vision
    5. Sore neck
    6. Irritability
    7. Headaches
    8. Sore shoulders
    9. Sleeplessness
    10. Eye irritation
    11. General feeling of stress
    12. Coughing
    13. Nose and throat irritations

24. Everything considered, how would you rate the effect of the physical characteristics of your work area on your ability to do your work? (Circle number)
    1. Very negative effect
    2. Negative effect
    3. No effect
    4. Positive effect
    5. Very positive effect

25. All in all, how satisfied would you say you are with your current job? (Circle number)
    1. Very satisfied
    2. Somewhat satisfied
    3. Not too satisfied
    4. Not at all satisfied

26. Is there anything else you would like to tell us about your office or the building as a whole which has not been covered by this questionnaire?

Thank you for completing this questionnaire. Your contribution to this research project is greatly appreciated. Your individual responses will be kept confidential.

Appendix C
Profiles of Mechanical and Electrical Systems —Toshiba Headquarters and NTT Twins Regional Headquarters

SCOPE

The scope of this project consisted of a walk-through survey of two buildings and on-site interviews with key Japanese personnel to determine the following:

1. Type, condition, thermal qualities, and integration, if any, with the mechanical, electrical, communication, data processing and building automation systems.
2. Type, condition, performance, characteristics of lighting, HVAC, power, plumbing, and intra-relationships, and with structure.
3. Standard, advanced, and innovative systems.
4. Possible systems and materials which are energy efficient and functional for these buildings but which were not used.

The existing conditions, innovations, and opportunities for further advances in mechanical and electrical systems are addressed below in terms of:

1. Building
2. Power
3. Lighting
4. HVAC
5. Controls

NTT TWINS REGIONAL HEADQUARTERS

Existing conditions:

NTT consists of twin towers — one an office tower, one a computer data center. The office tower was analyzed. It consists of 14 stories above grade plus 2 level below grade. Total floor area is 128,000 square meters, about 9,000 square meters per floor. Floor-to-floor height is 3.5 meters, floor to hung ceiling is 2.6 meters.

1. Building

• Single-paned, tinted glazing — transmission.
• Motorized operable windows.
• There is 1" fiberglass insulation in opaque walls.
• Solar shading consists of 60-cm window reveal plus internal pull-down combination solar shade/venetian blind.
• Stairways in corner are equipped with full length glass providing very good daylighting of the staircases in the four exterior corners of the building.
• The office layouts consists primarily of open landscape planning, with desks; few workstations. Vertically no task lighting.
• There are very few offices on the east and west exposures. The reveals do not eliminate all solar penetration on the south facades.
• An atrium provides lateral daylighting, but with the sun screen/louvers closed, there is no appreciable daylighting, and all overhead fluorescent lights were in operation.
• Ratio of net rentable area to gross floor area — 70% typical floor.
• Insulation type thickness in wall. 15 cm present with poured concrete panel inside (minimum 15-25 cm) separated by isolation paper for seismic.

2. Power

- Connected load - 3,750 Kw, but maximum usage is about 1,800 Kw.
- Primary voltage is 66 Kw. Secondary voltage is 6,000 volts, with step down transformers to 400 volts for motor, 200 volts for lights, and 100 volts to convenience outlets.
- Energy-efficient motors are used throughout.

3. Lighting

- Lighting for offices - uniform 1'x4' - 3 tubes supply and return air troffers, in rows approximately 9' center-to-center and 7' center-to-center in each row. Tubes are 40 watt, mellow white.
- Light troffers, speaker, and fire detectors are integrated in one panel.
- Lobbies, corridors, other public spaces have many down lights, and some bare-bulb fluorescent tubes. All office fixtures (luminaires) are bare tube without lens or diffusers.
- There is a large number of 150-watt incandescent down lights in public areas, large conference rooms, some passageways.
- There are local switches to control rows of fluorescent lights, but not separate perimeter lights.
- We could not locate any photocells, although management stated that there are some.
- There is an experimental office equipped with free-standing cylindrical units incorporating HID (high-intensity discharge) multi-Halogen uplights and an air conditioning DX evaporator and fan for cooling. Each lamp is 250 watts, providing 10,500 lumens, or 40 lumens per watt. They had tried more efficient metal halite lamps but objected to the color rendition. The air-cooled compressors are located outdoors. The H.I.D. uplights are shielded from direct view. Some units were malfunctioning and warm air instead of cool air was being discharged into the room. There are supplementary ceiling recessed down lights equipped with 17-watt screw-in fluorescent lamps and lens.
- There is an active solar energy system for heating hot water for the kitchen and cafeteria use. There are 270 solar collectors, each 4'x8' ar-

ranged two rows deep on the roof. Piping is reverse return. There are Dakin fan-coil units to dissipate excess heat to prevent overheating in the collectors.
- NTT claims that building uses 17.5% less energy than a conventional building.

4. HVAC

- HVAC system consists of a central chiller plant, located in a separate data center building to serve the data center and the NTT office building. The central plant consists of 5 centrifugal chillers and one gas/oil fired absorption chiller. Central cooling tower, ground mounted, provides condensing for all units. All chillers are Mitsubishi-York, each rated at 500 tons.
- All heating of the NTT office building is provided by recovered condenser heat, with the hot water piped to air handling units and fan-coil units in the office tower.
- Horizontal fan-coil units mounted above the hung ceiling provide heat to the perimeter with ceiling down-blow diffusers. A 4-pipe system with a common heating and cooling coil serves the south perimeter units, and a 2-pipe system with one coil for heating or cooling serves the north perimeter units.
- Chilled water cooling storage with 6,000 cubic meter storage tank operates at night. Tank has internal baffles to prevent diluting chilled water generated at 9°C with return water at 17°C.
- Two chillers are dedicated to the office tower, and 4 to the data center, but are interconnected for reliability.
- No outside air is supplied to the perimeter fan-coil units.
- Outside air-to-air handling units are constant at 30 cubic meter per hour.
- The present connected air conditioning load is 30% of installed capacity and is expected to rise to 100% in a 5-year period and level off for the next 10 years.
- Multiple groups of fan-coil units are controlled by one thermostat and one motorized chilled water value. Each fan-coil has additional three-speed manual control.

- At present there are 7 innovative thermosiphon cooling units with the evaporator installed inside on the tenth floor computer center, and the condenser mounted outdoors at a higher level. Dedicated mechanical refrigeration units back-up and supplement the thermonsiphon units. It is expected that there will eventually be 100 thermosiphon units. The minimum vertical distance between evaporator and condenser is 4 meters, the maximum 30 meters. Liquid line is 1.5 cm diameter, the suction line 2.5 cm. Air delivery is 70 cubic meters/minute per unit. The computer room is 1,200 square meters, with a load of 500 watts per square meter. The supplementary cooling units have a 15 kW compressor. The capacity of each thermosiphon units is 1,200/kcal/hr, and operates at 20 TD. Units are charged with F-22 refrigerant.
- Full use is made of economizer cooling, but not enthalpy cooling.

5. Controls

- A central energy management and control system incorporates lighting schedule, fan-coil and air handling units duty cycle, and can handle peak load control.
- The central control system consists of 16,000 points.

Innovations

1. Building

- Mechanized sliding operable windows, controlled individually by a switch.
- Combination solar screen/venetian blind.
- 60-cm window reveals for solar control.
- Corner stairways with glazed corners to provide daylighted stairways.
- Experimenting with a heat transfer wall to expel excess heat through the exterior wall.
- Cashless cafeteria.

2. Power

- Gas-operated main circuit breakers.
- Electronic ballasts with 50-cycle power.
- Clean power to computers with static voltage/frequency regulation.

3. Lighting

- Combination HID uplight/air-conditioning unit enclosed in free-standing floor mounted circular element.
- 17-watt, screw-in fluorescent down lights — advanced product.
- Solar water heating with heat dissipation units — advanced product.
- Return air troffers which cool fluorescent tubes — advanced product.
- Literature claims glare-free lighting, but bare bulbs create glare.
- HID uplight in cafeteria.

4. HVAC

- Thermosiphon cooling.
- Cooling storage, with chilled water tanks baffled to prevent dilution.
- Frequency controller for VAV fan systems — advanced product.
- Heat recovery, double bundle condensers in data center to provide all heat for the office tower.
- 4-pipe system to south perimeter fan-coil units, and 2-pipe system to north perimeter fan-coil units.

5. Controls

- Central condenser system for power factor control.
- Integrated diffuser, luminaires, sound speaker, fire detector.
- Building automation system.
- Under window, telecommunications and data service cabinets with under-carpet, fiber-optic feeders.

**Opportunities for Further Advances in
Mechanical and Electrical Systems**

1. Building

- Electro-chromatic glazing.
- Use more raised floors; eliminate hung ceilings.
  Raised floors can carry cool air as well as cables,
  conduits, and wire.
- Develop organic walls to change thermal characteristics as needed.
- Utilize the wide corridors for small gatherings
  and meeting places. Vary colors; now they are
  too dull and uninteresting.

2. Plumbing

- Use more effective water-saving fixtures.

3. Lighting

- 30-, 32- and 35-watt fluorescent tubes in place of
  40-watt tubes.
- Reflector installed in luminaires which permit
  use of fewer tubes in a luminaire, with a linear
  corresponding reduction in wattage, with only
  10% reduction in light output.
- Photo-voltaic light cells to generate electricity.
- Greater use of HID indirect lighting.
- Photocells and personnel sensors to control lighting (and in some cases air conditioning to match
  room occupancy).
- Greater room control to be able to shut off
  perimeter lights when daylighting is adequate.
- Provide light shelves and better glare control at
  perimeter.

4. HVAC

- Enthalpy control.
- Ice cooling storage with ice water distribution in
  place of chilled water to reduce pipe duct and
  fan sizes. Colder air distribution to room would
  be mixed with room air (induction diffusers) to

prevent cold drafts. (NTT plant on premises
only, not Toshiba.)
- Chilled water temperature reset to raise chilled
  water at lighter loads.
- Solar pond on site to provide hot water for
  power generation or absorption refrigeration.
- Desiccant dehumidification.
- Solar cooling with absorption refrigeration units.
- Recover energy from exhaust air.
- Use modular pumps sized for one third and two
  third of the load.
- Fan powered VAV system to control indoor air
  quality and also to transfer heat from ceiling
  where they are hard to service and create cold
  down drafts to the perimeter and incorporate
  with existing communications data cabinet (NTT
  only).

5. Controls

- Monitor indoor air quality and control outdoor
  air intake supply as needed, rather than fixed
  percentage of outdoor air.
- Integrate the building automation system —
  specifically air delivery, air temperature, chilled
  water temperature, chilled water quantity, cooling tower operation — to optimize energy conservation.
- Provide additional zone control to meet varying
  internal loads.
- Investigate electronic noise suppression for
  acoustical control.
- Provide more environmental control for the
  individual workstations.

General Comments

- The very large glass areas do provide views, but
  create heating, cooling, and glare problems.
- Complaints were registered about cold down
  drafts in winter, and some overheating in summer where direct sunlight penetrates the fenestration.
- The HVAC system comprising zones served by
  air handling units were not balanced to provide
  indoor temperature settings within zones.

TOSHIBA HEADQUARTERS

Existing Conditions

1. Building

- Single clear glazing.
- Fixed sash non-operable windows.
- Corridors are 3 meters wide.
- Smoke-free lobbies at both ends of corridors each floor face exterior air to minimize smoke inhalation.
- Lightwell in the center of the two "O" shaped floors at top, for view and daylight.
- Reflective glass was described in building literature, but did not seem apparent; may have light tint.
- Aluminum curtain walls.
- Building is 70% owner-occupied and 30% rental.
- Cashless cafeteria.
- 6-foot-high continuous glazing (fenestration) creates uncomfortable glare and contrast. Combination venetian blind/solar screen cuts glare, but also eliminates daylighting. All lights were on full. Solar control at windows does little to keep out heat since blinds are internal.
- There are 7,000 occupants, in 162,612 square meters, or an average of 230 square feet per person. Occupancy is increasing. Elevator capacity is limited; long waiting periods for elevators.
- Monochromatic colors are dull and uninteresting. Suggest more color, art, and more use of the wide corridors for meeting areas, rest and relaxation, social interaction.

2. Power

- Demand is 5,500 kW.
- 66 kV primary.
- 6,000 V secondary.
- Three phase: 415 V motors, 240 V lights, 105 V convenience outlet.
- Two 7,000 VA transformers.
- Gas circuit breakers.
- 2,000 kVA emergency diesel, not used for load shaving.

- Consumption 77,000 kW/hour/day.
- Night demand 800 kW.
- Energy-efficient motors are used throughout.
- Tenants supply their own UPS system as needed.
- Toshiba has a UPS system with batteries.
- There are four vertical shafts, one per quadrant, to handle power, communications, and data cable systems.

3. Lighting

- Uniform 2 lamp troffers in offices in continuous rows, 10'6" on center.
- 40-watt fluorescent tubes.
- No lens or louvres — glare.
- Lighting averages 2.5 - 3.5 watts/sq.ft.
- 80 footcandles below luminaire, 60 footcandles between luminaires.
- Air supply and return through alternate fixtures, with return only through alternate fixtures.
- Very uneven air distribution quantities and return air quality.
- Lights, sprinklers, fire detectors, and air diffusers are integrated in each row.
- Lobbies, public areas have many incandescent down lights, 75 10-watt, some 20-watt fluorescent lamps.
- Corridors are mainly lighted by two continuous rows of 40-watt fluorescent lamps, with every other lamp on separate switch to save energy.

4. HVAC

- Chilled water, and steam supplied from central municipal (or other ownership) off-site cooling and heating plants (not visited).
- Steam and chilled water distributed under ground to two basement-level equipment rooms. In the Toshiba building, chilled water is billed based on square meters of building (not metered). Steam condensate is metered.
- Chilled water delivered at constant temperature regardless of load.
- Main HVAC system consists of one air handling unit per 6 floors, per one quadrant (4 quadrants

total for each floor) to supply air to perimeter areas, and 2 air handling units, per 6 floors, per quadrant, to supply interior areas.

- Outdoor air intakes at perimeter of each air handling room.
- Interior zones are constant volume, perimeter zones are variable air volume with frequency controllers.
- Chilled water supplied at 7°C, return at 14°C. Peak load is 11,100 Meg.cal/hour. Peak steam load is 9,200 Meg.cal/hour. Condensate returns at 80°C.
- Cooling energy storage is only that volume in piping system not operated for night or weekend storage.
- Separate self-dedicated contained chiller for small computer room. Unit is located in the conditioned space.
- Outdoor air intakes set for 30% to 100% for economizer cooling. Air is prefiltered and also passed through fine mesh after filters.
- Smoking is prevalent and generally allowed everywhere. Some electrostatic filters are used for smoking areas. No outdoor air quality is maintained, but generally air is kept under 1,000 ppm CO_2, and dust 0.15 Mg/cubic meter or less.
- Exhaust return air fans are used with economizer cooling.
- Enthalpy control is not used.

5. Energy Management & Control System

- Sitimizu BECSS System
- Controls peak demand, but could not determine which circuits were shed.
- Equipment monitoring
- Scheduling of equipment operation
- Data collection
- Printing
- Temperature humidity control
- Trend plotting
- Demand control
- Lighting control
- Heat source control
- OA cooling control
- Fire control

- Each ahu for perimeter zones handles 30,000 cubic meters of air per hour.
- All heating and cooling loads are computer generated.
- Smoke exhaust control system by zones.

6. Plumbing and Sanitary System

- Gray water recycling 500 tons/day from kitchen; miscellaneous — 697 cubic meter/day.
- Low-flow toilet fixtures.
- Domestic hot water is generated from steam/hot-water heat exchanger.

Innovations

- Advanced building automation system.
- Advanced energy efficient motors.
- Integrated lighting, air, fire, and sound panels.
- Some low wattage (9-18 watt) fluorescent fixtures.
- Chilled water and steam supplied from district plant.
- Central/decentralized HVAC.
- Gray water recycling system.

Deficiencies

- Inadequate solar heat control.
- Inadequate building insulation.
- Too many incandescent light areas.
- Direct and indirect glare from windows and lighting fixtures.
- Inadequate lighting control zones.
- Lack of control of smokers — no areas designated for non-smoking.
- Economizer, but no enthalpy control.
- No continuous monitoring of air quality with control of outdoor air geared to indoor air quality.
- HVAC air distribution balance.
- Chilled water temperature control.

Appendix D
Profiles of Telecommunications Systems — Toshiba Headquarters and NTT Twins Regional Headquarters

Both the Toshiba Headquarters and the NTT Twins Tokyo Regional Headquarters serve two purposes. First, both are key operation centers for their businesses, with the general office floors configured for that purpose. Second, both organizations have reserved a portion of their facilities to showcase the products, technology, and services they offer to the public. Each purpose provides a different perspective for a telecommunications analysis. Because of this, the facts and evaluations in this appendix (for Toshiba and NTT) are separated into two sections: General Office Floors and Showcase Area.

In both the Toshiba and NTT buildings there is far more telecommunications technology in use and on display in the showcase areas than in the general offices. Also, the cost of configuring telecommunications in the showcase areas, and maintaining these areas during equipment migration and personnel relocations, is probably somewhat less than the general office floors. More importantly, although neither organization is concerned with relocation costs in their internal office operations, clearly both understand that their customers have a very real concern about relocating personnel, equipment, and services; and the showcase areas demonstrate that both organizations are addressing relocation cost issues through the use of innovative building technology.

NTT TWINS REGIONAL HEADQUARTERS

The NTT Twins complex, which is comprised of two distinct buildings, has one building that serves as both the Tokyo Regional Headquarters for the NTT telephone operation, and another building that is a service bureau data center for a for-profit subsidiary of NTT that processes major data processing applications, such as weather forecasting models for external customers. The tour and review focused only on the building serving the telephone operation, although the building systems and other support facilities, such as the security system, serve both buildings.

General Office Floors

The telecommunications services seen at NTT generally support a sophisticated form of office automation based on electronic mail and enhanced telephone services using the NTT Twins local area network and telephone cable plant. Personnel sign on to their systems using identification cards, create documents through word processing, and send them electronically to various addresses both inside the complex and to remote locations. These documents include manufacturing and sales orders, and memoranda that lend themselves easily to electronic mail applications. Also, the heavy emphasis on meetings with large groups of attendees further utilizes the mail system for agendas, meeting minutes, and discussion and position papers. There are also a number of ancillary systems to the electronic mail operation, such as directories, remote printing services, and a supplies requisition system. The files for these applications reside on processors both locally and at the various data centers around Tokyo and other distant locations.

Data transmissions come into the NTT Twins to one or more of the main computer rooms via microwave, a satellite digital communications network, and several value-added high-speed digital data networks. Rather than each department or computer having individual modems, virtually all dial-up-equivalent traffic is routed to and from the main computer center. Data networking within the building is accomplished via fiber-optic backbones that loop through the main riser closets, at speeds of up to 32 megabits. For data services, fiber-optic multiplexers and modems located in the main riser closets reduce the data rates from 32 megabits to 10 megabits for distribution to the departments. Fiber-optic cables are marked with appropriate designations, and a one-line diagram is taped to each distribution closet for reference.

Two main, multi-purpose riser closets are found on each floor. Each measures about 24' x 14' and houses electrical, telephone, and data services without crowding.

1. Telephone Service

Telephone service comes into the complex over standard trunks and multiplexed facilities from other NTT locations, along with the data services. It is then distributed to these main riser closets on various floors in 500-pair and larger shielded cables. The telephone cables are mounted within the closets on cross-connect blocks housed in large metal cabinets. They are then cut down to smaller shielded, twisted, vinyl-sheathed cables and fed out to the office areas through the building's three-partition cellular deck cable distribution system to the departmental distribution closets in the core wall and window wall. Telephone cable is well organized, and labeling conventions include pair designation and extension numbers in the closets; however, there is little labeling in trenches or under the raised floors.

Horizontal telephone distribution is accomplished via under-carpet, flat-wire, four-conductor cable to the closet at either the window or the core wall

for service access, rather than through the cellular deck system. The transition from flat cable to standard telephone cable at the desk is provided by a small plastic device that fits poorly between the carpet squares, causing it to buckle; many were kicked and broken.

2. Electrical Service

Electrical power for telecommunications devices and services comes from the standard utility lines, without any type of UPS or power conditioning for the general office floors. Distributed wiring closets on the core and on the window wall within the office areas house electrical distribution panels, as well as fiber-optic modems that convert the data services to copper. Also located in these closets are small departmental digital PBXs which serve a portion of a particular floor. These PBXs are generally in 32- and 64-port sizes; however, in several areas there are additional 5- and 8-port units to accommodate the overflow due to more personnel and, therefore, more telephones. The PBXs are fully functional, with trunking ratios from 2:1 to 5:1. Electrical switch panels are located in the main riser closets. The 100-volt service feeds through the trench system to the distribution closets in the departments.

The horizontal data and electrical cable distribution runs through separate compartments of the cellular deck system, which is accessible from the core wall and window wall closets. It features plug-in rather than hard-wire connections.

There is a building-wide CATV network that uses standard industry connectors, splitters, amplifiers, and fittings, and also terminates in the main riser closets. Distribution to the office areas follows the data distribution plan.

Several monument and tombstone configurations are used for electrical power. Terminals are plugged into the same receptacles as other electrical devices. Data services are fed from similar monument types as electrical services, using a separate compartment of the cellular trench for distribution from the core and window wall closets.

3. Data Processing Areas

Departmental data processing equipment, both terminals and processors, is generally located behind low partitions in an open area near the user community, with terminal-to-user ratios of 1:10 not uncommon. Personnel complained about not having access to equipment, and many bring in their own personal computers to use when the departmental equipment is not available.

Cabling to the departmental terminal area is accomplished via copper cable (coaxial or RS-232-type cabling) from the fiber-optic modems in the distribution closets. Devices include standard terminals, personal computers, multi-function workstations, one or more types of impact printers and file storage devices. Most have NTT labels, although NTT manufactures very little equipment; however, the NTT local area network is advertised as being able to accommodate most standard Japanese interfaces. NTT is a heavy user of facsimile services, and fully featured fax machines are numerous.

The area around the data processing terminal area is fairly noisy, especially when the printers are running. Some printers have acoustic covers and shrouds, which helps somewhat, but the clatter of the impact printers is still noticeable. There is no special air conditioning or other environmental services for the data processing equipment on the general office floors; nonetheless, the building HVAC system appears to dissipate the heat load adequately.

The NTT office floors are configured in typical Japanese fashion — rows of steel desks occupied by staff personnel ordered in ascending seniority from back to front, headed by the supervisor at the front of the group. Technology at the typical desk at NTT is limited to a fairly well featured telephone, with four-way conferencing, speed dialing, camp-on, speakerphone capability, a message-waiting lamp, and some LCD display capability found on most instruments.

4. Maintenance Services

Maintenance services for the data and electrical systems at NTT are supplied by Nihon Intelligent Building Systems, a joint venture group owned by NTT, Mori, and others. NTT technicians service the telephone equipment and cable plant. Wire installation in both facilities is done neatly in all closets, but wire management on the office floor areas is messy and clearly not monitored. Tombstones are abandoned rather than removed when personnel are relocated. Assignment records are maintained on drawings and microfiche. Maintenance personnel felt that this method is adequate and much easier than using CAD or any type of computer-aided wire management.

Costs associated with relocating personnel, including telecommunications equipment and services, do not appear to be an issue, but are accepted as an unavoidable cost of doing business. NTT was not able to provide the average cost of relocating a terminal, outlet, or workstation, or to determine the effect that relocation had on office productivity. However, there is clearly an understanding of the impact of relocation costs to their customers as evidenced in the planning and configuration of the showcase area (see "Showcase Area" summary).

5. Miscellaneous

Security at NTT is controlled by card reader identification badges. Guard services are used and IDs are checked at the main entrances. Workers use their badges to report to their departments, sign on to their terminals, and even charge their lunches.

All reception and conference room reservations are handled by a variation of the electronic mail system. Conference rooms had telephones, but no data outlets were activated.

Although the tour did not include any of the primary data centers, the building control center for the Twins is physically configured and equipped similarly to the computer rooms. An asbestos cement raised floor with a vinyl surface is installed in the building control center, with cable tray wire management under the floor where needed. Both ionization and photoelectric smoke detectors are used, as well as Halon extinguishing systems and remote annunciation of building fire alarm and detector status.

Showcase Area

NTT's demonstration area serves a dual role. First, it showcases telecommunications products that NTT sells; second, it serves as the offices of the NTT Intelligent Building Design Service Department, which offers architectural, engineering, and planning services similar to those of U. S. Regional Bell Operating Company Building Industry Consulting (BIC) groups. A major part of their service is designing office space that can be easily and cost-effectively renovated from a telecommunications point of view.

The demonstration area makes use of core wall and curtain wall wiring closets for small departmental digital PBXs, fiber-optic electronics, and small processors as in the general office areas. However, the actual usage of technology is much higher in the showcase area than in the general office areas.

To provide further flexibility, NTT has installed a raised floor and modular workstations that contain office automation equipment including terminals, printers, and other peripherals much more accessible to the occupants than in the general office areas. The terminal-to-personnel ratio is close to 1:1, with facsimile, local printers, CAD design equipment, and other office automation both in evidence and in use.

Although there were no office relocations in process during the tour, relocating personnel and services appears to be quite easy from a telecom-

munications perspective. The raised floor and densely distributed wiring closets require fairly short cable runs, and virtually all cabling is modular plug connected.

Innovative Trends

No significant telecommunication innovations were observed in the NTT Twins building. Completed in 1986, the NTT Twins telecommunications services and their impacts on the building design are similar to those found in most modern buildings in the United States of the same period, especially if compared to the showcase area. However, there are several very good applications of telecommunications and building technology at the NTT Twins building.

1. Curtain Wall Wiring Cabinets

Wiring closets are provided throughout the building in the spandrel area between the columns in the curtain wall. These are used for PBXs, electrical panels, and fiber-optic electronics. Most of the small departmental telephone switches and modems for the fiber-optic equipment are sized for installation in these closets, and are mounted on the curtain wall, with small openings to the trench system (or access floor in the demonstration area) for cable distribution. One unanswered concern regarding this application is a possible condensation problem in the cabinet due to its proximity to the outside.

2. Access Floor

The NTT Twins building utilizes two access floors that are good applications of building technology. First, in the showcase area, NTT has installed a raised asbestos cement access floor. The 45-cm (17.8 inch) square panels sit on integral pedestals at each of the four corners, providing a 45-mm (1.78 inch) clear space for electrical wiring and some office automation cabling. The panel material is fairly lightweight, yet gives the effect of a solid floor, and is easily removed to access the cabling underneath. This panel system provides minimal wiring space, but is appropriate for conference rooms or other areas where the feel of a solid floor is important, and where cable access is needed in the middle of the room, and is subject to change.

Second, there is a raised floor system which sits on metal pedestals, with the panels also 45-cm square. It is screwed down to the pedestal system in the middle of the panel, where lateral braces are installed. The panels are leveled by adjusting the pedestals. The lateral bracing provides good seismic reinforcement, as well as stability — an important consideration in Tokyo. The concept appears to be effective for a fairly large amount of wire management distribution, such as a dense, heavily automated office floor; however, the clear space under the panel is not large enough or easily accessible enough for a data center cable distribution plan.

3. Pop-up Electrical Monument

Although there were many types of fixtures available to access the trench system at the NTT Twins building, one in particular appears to be very functional.

The fixture is used only in an electrical configuration, but can be easily adapted to data or voice connectors. It is circular, fashioned of stainless steel, and fits flush with the carpet squares. It has a spring release that pops the fixture up for use; closing the top activates the closing mechanism which locks the unit. The difference between this fixture and similar fixtures observed in other applications is the flatness of the closed unit and the overall workmanship of the fixture.

TOSHIBA HEADQUARTERS

The Toshiba Headquarters is essentially a tenant building, with Toshiba occupying a significant portion of the complex; all floors are configured as if they were tenant space.

The floors are divided into quadrants, with departments located in the four corners. All base building risers, including HVAC, standard electrical, and telephone distribution are located in the public corridor areas instead of in the departmental spaces. Toshiba, as a major tenant with a large population, had to dedicate riser space for its large amount of proprietary telecommunications service cabling to avoid competition with the other tenants for shared riser space. They elected to design risers and specialized wireways within their leased space, and provided a significant amount of flexibility in telecommunications growth with minimal impact on the ability to relocate equipment and personnel.

General Office Floors

Toshiba's basic computer applications include electronic mail with ancillary directory, document filing, printing services, and various types of order control for product development and manufacturing, all supported by a sophisticated long-distance private telephone network that links the various Japanese offices and plants to the headquarters. Much of the strategic planning and product development for their microelectronics and consumer products business segments are managed from this complex; information generated there is used throughout the Toshiba organization worldwide. These applications reside on mainframe computers located at the data center several buildings away in the same complex, and to a lesser extent on the various office automation minicomputers in the departments.

Data communications services reach the corporate headquarters on 100-megabit fiber-optic lines (the LAN Ring) looped between the main building and the data center. A coaxial broadband CATV system links other Toshiba locations on microwave and standard CATV circuits. As at NTT, there is virtually no dial-up low-speed data service needed on the general office floors, as communications are centralized on the main processors in the computer centers. The 100-megabit LAN Ring is tapped at the OA room, where fiber-optic electronics converts the signal to 10-megabit coaxial service (the LAN Bus), which is routed overhead in cable trays to core wall closets. The LAN Bus is then tapped again and feeder cable is fed into another level of the three-level cellular trench to the equipment.

1. Telephone Service

Telephone service enters the building in the basement and is distributed to the floors in an elevator corridor riser on multi-pair sheathed bundles. There are a number of PBXs and telephone switches throughout the complex. Telephone cable runs from these switches again through the elevator corridor riser system to one of four small telephone closets per floor. Each of these closets has cross-connect blocks for approximately 200 two-pair connections. Two-pair shielded bundles are then fed into one level of a three-level cellular trench, and are distributed into the departmental spaces to the desks and work areas.

2. Electrical Services

Toshiba provides "clean" power for the OA equipment and services on a separate line from the main building bus. This power feed is not in any way conditioned, but simply isolated from the electrical and mechanical loads of the building.

In order to accommodate most of their proprietary cabling, Toshiba designed a riser system in the middle of each side of the building rather than use the building riser system in the elevator corridors. Surrounding the risers are small computer rooms (called OA rooms), one for each wing. These risers have condenser water for air conditioners (no water-cooled processors were observed on the general office floors), the electrical riser for "clean" power for the OA equipment and terminals, and the LAN Ring fiber-optic backbone.

Electrical power for Toshiba terminals is obtained from a separate fixture that accesses the third level of the cellular trench in the floor, with electricity for terminals identified with a special receptacle that does not accommodate a standard plug. The "OA" power runs in the same trench as utility power, but wired to the special receptacle where needed. The trenches themselves are easy to locate, as the access covers to the distribution system are always aligned with the lighting fixtures on the general office floors.

Toshiba technicians maintain all the cable plants and equipment in the building. As with NTT, wire management is maintained by hand on drawings and microfiche.

3. Data Processing Areas and Equipment

The physical layout of the general office floors is similar to NTT, with standard rows of steel desks and very poor ratios of terminals to personnel. Certain departments, however, specifically the travel agency and the advertising design department, feature slightly more desktop automation. Nevertheless, most equipment is found in either the OA rooms or in centralized departmental terminal areas.

These OA rooms are not in use on all floors. In several areas they were completely abandoned because the amount of equipment the departments need did not fit in the room. In these cases, the equipment was placed in the open, near the workers.

The noise in the OA rooms is fairly intense, especially when the air conditioners, peripherals, and printers are active. The departmental terminal areas are somewhat less noisy, due to the open area, but impact printer chatter was noticeable at some distance. Toshiba personnel in the areas observed appeared to be more active than those at

NTT. There was a general buzz in the room, which made the overall noise created by the departmental systems much less noticeable after a short time.

Telephones instruments at Toshiba have standard features including four-way conferencing, speed dialing, messaging-waiting indicators, camp-on, and LCD displays. Some personnel had speakerphones, but not all. As with NTT, Toshiba is a heavy user of facsimile services; fully featured fax machines are numerous. In fact, there are two PBXs in the headquarters dedicated to Group IV speed fax equipment for transmission outside the complex. In addition, Toshiba is a pioneer of optical disk storage, and although optical disk equipment is in use on some of the office floors, paper still prevails for virtually all applications.

4. Miscellaneous

The Toshiba security system is based on a card reader identification badge system. Guard services check IDs at the main entrances. Workers use the badges to report to their departments, sign on to their terminals, and charge their lunches.

As with NTT, the building control center is on an asbestos cement raised floor with both ionization and photoelectric smoke detectors in use as well as Halon extinguishing systems and remote annunciation of the fire situation.

Costs associated with relocating personnel, including telecommunications equipment and services, are not an issue with Toshiba; however, there is an understanding as to the impact of the cost of relocation to their customers, which is seen in the showcase area and in some of the building technology applications used in the showcase area.

Showcase Area

Toshiba's product line demonstration room, known as TotalNet Plaza, is named after their flagship product called "TotalNet" (Toshiba Office automation Telecommunications Architecture

and Logistics Network), a high-speed local area network based on their 100-megabit fiber-optic network. Toshiba manufactures the fiber-optic electronics, as well as the interface devices and terminal equipment which includes high- and low-speed terminals, display devices, optical disk storage, and the AT&T/Toshiba PBX, all of which are somewhat integrated on the network with gateways. Toshiba's product line direction is interconnectivity with any number of multi-vendor products on the network.

Physically, the TotalNet Plaza features a two-level raised floor for wire management. The overall look and function resemble the information center or automation demonstration area of a relatively sophisticated U. S. company. The TotalNet Plaza features are not used throughout the building, only in the demonstration area.

Innovations

The Toshiba building features several good applications of building technology as they relate to telecommunications.

1. Raised Floor

The TotalNet Plaza demonstration room at the Toshiba Headquarters utilizes a two-level raised floor to accommodate the myriad of telecommunications and electrical cabling necessary in that room. The panels are made of an asbestos cement and are fairly lightweight, yet solid. They rest on a stringerless pedestal system, approximately six inches high, which is fastened to the slab with an epoxy. Below the asbestos cement panels is a translucent panel that rests on the same pedestals, but about three inches below the top panel.

Electrical services are installed on the slab, and are clearly visible through the translucent panel. Data services and some fiber-optic electronics are then installed on the translucent panels, thereby providing a separation and wire management method. If the cable on the translucent panel is fairly rigid, these panels can be installed on every other panel, or every third panel, to give support to the cable and fiber-optic electronic devices.

2. Modular Cabinet and Wiring Closets

To best utilize the space along the large core wall area within the office wings, the Toshiba project team designed a series of cabinet units to be used interchangeably for storage, file space, wire pathways, and building system control locations.

The units are approximately nine feet tall (to the ceiling), and one meter (3.2 feet) wide. Configurations vary from standard coat closets with either storage or a blank panel above, to a full width of wireway behind optionally lockable doors that accommodate cable coming down from the ceiling. On all units, the bottom three inches of the cabinet conceals an accessible pathway for cable, thereby providing access to the cellular trench manholes under the cabinet.

This approach provides abundant wiring flexibility as well as additional storage along a corridor area that might otherwise be unused.

3. Electronic Board Room

The main boardroom of the Toshiba Headquarters is one of the few observed that can be considered an "electronic" boardroom. There are two large display screens capable of projecting video from VCRs, commercial television, or Toshiba's in-house CATV network, or any one of a number of computer outputs controlled from a main panel at the side of the room. In addition, a voice enhancement system that resides in the large (approximately 40 feet in diameter) conference table, controls the volume of the speaker's voice and maintains a constant level of audio to each seat.

Appendix E
ABSIC Field Evaluation Team

The ABSIC Field Evaluation Team collectively embodies expertise in various performance areas, as is evident from these profiles of the team members.

PLEASANTINE DRAKE
Principal
Architectural Diagnostics

Pleasantine Drake holds two architectural degrees and has been involved in all aspects of building programming, design, construction, and evaluation. Since 1982, she has been Principal of Architectural Diagnostics, which she established and which provides expertise in functional, behavioral, and technical aspects of building programming, design, operation, and use. It focuses upon problems of total building performance — the integration of decisions regarding building component and system design with those of quality assurance, occupant needs and behavior, space planning and fit-up, and maintenance programs and practices. Ms. Drake is affiliated with the Centre of Building Diagnostics (Cantech) Ltd., of Ottawa, Ontario, and the Centre of Building Diagnostics (Scotland) Ltd., in Dundee, Scotland.

Ms. Drake's recent work has focused upon the design, operation, management, and evaluation of office environments, and particularly on the challenges inherent in the introduction of new technologies into the office workplace. She has also conducted research on environmental issues as they relate to quality of working life and performance of occupants. She has coauthored user manuals and helped design and implement joint planning processes which involve staff in facility planning projects.

Ms. Drake has taught at universities, including the University of Calgary where, as Associate Professor of Architecture, she was responsible for developing the first Canadian graduate curriculum in facility/environmental programming. Ms. Drake has served on the following three committees of the Building Research Board of the U.S. National Academy of Sciences: Building Diagnostics, 1982-84; Improved Preliminary Planning/Programming in the Building Delivery Cycle, 1984-85; and Office Planning for the Public Sector 1986-87. In 1987-88, she was a member of the Steering Committee, and a topic group leader and rapporteur for the International Symposium on Advanced Comfort Systems for the Work Environment organized by Rensselaer Polytechnic Institute. Ms. Drake is also a member of the research team for the Impact of Advanced Technology Project at Carnegie Mellon University, which is studying the impact of advanced technologies on buildings in various countries.

FRED DUBIN, P.E.
President
Dubin-Bloome Associates, P.C.

The late Fred Dubin, P.E., was president of Dubin-Bloome Associates, P.C., a consulting engineering and planning firm established in 1946, and a partner in Fred S. Dubin International in Rome. Major design projects by Mr. Dubin include the Salk Institute for Biological Studies; management consulting contract for HUD's Solar Energy Demonstration Project; phytotrons at Duke University and North Carolina State University; and United Nations Environmental Headquarters in Nairobi, Kenya. For the Veterans Administration, he prepared the standards and design guidelines for all existing VA hospitals. He prepared the first energy construction and design standards for Jamaica in 1983; and in 1988, under contract to the World Bank, he collaborated with a team from Jamaica to complete the final draft of the Jamaica Energy Efficient Building Standards and Code.

His research has been supported by agencies such as the U.S. Departments of Energy, Housing and Urban Development, and the Interior; the Agency for International Development; the World Bank; and Public Works Canada.

He served on the Building Research Board of the National Academy of Sciences and was a member of the Steering Committee; he was a topic group leader and rapporteur for the International Symposium on Advanced Comfort Systems for the Work Environment, organized by Rensselaer Polytechnic Institute. Among his professional affiliations, he was a fellow in the American Consulting Engineers Council, the American Society of HVAC Engineers, and the Scientist's Institute for Public Information.

Mr. Dubin authored several books and more than 200 articles on engineering, architecture, and energy. He served on the faculty of several universities, including the University of Arkansas, Carnegie Mellon University, Columbia University, University of Southern California, Massachusetts Institute of Technology, and New Jersey Institute of Technology. He developed curricula and conducted classes, symposia, workshops, and studio programs on energy conservation in buildings. He held a B.S. in mechanical engineering from Carnegie Institute of Technology (now CMU) and a Master of Architecture from Pratt Institute.

Mr. Dubin forged substantial links to the People's Republic of China. In 1983, he was a featured speaker at the first U.S.–China conference on energy and environment; in 1986, he participated in a Citizen's Ambassador technical exchange program with the Chinese; he also served as a U.S. delegate to a 1988 workshop addressing China's energy policy. At the time of his death, he had just opened a joint venture office in the People's

Republic of China, and was developing a seven-part energy program for China, which includes a comprehensive building energy code and design manual.

VOLKER HARTKOPF
Professor of Architecture
Director, Center for Building
Performance and Diagnostics
Carnegie Mellon University

Volker Hartkopf is a Professor of Architecture and Director of the Center for Building Performance and Diagnostics at Carnegie Mellon University, where he teaches design and building performance in professional, Master of Science, and Ph.D. programs. He holds a Diplom Ingenieur degree and a Doctor Ingenieur degree (Ph.D.) from the University of Stuttgart and a Master of Architecture with a minor in Business Administration from the University of Texas at Austin. He practiced and taught architecture in Germany before coming to the U.S. on a Fulbright Scholarship in 1970.

Professor Hartkopf came to Carnegie Mellon University in 1972. He has completed research and demonstration projects in Bangladesh, Canada, Germany, Peru, and the U.S. in industrial architecture, housing, commercial buildings, energy conservation, and total building performance. He was instrumental in establishing North America's first multidisciplinary graduate program in architecture, civil engineering, and urban affairs in 1975 with grants from the National Science Foundation (NSF) and the building industry.

In addition, his extensive research was supported by the U.S. Departments of Energy, Housing and Urban Development, and Interior; the U.S. Agency for International Development; the City of Pittsburgh; the German Marshal Fund; the National Endowment for the Arts; the National Academy of Sciences; and Public Works Canada. His work received the Award for Applied Research in *Progressive Architecture* in 1986. Professor Hartkopf has contributed over 60 technical publications in books, journals, reports, and conference proceedings.

Between 1981 and 1985, Professor Hartkopf spent two and a half years in the Executive Interchange Program with Public Works Canada in the Architectural and Building Sciences Directorate as the team member charged with developing a comprehensive methodology for total building performance evaluation.

VIVIAN LOFTNESS
Associate Professor
Department of Architecture
Carnegie Mellon University

Vivian E. Loftness is a principal of VLH Associates and Associate Professor at Carnegie Mellon University in Pittsburgh, Pennsylvania. Ms. Loftness, an international energy and building performance consultant for commercial and residential building design, has edited and written numerous publications on energy conservation, passive solar design, climate and regionalism in architecture, as well as design for performance in the office of the future. While at the American Institute of Architects Research Corporation, she was technical project manager for the HUD Solar Energy Demonstration Program, chairman of the "Climate and Architecture" working conference with the Departments of Energy and Commerce, and technical consultant to the DOE Passive Solar Program. Her technical consulting and research in energy conservation, passive design, and building climatology continues today for such institutions as the Department of Energy, National Academy of Science, National Science Foundation, and the World Meteorological Organization.

In the private sector, her work with Dubin-Bloome Associates as architectural project manager led to the design and construction of numerous energy conserving buildings. Under contract to the Greek and German governments, she completed the energy conservation and passive solar design of a 400-unit low-income community, now under construction in Athens, Greece. In 1982, Ms. Loftness began work with the Architectural and Building Sciences division of Public Works Canada, researching and developing the issues in the areas of total building performance and building diagnostics. In the past few years, this work has led to advanced architectural research in the performance of a range of building types, from museums to high-tech offices, and the innovative building delivery processes necessary for improving quality in building performance.

PETER A.D. MILL
President
Centre of Building Diagnostics (Cantech) Ltd.

Peter A.D. Mill is the founder and president of the Centre of Building Diagnostics (Cantech) Ltd. in Ottawa, Canada, which was established in 1988, and the Centre of Building Diagnostics (Scotland) Ltd. at Dundee University of Scotland. Mr. Mill is internationally acclaimed for his work on the development of total building performance assessments and non-destructive testing methodologies, ranging from thermography to occupancy use analysis. The Centre of Building Diagnostics (known as CBD) provides architectural and building science consulting in design, construction research, and performance diagnostics of existing buildings. CBD is also actively involved in the design and development of innovative building products.

Recent projects include consulting with Lloyd's of London on retrofits to both the new and the old buildings, the design consultation and quality control on the proposed Ohio Aerospace Institute, and the Canada Museums Construction Corporation for construction quality control testing on the new National Gallery of Canada and the new Canadian Museum of Civilisation. From 1987–90 Mill was an Executive Architectural and Building Science Consultant to Johnson Controls, in Milwaukee, Wisconsin, where he led the development of the Personal Environments System™.

Prior to the establishment of CBD, Mr. Mill was Director of Architectural & Building Sciences at Public Works Canada. In 1987–88, Mr. Mill was on an executive interchange sponsored by Carnegie Mellon University in Pittsburgh, and a research fellowship with the British Social Sciences and Engineering Research Council to do development and training work in Britian.

Mr. Mill is a Research Fellow of the Center for Building Performance and Diagnostics, an Associate Fellow of the Institute of Building Sciences at Carnegie Mellon University, and a consultant to ABSIC. From 1973–76, Mr. Mill was Associate Professor of Building Sciences in the graduate programme in the Faculty of Environmental Design at the University of Calgary, Alberta.

His degrees include an A.A.DIP. from the Architectural Association School of Architecture, London, England, and a Master of Architecture from the State University of New York, Buffalo. He has published numerous professional papers and co-authored chapters of several books. He is co-inventor on the patencies of various innovative building products.

JAMES D. POSNER
Executive Vice President
COMSUL, Ltd.

Mr. Posner is Executive Vice President of COMSUL, Ltd., a telecommunications planning and consulting firm founded in 1967. He has extensive experience in voice and data network planning, design, and implementation, and has developed integrated voice and data communication systems for major computer and communications equipment manufacturers, including IBM, DEC, Wang, Hewlett Packard, and AT&T.

Since joining COMSUL in 1975, Mr. Posner has served as project manager for many large planning projects involving voice and data systems, both in the U.S. and abroad. He has designed and

implemented systems ranging from multipoint PBX complexes with tie-line networks to Centrex systems of over 1,000 lines. These projects have included strategic and tactical planning, applications concept development, technical specifications preparation, equipment and vendor evaluation, and full responsibility for installation management. Many projects have involved facility planning and have focused on integrating technology with the base building disciplines in buildings that exceed two million sq. feet.

Prior to joining COMSUL, Mr. Posner was with Pacific Telephone, where he was responsible for developing its competitive strategy, necessitated by the deregulation of the industry. He developed procedures and guidelines for telephone system design and sales tools, including a computer program to analyze the financial implications of private system procurement. These tools remain in use today.

He also has experience with military combat radio systems deployment and operation, and was an instructor at the Fort Ord Radio School while serving in the U.S. Army.

He serves on the Board of Directors of the Society of Telecommunications Consultants and the AT&T National Consultants Council. He also serves as the technical consultant to the Northern District Federal Courts. He has presented numerous seminars and authored several articles, most recently an issues paper focusing on the new levels of relationship between the corporate real estate/facilities and the technology systems/MIS officers.

GEORGE RAINER
Principal
Flack & Kurtz Consulting Engineers

George Rainer, a principal at Flack & Kurtz Consulting Engineers, has extensive experience in the design of building mechanical systems for a wide variety of facilities, including universities, office buildings, laboratories, and military bases.

He directed an upgrade of AT&T Bell Laboratories at Murray Hill, NJ, which provided state-of-the-art infrastructure to serve the Laboratories well into the 21st century, and included the installation of a central supervisory control system containing more than 6,000 points.

His work in energy conservation and management includes the development of energy audit manuals for the U.S. Navy and the U.S. Department of Health, Education, and Welfare; energy studies on housing and colleges in New York State; the implementation of numerous energy retrofit applications; and cogeneration studies for projects such as Metrotech Development in Brooklyn and the Brooklyn Naval Yard.

His work on the preparation of utility master plans includes facilities such as the U.S. Military Academy at West Point and the law school campus of the University of Connecticut; new towns such as Harbison, South Carolina, and Grand Valley, Colorado; and urban development projects such as Roosevelt Island and Battery Park City in New York.

Mr. Rainer holds a B.S. degree in mechanical engineering and a master's degree in urban planning, both from New York University. He is registered in six states, and lectures at Pratt Institute, where he developed a course on Urban Infrastructure for architects, planners, and urban designers. His book, *Understanding Infrastructure*, was published by Wiley Interscience in 1990.

HERBERT ROSENHECK
President
Technology Planning Associates

Herbert Rosenheck is president of Technology Planning Associates (TPA), a consortium of specialists in information systems and services, communications, and engineering that provides a broad, integrated range of business and technical skills to major Fortune 100 industrial and financial firms and government agencies, ensuring that current and projected office automation, distributed data processing, communications, and other functional requirements are satisfied.

He has been Vice President and General Manager for TRW Inc., where he was responsible for development and operations of the high-technology Information Services Division, developing and operating one of the nation's largest computer network systems. He has participated on Building Resource Committees at the National Academy of Sciences, and the Energy and Power Research Institute (EPRI).

Mr. Rosenheck was a member of the data and telecommunications team of OCNET (in Orange County, California) — one of the largest private systems in the country. At American Greetings in Cleveland, Ohio, he conducts project design reviews and provides management advisory services related to the development of a multi-million dollar order control and distribution system, which encompasses state-of-the-art nationwide data/voice communication networks.

His technical strength lies in the integration of information and data services with the operation of the office environment and understanding the processes, operational work flows, and facilities requirements. He managed the development of requirements and implementation of the voice, data, image, and text information systems and related facilities planning for the TRW World Headquarters as well as for other organizations.

His knowledge of MIS operations and strategic planning, budgets, and schedules gained in more than 30 years' experience is critical to helping MIS and telecommunications departments plan, budget, and schedule resources for major projects.

GEORGE R. ZIGA
President
Planning & Design Associates, Inc.

George R. Ziga is president of Planning & Design Associates, Inc., a consulting firm located in Cleveland, Ohio, that specializes in providing information systems, telecommunications planning, and project management services to companies that are building or renovating offices and facilities. Since 1983, he and his organization have provided services to a number of Fortune 100 companies as well as members of the banking, pharmaceutical, and public sector industries throughout the United States.

Prior to founding PDA, Mr. Ziga was a senior manager on the Ernst and Young management consulting services staff specializing in information systems planning and design, working primarily in the healthcare, energy, and telecommunications industries.

Mr. Ziga holds a bachelor's degree in physics and mathematics, and has studied accounting and business. He has conducted numerous training classes and seminars in telecommunication and information systems and has significant experience in developing project plans, technical documentation, and procedures.

MAO-LIN CHIU
Postdoctoral Researcher
Department of Architecture
Carnegie Mellon University

Mao-Lin Chiu, originally from Taipei, Taiwan, R.O.C., is a postdoctoral researcher at the Center for Building Performance and Diagnostics at Carnegie Mellon University. He earned a Ph.D. in Architecture from CMU in 1991, an M.S. in Architecture and Public Management and Policy from CMU in 1987, and a B.S. in Architecture from the National Cheng-Kung University in Taiwan in 1982.

His professional experience includes working for the Architectural Engineering Group in the civil service, and as a project designer for office buildings and housing projects at Forum Architects and Associates in Taipei. At Carnegie Mellon University, he was awarded a Richard King Mellon Fellowship and worked in the Department of Architecture from 1987 to 1991.

His research includes the energy consumption and the use of computers in electronic offices, the physical configuration of intelligent office buildings, office investment decisionmaking processes and interrelationships with building performance and building economics. His doctoral dissertation was entitled "Office Investment Decisionmaking and Building Performance."

Appendix F
ABSIC Mission Statement and Profiles of Industry Members

The ABSIC Mission

The Advanced Building Systems Integration Consortium (ABSIC) is a university-industry partnership established in July 1988 at Carnegie Mellon University. The Consortium was created for the advancement of the North American building industry. It conducts research, development, and demonstrations for the purpose of increasing the quality and user satisfaction of commercial buildings and integrated building systems, while improving cost, time, and energy effectiveness. Its members are prominent leaders in the market for high-performance buildings, and they intend to drive the market rather than follow it. A primary ABSIC mission is to effect a positive change in the building industry. The Consortium believes that high-performance buildings must provide appropriate physical, environmental, and organizational settings to accommodate changing technologies and workplace activities. Ultimately, the work of ABSIC will contribute to the enhancement of worker effectiveness, communication, comfort, and overall productivity.

ABSIC Membership

ABSIC is composed of prominent corporations of the North American building industry, together with the Center for Building Performance and Diagnostics (in the Carnegie Mellon University Department of Architecture). ABSIC is funded by the National Science Foundation, and is designated an NSF Industry/University Cooperative Research Center (I/UCRC). Along with the support of the North American corporations, ABSIC also has attracted the support of several prominent members of the European building industry — in particular, Josef Gartner & Co., of Gundelfingen, Germany; Mahle GmbH, of Stuttgart-Bad Cannstatt, Germany; and Siemens Solar, of Munich, Germany.

The organizations involved in ABSIC are profiled below:

AMP Incorporated

AMP Incorporated, based in Harrisburg, Pennsylvania, is the world's leading producer of electrical and electronic connectors and interconnection systems. In addition to supplying a vast array of connection products used in computer and telecommunications equipment, AMP offers voice, data, and power interconnects for networking and intelligent building applications. Products include under-carpet wiring systems; connectors for twisted-pair, coaxial, and fiber-optic cable; modular wall and floor outlets; patch panels and portable wiring closets; cable taps and baluns; and related accessories and tooling. All components have been designed to support flexible, vendor-independent premise wiring systems.

American Bridge Company

American Bridge Company, an affiliate of the Continental Engineering Corporation, is engaged in the structural erection of office buildings, hotels, sports arenas and stadiums, bridges, industrial facilities, and other steel and prestressed concrete structures requiring complex erection methods and procedures. Incorporated in 1900 with the merger of 28 bridge and structural companies,

American Bridge uses a wide range of management methods and engineering technologies to provide comprehensive engineering and construction services. The company is headquartered in Pittsburgh, Pa., with regional offices throughout the country, and employs more than 100 full-time employees, with another 200 to 300 field employees involved in specific projects.

Armstrong World Industries

Armstrong is a multinational manufacturer and marketer of products for the interiors of residential, commercial, and institutional buildings. Its products include floor coverings (resilient flooring and ceramic tile), building products (primarily acoustical ceiling systems and wall panels), and furniture. In addition, it supplies a variety of insulation materials and adhesives products worldwide. Armstrong manufactures products at 91 plants in 13 countries around the globe and has approximately 25,000 employees.

Bechtel Civil Company

Bechtel Civil Company operates as a unit of Bechtel Corporation. It consists of six business lines: Mining & Metals, Waste-to-Energy, Water Resources, Buildings & Infrastructure, Surface Transportation, and Aviation Services Transportation. Through a shared worldwide global network of regional offices, Bechtel Civil Company provides a full range of planning, feasibility studies, engineering, construction, management, and operation and maintenance services in its business lines worldwide. Currently, Bechtel Civil Company, which concentrates on community and commercial facilities, employs over 3500 persons. Of these 3500, there are 120 architects and over 450 engineering professionals.

Bell of Pennsylvania

Bell of Pennsylvania offers its customers the vast resources of its parent company, Bell Atlantic Corporation, a leading international communications and information management company. Daily, Bell of Pennsylvania's four million customers enjoy the advantages of technologies that are driven by state-of-the-art processes such as computer-based switches (now present in virtually 100 percent of Bell of Pennsylvania's switching centers); Signalling System 7, the software "brains" to manipulate the network; and fiber-optic cable, the high-capacity (or broadband) highway for transmission of digital signals, which now links most of the company's switching centers and is being extended through the network to customers. These technologies are the key to high-definition television and full-motion interactive video, and present enormous potential benefits to education, business, healthcare, and economic development. Bell of Pennsylvania continues to lead the telecommunications industry in the early and aggressive deployment of this intelligent network of the future.

Duquesne Light Company

Duquesne Light Company supplies electricity and other energy services as the principal subsidiary of DQE. With a strong commitment to economic development for the retention and growth of jobs in the area, Duquesne Light delivers quality service and superior customer satisfaction. Their active participation in the development and application of new technologies distinguishes their position within the energy service marketplace.

Johnson Controls, Inc.

Johnson Controls, Inc. is a $4.5 billion diversified company headquartered in Milwaukee, Wisconsin. The company is a global leader in control systems and services for non-residential buildings, automotive seating, automotive batteries, and plastics packaging. Some 43,000 employees work at approximately 500 locations worldwide. The mission of Johnson Controls is to exceed the expectations of its customers through continuous improvements in quality, service, productivity, and time compression.

The Knoll Group

The Knoll Group, a subsidiary of Westinghouse Electric Corporation, is a New York–based office furnishings company committed to delivering intelligent workspaces worldwide. The unique Knoll combination of superior design, innovative technology, and reliable services makes such workspaces possible. The company offers a variety of open office systems, seating, files and storage, desks and casegoods, executive furniture, contract textiles, and office accessories for the intelligent workspace. Each product is inspired by the Knoll devotion to quality, produced by world-class manufacturing, and backed by the industry's highest standard of service.

Miles Inc.

Miles Inc. is a Fortune 100, research-based company with major businesses in chemicals, health care, and imaging technologies. Headquartered in Pittsburgh, Miles employs some 30,000 people at its operations throughout the United States and Canada. In 1991, the company's sales were $6.2 billion.

Miles products are in evidence in many areas of the architectural market. Miles inorganic pigments are found in concrete roofing, paving, and block as well as paints; organic pigments are used in architectural coatings; polyurethanes are used in insulation, doors, window frames, and furniture; thermoplastic resins find applications in glazing and furnishings; and polyurethane resins are used in formulating high-performance coatings.

PPG Industries

PPG Industries is a global producer of flat glass, fiberglass, coatings and resins, chemicals, and medical electronics. The company has about 60 production facilities in the United States and more than 100 worldwide, including subsidiaries, joint ventures, and minority interests. PPG employs 35,500 persons and is owned by 41,700 shareholders.

PPG is one of the world's largest manufacturers of flat glass and continuous-strand fiberglass, the world's largest producer of automotive and industrial coatings, and a leading maker of chlor-alkali and specialty chemicals, medical electronics, and trade paints.

Westinghouse Electric Corporation

Westinghouse Electric Corporation is a premier technology-based manufacturing and service company. Its 122,000 employees create ideas and solutions to meet the needs of customer and to help improve the quality of life around the world. Dedication to quality and market leadership characterize the 104-year-old corporation as it works worldwide to enhance shareholder value. Focused growth and diversity are other hallmarks. Principal markets include the industrial, construction, and electric utility industries, environmental services, defense and commercial electronic systems, broadcasting, and financial services. Other operations serve specialized markets, such as transport refrigeration, office furniture (see The Knoll Group), and business communications.

ABSIC European Partners

Four European organizations have joined ABSIC in the development of the Intelligent Workplace, a research and demonstration project under construction at Carnegie Mellon University that builds on the experience gained from the international case studies. These companies, which will be donating materials and professional services to the project, include: Josef Gerner & Co. of Gundelfingen, Germany (facades and enclosure systems); Mahle GmbH, of Stuttgart, Germany (raised floors); Siemens Solar, of Munich, Germany (photovoltaic panels); and Krülland, of Neuss, Germany (sun protection devices).

Appendix G
Bibliography

ABSIC, *ABSIC News*, Vol.1, No.1, 1988-1989.

ABSIC, *German Building Studies*, research report presented at the February 14, 1989, meeting of the Advanced Building Systems Integration Consortium, Pittsburgh, PA.

ABSIC, *Japanese Building Studies*, research report presented at the October 4, 1988, meeting of the Advanced Building Systems Integration Consortium, Pittsburgh, PA.

"The ABSIC Mission," *ABSIC News*, No.2, 1989-1990.

ABSIC, *North American Building Studies I*, research report presented at the May 30, 1990, meeting of the Advanced Building Systems Integration Consortium, Pittsburgh, PA.

ABSIC, *North American Building Studies II*, research report presented at the March 6, 1991, meeting of the Advanced Building Systems Integration Consortium, Pittsburgh, PA.

ABSIC, *U.K. Building Studies*, research report presented at the July 20, 1989, meeting of the Advanced Building Systems Integration Consortium, Milwaukee, WI.

ARK Hills, Tokyo, Japan: Kogyo Chosakai Publishing Co., Ltd., 1987.

Barron, Janet J., "Will TRON Succeed?" *Byte*, April 1989, p. 301.

Becker F., *The Total Workplace: Facilities Management and the Elastic Organization*, New York: Van Nostrand Reinhold, 1990.

Bennett, J., R. Flanagan, and G. Norman, *Capital & Countries Report: Japanese Construction Industry*, Reading, U.K.: Centre for Strategic Studies in Construction, University of Reading, 1987.

Brill, M., with S. Margulis, E. Konar, and BOSTI, in association with Westinghouse Furniture Systems, *Using Office Design to Increase Productivity*, Vol. 1, Buffalo: Workplace Design and Productivity, Inc., 1985.

Building Report: IBM Hakozaki Office, Tokyo: IBM Japan, Ltd., 1989.

Chiu, Mao-Lin, *Office Investment Decisionmaking and Building Performance*, Ph.D. thesis, Department of Architecture, Carnegie Mellon University, Pittsburgh, PA, May 1991.

CIB Working Commission W60, "Working with the Performance Approach in Building," International Council for Building Research Studies and Documentation, Publication 64, January 1982.

Cohen, Charles L., "Update: TRON Moves In — To Real-Time Control," *Electronics*, January 1989, p. 168.

Cohen, E., and A. Cohen, *Planning The Electronic Office*, New York: McGraw-Hill Book Company, 1984.

Dambrot, Stuart M., "Open Systems, Oriental Style," *Datamation*, August 1, 1989, pp. 3-4.

Davis, G., F. Becker, F. Duffy, and W. Sims, *ORBIT-2™ Overview Report*, Norwalk: Harbinger Group, Inc., 1985.

deCourcy Hinds, Michael, "Finding New Ways to Make Smell Sell," *The New York Times*, July 23, 1988, p. 16.

Development Opportunities for Integrated Building Management Systems, Amersham: ProPlan, 1990.

Duffy, F., and A. Henney, *The Changing City*, London: Architecture Planning Design (DEGW), 1988.

"First TRON Microprocessor Gets Japan into the 32-bit Fray," *Electronics*, January 21, 1988, pp. 31-32.

Gillin, Paul, "Mixing High Tech and High Rises," *Computerworld*, August 13, 1990, pp. 25-26.

GSA Peach Book, or *The PBS Building Systems Program and Performance Specification for Office Buildings, Third Edition*, Washington, DC: Public Buildings Service, General Services Administration, 1975.

Hartkopf, V., "The Office of the Future: Intelligence in Office Design," presented at the International Building Symposium, University of Karlsruhe, Germany, October 14, 1989.

Hartkopf, V., V. Loftness, and P. Mill, "The Concept of Total Building Performance and Building Diagnostics," in *Building Performance: Function, Preservation, and Rehabilitation*, Philadelphia: ASTM, STP 901, 1986.

Hartkopf, V., V. Loftness, and P. Mill, "Integration for Performance," in *The Building Systems Integration Handbook*, ed. Richard Rush, New York: John Wiley & Sons, 1986.

Hartkopf, V., Loftness, V., Mill, P.A.D., Siegel, M., "Architecture and Software for Interactive Learning About Total Building Performance," presented at the 3rd International Buffalo CAD Symposium, Buffalo, NY, March 23-25, 1990.

High-Technology Workplaces, ed. Pierre Goumain, New York: Van Nostrand Reinhold, 1989.

Hirata, Shinichi, "System Engineers and Office Amenity," *NAND, Quarterly Magazine of Facility Planning for Yutori*, July 1991, pp. 30-33.

Hi-Touch Research Parks Cooperative Association, "Hi-Touch Research Parks — Research Parks in Japan (10)," *JETRO*, March 1991, pp. 6-9.

IBMS-Manufacturer/SupplierAnalysis, Amersham: ProPlan (undated).

Intelligent Building, brochure published by the Shimizu Construction Co., Tokyo, Japan, 1986.

Intelligent Building, ed. Intelligent Complex Promotion Committee, Tokyo, Japan: Kabin Publishing Co., 1986.

Intelligent Building Definition Guideline, First Edition, ed. Richard Geissler, Intelligent Building Institute, Washington, DC, 1987.

The Intelligent Building Sourcebook, ed. Bernaden J. and Neubauer R. (Johnson Controls, Inc.), Lilburn, GA.: Fairmont Press, 1988.

Intelligent Buildings, ed. B. Atkin, New York: Halstead Press, (div. of John Wiley & Sons, Inc.), 1988.

Intelligent Controls in Buildings: The UK Market 1989-94, Amersham: ProPlan, 1990.

Jerome, Marty, "TRON's Global Net," *PC-Computing*, December 1989, pp. 175-176.

Kallan, Carla, "Focus on Fragrance," *USAir Magazine*, October 1990, pp. 114-119.

Kitamura, Atsushi, "The Implications of Intelligent Buildings," *NAND, Quarterly Magazine of Facility Planning for Yutori*, July 1991, pp. 18-19.

Lecht, Charles P, "There's No Place Like TRON City," *Computerworld*, May 29, 1989, p. 19.

Lemer, A.C., and F. Moavenzadeh, "Performance of Systems of Constructed Facilities," in *Proceedings, Performance Concept in Buildings*, NBS 361, Gaithersburg, MD: National Bureau of Standards, 1972.

Levin, D., "Smart Machines, Smart Workers — 'Gold Collar' Force Vital to Automation," *The New York Times*, October 17, 1988.

Loftness, V., "Trends in Intelligent Buildings," presented at Future Build 2000: The Globalization of Intelligent Buildings, sponsored by the Intelligent Buildings Institute, New York, NY, October 30-31, 1990.

Loftness, V., and V. Hartkopf, *The Electronically Enhanced Office*, Carnegie Mellon University Technical Report, Pittsburgh, PA, 1989.

Loftness, V., V. Hartkopf, and P. Mill, "Critical Frameworks for Building Evaluation: Total Building Performance, Systems Integration, and Levels of Measurement and Assessment," in *Building Evaluation*, New York: Plenum Press, 1989.

Loftness, V., V. Hartkopf, and P. Mill, "The Intelligent Office," *Progressive Architecture*, September 1990.

Mallery Stephen, "Catching Some Rays: New Device Delivers Filtered Sunlight Indoors," *Architectural Lighting*, October 1987.

Methods in Environmental and Behavioral Research, ed. Robert B. Bechtel, Robert W. Marans, and William Michelson, New York: Van Nostrand Reinhold Co., 1987.

Mill, P., V. Hartkopf, and V. Loftness, "Evaluating the Quality of the Workplace," in the *Ergonomic Payoff: Designing the Electronic Office,* ed. Rani Lueder, New York: Nichols Publishing Co., 1986.

Nakatsu, Moto, "Office Innovation at Hakozaki IBM Japan," IBM Asia Pacific, photocopy, August 1990.

NEC's New Head Office Building, NEC brochure, undated.

National Academy of Sciences, Building Research Board, *Electronically Enhanced Office Buildings,* a joint report by the Committee on Technologically Advanced Buildings and the Committee on High Technology Systems for Buildings, Washington, DC: National Research Council, 1988.

National Research Council, Building Research Board, Commission on Engineering and Technical Systems, *Building Diagnostics: A Conceptual Framework,* Washington, DC: National Research Council, 1985.

NOPA, *Results of Survey on Office Environments in Japan,* Tokyo, Japan: New Office Promotion Association, 1988.

NTIS, "Panel evaluates Japanese construction technologies," *Foreign Technology,* Nov. 30, 1990, p. 1.

NTT Twins, brochure published by NTT, Tokyo, Japan, 1986.

OA Furniture & Supplies '88, product catalog published by KOKUYO, Tokyo, Japan, 1988.

Office Renaissance, Beyond the Intelligent Buildings, ed. J. Lin, Tokyo, Japan: Sho-Koku Sha, 1986.

Office Today — Searching for a Richer and Better Environment, Takenaka-Komuten Co., Osaka, Japan (undated).

Officing: Bringing Amenity and Intelligence to Knowledge Work, Osaka, Japan: Matsushita Electric Works and CRSS, 1988.

Performance Standards in Buildings: Contents and Presentation; ISO 6240, Geneva, Switzerland: International Standards Organization, 1980.

Performance Standards in Buildings: Principles for Their Preparation and Factors for Inclusion, ISO/DP 6241, Geneva, Switzerland: International Standards Organization, 1981.

Planning and Designing Guidebook for Intelligent Buildings, First Edition, Tokyo, Japan: NTT Telecommunications and Architectural Research Division, 1987.

Planning and Detailing of Intelligent Buildings, Tokyo, Japan: Sho-Koku Sha, 1987.

Planning of Intelligent Building, Tokyo, Japan: Kajimi Publishing Co., 1986.

Poe, Robert, "Japan's TRON Tactics," *Datamation*, October 1, 1987, p. 21, 24.

Preiser, W., H. Rabinowitz, and E. White, *Post-occupancy Evaluation*, New York: Van Nostrand Reinhold, 1988.

Project Delivery System, Stages 1-10, Ottawa, Canada: Departmental Planning and Coordination Branch, Public Works Canada, 1983.

Public Works Canada, Architectural and Building Sciences Division, *Stage I in the Development of Total Building Performance, Summary Report*, Vol. 1, 1983.

Pulgram, W., and R. Stonis, *Designing The Automated Office: A Guide for Architects, Interior Designers, Space Planners, and Facility Managers*, ed. Stephen Kliment and Susan Davis, New York: Whitney Library of Design, 1984.

Rubin A., *Revised Interim Design Guidelines for Automated Offices*, NBSIR 86-3430, Washington, DC: U.S. Department of Commerce, National Bureau of Standards, 1986.

Rubin, A., *Office Design Measurements for Productivity — A Research Overview*, NBSIR 87-3688, Washington, DC: U.S. Department of Commerce, National Bureau of Standards, 1987.

Rubin, A., *Intelligent Building Technology in Japan*, NISTIR-4546, Washington, DC: U.S. Department of Commerce, April 1991.

Rubin, A., and Jacqueline Elder, *Building for People: Behavioral Research Approaches and Directions*, Special Publication 474, Washington, DC: National Bureau of Standards, 1980.

Sakamoto, Nobuyuki, "The Intelligent Revolution Comes to Japan," *Japan Update*, Winter 1988.

Sakamura, Ken,"The TRON Project," *Microprocessors and Microsystems*, October 1987, pp. 493-502.

Sakamura, Ken, and James J. Farrell, *TRON Project* (brochure),1990.

Sakamura, Ken, and Richard Sprague, "The TRON Project," *Byte*, April 1989, pp. 292-301.

Schwanke, D., *Smart Buildings and Technology-Enhanced Real Estate*, 2 volumes, Washington, DC: Urban Land Institute (ULI), 1985.

Shimizu Corporation Brochure, Tokyo, Japan (undated).

Steele, Fritz, *Making and Managing High-quality Workplaces: An Organizational Ecology*, New York: Teachers College Press, 1986.

Sundstrom, E., and M. G. Sundstrom, Work Places: *The Psychology of the Physical Environment in Offices and Factories*, ed. Daniel Stokols and Irwin Altman, Cambridge: Cambridge University Press, 1986.

"Sunlight Collection and Transmission System of the Himawari," brochure by La Foret Engineering and Information Service, Tokyo, Japan (undated).

Suzuki, Etsuro, "The View from Japan of Future Building Programs," presented at the Fall Symposium of the Advisory Board on the Built Environment, Washington, DC, November 1983.

Takenashi, M., "Intelligent Buildings in Japan," presented at the ASHRAE Forum on Advances in HVAC Systems in Japan, in Atlanta, GA, February 1990.

Toshiba, brochure published by Toshiba Corporation, Tokyo, Japan (undated).

The Total Environment City — ARK Hills, Tokyo, Japan: Mori Building Co., Ltd., 1986.

"TRON-concept Intelligent House," *The Japan Architect*, April 1990, pp. 37-40.

"TRON Takes Hold," *Scientific American*, June 1988, p. 114.

Umeda Center Building, brochure by Takenaka-Komuten Co., Ltd., Tokyo, Japan, 1987.

Umeda Intelligent Building: Planning and Application, ed. Takenaka-Komuten Co., Tokyo, Japan: Sho-Koku Sha, 1988.

"Uncovering the Hidden Costs," *Wall Street Journal*, June 12, 1987, Northeast edition.

Valigra, Lori, "TRON Inventor Decries Growing U.S. Fear of Japan Infiltration," *Computerworld*, May 22, 1989, p. 99.

Ventre, Francis T., *Documentation and Assessment of the GSA/PBS Building Systems Program: Final Report and Recommendations*, Washington, DC: National Bureau of Standards, 1983.

Watanabe, Teresa, "House of Controversy," *Los Angeles Times*, July 2, 1990, sec. D, p. 1.

Wilson, S., and A. Hedge, *The Office Environment Survey: A Study of Building Sickness*, London: Building Use Studies Ltd., 1987.

"The Wizard of TRON," *The Economist*, February 27, 1988, pp. 73-74.

Wright, Gordon, "Robots tiptoe onto the job site," *Building Design & Construction*, Vol. 30, No. 13, November 1989, p. 64.

Zeisel, J., *Inquiry by Design: Tools for Environment-behavior Research*, Monterey: Brooks/Cole Publishing Co., 1981.